D1131701

BOOK 11

WORDLY WISE 3000®

Direct Academic Vocabulary Instruction

Teacher's Resource Book

Fourth Edition

Kenneth Hodkinson • Sandra Adams • Erika Hodkinson

EDUCATORS PUBLISHING SERVICE
Cambridge and Toronto

© 2018 by School Specialty, Inc. All rights reserved. Except as authorized below, no part of this book may be reproduced or utilized in any form or by any electronic or mechanical means, including photocopying, without permission in writing from the publisher.

The purchase of this book entitles the buyer to reproduce designated pages for instructional use. Reproduction for an entire school system or for commercial use is prohibited without written permission.

Printed in Newburyport, MA, in June 2017
ISBN 978-0-8388-7724-1

3 4 5 BRB 22

Contents

Welcome to *Wordly Wise 3000*

We have to stop thinking of vocabulary as a supplemental activity. We must put it where it belongs, at the very core of the curriculum.

—Ken Hodkinson

Words are not just words. They are the nexus—the interface—between communication and thought. When we read, it is through words that we build, refine, and modify our knowledge. What makes vocabulary valuable and important is not the words themselves so much as the understandings they afford.[1]

—Marilyn Jager Adams

For over fifty years, *Wordly Wise* has provided students with systematic, direct instruction in academic vocabulary. Research has proven that a rich and varied vocabulary provides a critical foundation for reading comprehension and academic achievement, which is why rigorous state and national standards have intensified efforts by educators to deliver more robust vocabulary instruction for students.

Wordly Wise 3000, Fourth Edition, now places greater emphasis on building independent vocabulary acquisition skills, such as determining meaning from context, and on reinforcing knowledge of the key academic words that students will find most useful across all content areas. In addition, engaging new activities involve students in actively applying word knowledge by discussing words with peers, writing their own sentences, acting out meanings, and even visually representing word meanings.

At the same time, *Wordly Wise 3000* continues to provide teachers and students with the same rigorous, high quality, flexible vocabulary instruction they have always relied on, while offering new strategies and resources for differentiation to meet the needs of today's increasingly diverse classrooms.

We hope you enjoy the *Wordly Wise 3000* family of products. If you are considering a digital solution to meet your vocabulary instruction needs, take a look at our new *Wordly Wise i3000*™, powered by Exploros, at epsbooks.com/ww3000.

For both print and digital formats, students can practice and master their vocabulary on Quizlet.com—an entertaining and engaging learning application that can be used anywhere at any time, adding value for both teachers and students. Quizlet activities and games provide fun practice and additional reinforcement of vocabulary words.

How *Wordly Wise 3000* Helps Build Academic Vocabulary

Wordly Wise 3000 focuses on improving students' vocabulary by furthering their understanding of new words and concepts as well as strengthening their independent vocabulary acquisition skills. Studies have shown that reading comprehension and vocabulary knowledge are strongly correlated,[2] and researchers have found that word knowledge in primary school can predict how well students will be able to comprehend the texts they read in high school.[3] Limited vocabulary prevents comprehension. As text complexity increases, the need for a more extensive academic vocabulary rises.

Poor readers often read less because reading is difficult and frustrating for them. They may not read widely enough to increase their knowledge of academic vocabulary, which could help them to comprehend more. This perpetuating cycle means that as students continue through middle school and high school, the gap between good and poor readers grows wider.

The good news is that direct vocabulary instruction can help break this cycle of failure. We know that good readers acquire much of their vocabulary indirectly—through wide independent reading. However, direct, explicit instruction can help students learn enough words to become better readers and thus acquire even more words as a result of reading.

Direct vocabulary instruction is useful for students at all levels, but it is particularly useful for students who have a limited English vocabulary or little exposure to incidental vocabulary learning outside of school. We know that students come to school with vastly different vocabularies and different levels of exposure to academic words. However, arriving in class with a limited vocabulary does not predict failure—it only highlights the need for direct and systematic academic vocabulary instruction in the school. As one researcher put it, "If we are serious about 'increasing standards' and bringing a greater proportion of schoolchildren to high levels of academic accomplishment, we cannot continue to leave vocabulary development to parents, chance, and highly motivated reading."[4]

Experts emphasize that vocabulary development is an attainable goal. If given the systematic opportunity to learn new words via effective direct instruction, most students can acquire vocabulary at rates that will improve their comprehension. This enables them to read increasingly complex texts with fluency, setting the foundation for college and career readiness.

On average, students learn about 3,000 words per year, all told, or six to eight words per day—a remarkable achievement! If students are taught new words at a rate of eight to ten words per week for 37 to 50 weeks, about 300 to 500 words per year can be taught through direct instruction.[5] This still leaves a large portion of words to be learned incidentally. Although the percentage of words learned through direct instruction may seem small, it is significant. Stahl has pointed out that for students at the lower end of the vocabulary range, who learn perhaps 1,000 words a year, a gain of 300 words equals a 30 percent increase, and that for average students, a gain of even 10 percent is educationally significant—especially if it is repeated year after year.[6] Experts agree that a combination of direct instruction of word meanings, discussions about words and word parts, and encouragement of wide reading is the best way to help students develop vocabulary.

Teaching the Words that Matter Most

Equally important to the sheer number of words students learn is the kinds of words they learn. Regardless of how many words students know upon entering school, most of them will have sufficient vocabulary for everyday tasks such as playing with peers and watching television. These are the words renowned vocabulary researcher Beck and her colleagues identify as Tier One words in their three-tier model.[7] But to do well in school, they must know the language of school—the words they find in books, from novels to textbooks, in online articles, and on tests. School, or academic, language—Beck's Tier Two words—also includes general instructional language, such as *summarize* and *develop,* as well as the words used in outside reading and those that are liable to have utility across various fields of study. Tier Two words are likely to have the most direct impact on students' academic lives. In addition to this general academic language, students also need content-area specific language. These are Tier Three words, and they are taught most effectively within the context of a content area, such as science or social studies. As Stahl and Nagy say, "The language of conversation, and of television, simply is not adequate preparation for the language that students will encounter in their texts."[8]

Wordly Wise 3000 is designed to teach primarily Tier Two words with a healthy smattering of Tier Three words. In the fourth edition of *Wordly Wise 3000,* specific Tier Two words that occur most frequently across academic disciplines are given special attention, as are words with roots and affixes that are common in academic texts.

The *Wordly Wise 3000* Approach to Vocabulary Instruction

What is the best way to teach students to acquire words? Best practice indicates that effective vocabulary instruction should include:

- both definitional and contextual information about a word;

- multiple exposures to the word in different contexts;

- encouragement of students' active participation in their own word learning.[9]

Traditionally, vocabulary instruction has not been instruction at all, but has focused on having students look up words in a dictionary and memorizing them. This approach rarely leads to students truly understanding word meanings or retaining them. Students who simply memorize definitions frequently have trouble applying the information and often make mistakes about the meanings.[10]

Word meaning is highly contextual, and word knowledge is built incrementally. To know a word, students need to encounter it multiple times, in several contexts. An approach that includes definitions as well as exposure to words in context generates a full and flexible knowledge of word meanings. When students are given several sentences in which a word is used in different ways, they begin to see how a word's meaning can change and shift depending on its context.

For example, consider the word *got* as it appears in the following sentences:

> *Joseph got a cold.*
>
> *Joseph got rich.*
>
> *Joseph got a note from Krishna.*
>
> *Krishna got in trouble.*

Although in most of these examples, *got* conveys the idea of receiving, the meaning is slightly different in each one. Based on the concept that students need to see words in different contexts to learn them, each lesson provides definitions of the vocabulary words—some with multiple meanings—and several examples of their use in context, as well as exercises in which they can be applied.

Context helps students make connections between and among words, and these connections can deepen understanding. For example, students may have difficulty understanding the definition of the word *symbol* (Book 4,

Lesson 15), because it is an abstract concept that is difficult to define. However, after reading the lesson's Vocabulary in Context passage about the bald eagle, America's symbol, students understand the word's meaning in a much more concrete way. Students begin to develop a deeper knowledge of the word as they think about what the bald eagle symbolizes and consider other symbols they are familiar with.

Students may think they know the meanings of words when they only have a partial understanding. The more exposure students have to a word in a variety of contexts, the more likely it is that they will know it well and deeply. Each lesson in *Wordly Wise 3000* asks students to use and apply several of the lesson's words in different and increasingly sophisticated contexts as they complete the exercises.

Active Application of Word Knowledge

Students remember words better when they connect new meanings to knowledge they already have and use words to express their ideas. This type of active processing occurs when students work with words in some of the following ways: producing antonyms and synonyms; rewriting definitions; identifying examples and non-examples of the word; using more than one new word in a sentence; creating sentences that contain the word.[11]

Each activity in *Wordly Wise 3000* reinforces definitional or contextual information about the word and gives students a chance to own the word for themselves. Activities that require students to apply word knowledge develop a richer, deeper and more flexible knowledge of words.

Practice Testing and Distributed Practice

Wordly Wise 3000 has partnered with Quizlet to provide complete study sets and games for every lesson to help your students challenge themselves and test their memories of words and meanings. Quizlet's learning application provides an entertaining and engaging twist on an incredibly effective learning strategy—practice testing. Research shows that calling information to mind, retrieving it from memory, strengthens the ability to recall that information long term.[12]

When students use Quizlet to study and play *Wordly Wise 3000* vocabulary games in at least two sessions at different times over the course of a week, they also use another learning strategy that is proven to be effective: distributed practice. Studying in intervals over time rather than all at once helps students retain information longer.[13] While students are playing games and having fun, they are embedding each word and meaning more deeply in their long-term memory.

Wordly Wise 3000: A Flexible Vocabulary Solution

Wordly Wise 3000 is designed for maximum flexibility. The lessons can be used in different settings and at different frequencies. Teachers have told us they use the program in several ways:

- as in-class activities
- as homework
- as independent study
- as preparation for standardized tests

In general, we recommend more in-class direct instruction at the primary grades, more student-centered guidance and coaching as students proceed through the upper elementary grades and middle school, and more independent work in high school. Of course, the way you use *Wordly Wise 3000* depends entirely on the needs of your students and on your goals as an educator.

Placing Students in *Wordly Wise 3000*

We recommend that, in general, you begin students in the *Wordly Wise 3000* book corresponding with their nominal grade level. The Vocabulary in Context reading passages included in each lesson are written in accordance with The Lexile Framework® for Reading to reach measures recommended by rigorous state and national standards.

Teachers tell us that the reading passages can present challenges to students who require support in reading. For this reason, we now include secondary passages in each Teacher's Resource Book. These secondary passages present the same rich content and context as the original passages, but are written at a lower Lexile® measure. The only substantive difference between a primary and secondary passage is the relative readability of the sentences.

Providing students with these secondary passages allows students who require support in reading to successfully learn and utilize the same grade-level vocabulary as their peers.

See the chart below for the Lexile ranges of Vocabulary in Context passages in *Wordly Wise 3000*. If you do not know your students' Lexile measures, you may want to visit the MetaMetrics®, Inc. website: www.MetaMetricsInc.com.

Level	Primary Passage Lexile Range	Secondary Passage Lexile Range
2	420L–650L	190L–530L
3	520L–820L	420L–650L
4	740L–940L	520L–820L
5	830L–1010L	740L–940L
6	925L–1070L	830L–1010L
7	970L–1120L	925L–1070L
8	1010L–1185L	970L–1120L
9	1050L–1260L	1010L–1185L
10	1080L–1335L	1050L–1260L
11	1185L–1385L	1080L–1335L
12	1185L–1385L	1080L–1335L

Note: It is also possible to teach different levels of *Wordly Wise 3000* within the same classroom to differentiate instruction for individual students or groups, using their Lexile measures as a guideline.

Worldly Wise 3000 Overview and Pacing Guide

Educators require instructional solutions that are adaptable to their individual teaching needs and the needs of their students. Many teachers have limited in-class time to devote exclusively to vocabulary and may spend the majority of that time working with students who require support. Regardless of how much in-class time you have for direct vocabulary instruction, you can use *Wordly Wise 3000* to build your students' vocabulary skills.

The following pacing guide shows three options for weekly teaching plans, but your unique classroom requirements and your students' needs should ultimately guide you in pacing instruction as you see fit.

In-class Instructional Minutes: 30–40 minutes, once a week				
Day 1	**Day 2**	**Day 3**	**Day 4**	**Day 5**
Students complete the Rate Your Word Knowledge worksheet. Introduce the word list with turn-and-talk activities. Homework: Students use the lesson's accompanying study set on Quizlet.	Homework: Students complete practice activities A, B, C, and D.	Homework: Students read the Vocabulary in Context passage and answer the comprehension questions.	Homework: Students complete the Vocabulary Extension activity. Students use the lesson's accompanying study set on Quizlet to prepare for the Lesson Test.	Students take the Lesson Test.

In-class Instructional Minutes: 15 minutes, 3 times a week

Day 1	Day 2	Day 3	Day 4	Day 5
Students complete the Rate Your Word Knowledge worksheet. Introduce the word list with turn-and-talk activities. Students complete practice activity A in class. Homework: Students complete the remaining practice activities.	Homework: Students use the lesson's accompanying study set on Quizlet.	Review answers to practice activities A, B, C, and D. Students read the Vocabulary in Context passage and answer the comprehension questions. Homework: Students use the lesson's accompanying study set on Quizlet.	Homework: Students use the lesson's accompanying study set on Quizlet to prepare for the Lesson Test.	Students complete the Vocabulary Extension activity. Students take the Lesson Test.

In-class Instructional Minutes: 10 minutes, 5 times a week

Day 1	Day 2	Day 3	Day 4	Day 5
Introduce the word list with turn-and-talk activities. Students complete practice activities A and B. Homework: Students use the lesson's accompanying study set on Quizlet.	Students complete practice activities C and D. Review answers to practice activities A, B, C, and D. Homework: Students use the lesson's accompanying study set on Quizlet.	Students read the Vocabulary in Context passage and answer the comprehension questions. Homework: Students use the lesson's accompanying study set on Quizlet.	Review answers to the comprehension questions. Students complete the Vocabulary Extension activity. Homework: Students use the lesson's accompanying study set on Quizlet to prepare for the Lesson Test.	Students take the Lesson Test.

Endnotes

[1] Adams, 180.

[2] Southwest Educational Development Laboratory, 14; Stahl, 3.

[3] Biemiller, 24.

[4] Biemiller, 28.

[5] Stahl, 9; Texas Education Agency, 5–6.

[6] Stahl, 30.

[7] Beck et al., 8.

[8] Stahl and Nagy, 41.

[9] Stahl, 30; Texas Education Agency, 20.

[10] Texas Education Agency, 8.

[11] Stahl, 31–32; Texas Education Agency, 21–23.

[12] Dunlosky et al., 29–35.

[13] Dunlosky et al., 35–40.

Bibliography

Adams, M. J. (2009). The challenge of advanced texts: The interdependence of reading and learning. In *Reading more, reading better: Are American students reading enough of the right stuff?* (pp. 163–189). New York, NY: Guilford Press.

Beck, I. A., McKeown, M. G., & Kucan, L. (2002). *Bringing words to life: Robust vocabulary instruction.* New York, NY: Guilford Press.

Biemiller, A. (2001). Teaching vocabulary: Early, direct, and sequential. *American Educator, 25*(1), 24–28, 47.

Common Core State Standards Initiative. (2010). *Common Core State Standards for English language arts & literacy in history/social studies, science, and technical subjects.* Washington, DC: National Governors Association Center for Best Practices and the Council of Chief State School Officers.

Dale, E., & O'Rourke, J. (1986). *Vocabulary building.* Columbus, OH: Zaner-Bloser.

Dunlosky, J., Rawson, K. A., Marsh, E. J., Nathan, M. J., & Willingham, D. T. (2013). Improving students' learning with effective learning techniques. *Psychological Science in the Public Interest,*14(1), 4–58.

Kelley, J. G., Lesaux, N. K., Kleffer, M. J., & Faller, S. E. (2010). Effective academic vocabulary instruction in the urban middle school. *The Reading Teacher, 64*(1), 5–14.

Marzano, R. J., & Pickering, D. K. (2005). *Building academic vocabulary: Teacher's manual.* Alexandria, VA: Association for School Curriculum Directors.

Schwartz, R. M., & Raphael, T. (1985). Concept of definition: A key to improving students' vocabulary. *The Reading Teacher, 39*(2), 198-205.

Southwest Educational Development Laboratory. (2000). *The cognitive foundations of learning to read: A framework.* Austin, TX. Retrieved from http://www.sedl.org/reading/framework/framework.pdf

Stahl, S. A. (1999). *Vocabulary development.* Cambridge, MA: Brookline Books.

Stahl, S. A., & Nagy, W. E. (2006). *Teaching word meanings.* Mahwah, NJ: Erlbaum.

Texas Education Agency. (2000). *Promoting vocabulary development: Components of effective vocabulary instruction.* Austin, TX.

Learning Objectives

Students will . . .

- become familiar with words, definitions, and sentences that place words in context.

- interact with peers to use words and to deepen their understanding of word meanings.

Guidance

Have students practice careful reading and active listening to prepare for turn-and-talk activities, which they will perform with a partner. Read the word list aloud to, or with, students, spending additional time on unfamiliar words. Ask pairs of students to complete the turn-and-talk activities before moving on to the next word.

Practice

Monitor students as they complete the turn-and-talk activities and correct any misconceptions they may have about word meanings.

Students Requiring Support

Students who require support, and English learners in particular, benefit from conversation with peers about word meanings. If possible, pair English learners with partners who share a home language and can help clarify meaning or deepen understanding.

Word List

Robust vocabulary instruction begins with introducing students to words they may or may not be familiar with. The contextual sentences provided in the word list increase exposure to words in context and help students fully grasp meanings.

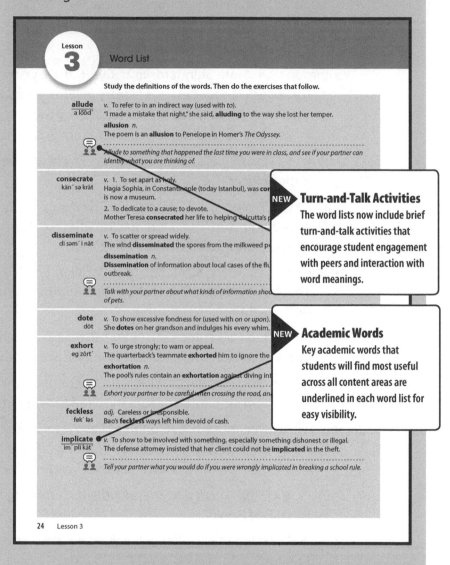

NEW ▶ Turn-and-Talk Activities
The word lists now include brief turn-and-talk activities that encourage student engagement with peers and interaction with word meanings.

NEW ▶ Academic Words
Key academic words that students will find most useful across all content areas are underlined in each word list for easy visibility.

NEW

Rate Your Word Knowledge

Before introducing the word list to students, have them complete a self-assessment of word knowledge, increasing their awareness that word knowledge is incremental and builds with each exposure to a word in context.

Use the information from these ratings to target in-class instruction as you introduce the word list, focusing most attention on the words students are least familiar with.

Learning Objectives
Students will . . .
- review words that will appear in the lesson.
- self-assess their understanding of each word's meaning.

Guidance
Explain to students that word knowledge builds gradually over time and that there are different levels to fully knowing a word. Tell students to rate their knowledge of each word honestly and accurately. Express confidence that by the time they finish the lesson, their understanding of each word's meaning will be complete.

Practice
Have students write each word from the lesson into the spaces provided and then complete the Rate Your Word Knowledge worksheet. Call on volunteers to either share the word they are least familiar with or the word they are most familiar with.

Target Instruction
Review the completed worksheets and note the words students are least familiar with. Target these words for extra attention when you introduce the lesson's word list.

Name _____ Date _____

Rate Your Word Knowledge

Write the words from Lesson _____ in the spaces provided.
Fill in the circle to rate your knowledge of each word.

1. _____
   O I've never seen this word before.
   O I've seen this word before, but I don't know what it means.
   O I think I know what this word means.
   O I know what this word means and can use it in a sentence.

2. _____
   O I've never seen this word before.
   O I've seen this word before, but I don't know what it means.
   O I think I know what this word means.
   O I know what this word means and can use it in a sentence.

3. _____
   O I've never seen this word before.
   O I've seen this word before, but I don't know what it means.
   O I think I know what this word means.
   O I know what this word means and can use it in a sentence.

4. _____
   O I've never seen this word before.
   O I've seen this word before, but I don't know what it means.
   O I think I know what this word means.
   O I know what this word means and can use it in a sentence.

5. _____
   O I've never seen this word before.
   O I've seen this word before, but I don't know what it means.
   O I think I know what this word means.
   O I know what this word means and can use it in a sentence.

6. _____
   O I've never seen this word before.
   O I've seen this word before, but I don't know what it means.
   O I think I know what this word means.
   O I know what this word means and can use it in a sentence.

7. _____
   O I've never seen this word before.
   O I've seen this word before, but I don't know what it means.
   O I think I know what this word means.
   O I know what this word means and can use it in a sentence.

© SSI • MAY BE DUPLICATED

Wordly Wise 3000 • Resource Book **27**

The Rate Your Word Knowledge worksheet is located with the Reproducible Masters.

Practice Activities

Understanding Meanings

This activity provides definitional information in sentence form, allowing students to read each sentence as either a true or false statement. First, students read sentences that define words. Then, if a sentence defines a word incorrectly, and thus is a false statement, students rewrite the sentence to express the word's correct meaning.

Learning Objectives

Students will . . .

- identify incorrect definitions.

- write sentences that define words correctly.

Guidance

Tell students that they may need to reread the word list to remind themselves of words and definitions. Model the activity by revising one incorrect sentence for students.

Practice

When students have completed the activity, review the correct answers as a class.

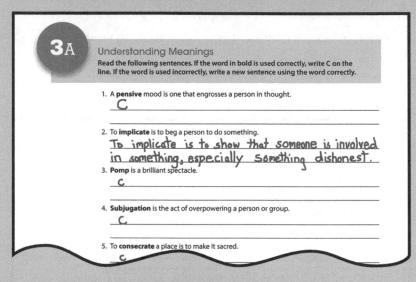

3A Understanding Meanings
Read the following sentences. If the word in bold is used correctly, write C on the line. If the word is used incorrectly, write a new sentence using the word correctly.

1. A **pensive** mood is one that engrosses a person in thought.
   C

2. To **implicate** is to beg a person to do something.
   To implicate is to show that someone is involved in something, especially something dishonest.

3. **Pomp** is a brilliant spectacle.
   C

4. **Subjugation** is the act of overpowering a person or group.
   C

5. To **consecrate** a place is to make it sacred.
   C

NEW

Determining Precise Meaning

This activity heightens awareness of context in determining word meaning. Students read a sentence in which a vocabulary word is used correctly, providing them with a specific contextual meaning for the word. Then they read two paraphrases of the sentence and select the one that accurately conveys the same contextual meaning.

Learning Objectives

Students will . . .

- determine the precise meaning of words in context.

- select sentences that accurately express precise meanings.

Guidance

Model the activity by completing one item with the class. First read the original sentence and then read the sentences with paraphrases aloud. Explain why only one of the paraphrases expresses the same meaning as the vocabulary word in the original sentence.

Practice

When students have completed the activity, review the correct answers as a class.

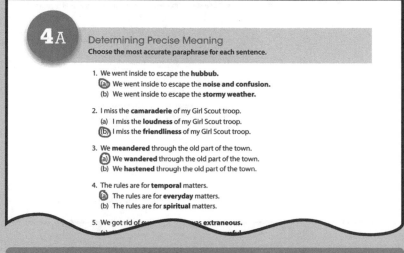

4A Determining Precise Meaning
Choose the most accurate paraphrase for each sentence.

1. We went inside to escape the **hubbub.**
   (a) We went inside to escape the **noise and confusion.**
   (b) We went inside to escape the **stormy weather.**

2. I miss the **camaraderie** of my Girl Scout troop.
   (a) I miss the **loudness** of my Girl Scout troop.
   (b) I miss the **friendliness** of my Girl Scout troop.

3. We **meandered** through the old part of the town.
   (a) We **wandered** through the old part of the town.
   (b) We **hastened** through the old part of the town.

4. The rules are for **temporal** matters.
   (a) The rules are for **everyday** matters.
   (b) The rules are for **spiritual** matters.

5. We got rid of ~~~~~~~~~~ was **extraneous.**

The Student Book Answer Key is located with the Answer Keys.

Using Words

This activity strengthens independent vocabulary acquisition skills by raising awareness of context and its role in determining meaning. Students decide whether a specific vocabulary word fits into each of three fill-in-the-blank sentences. Students use their knowledge of the word's meaning to assess whether or not it should be placed into a sentence.

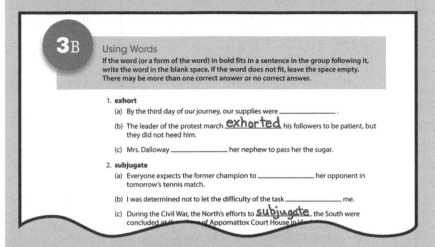

NEW ## Understanding Word Relationships

This activity deeply embeds vocabulary words in students' memory by requiring them to relate new words with words they already know. Linking new words with familiar words helps students own new terms and retain them better. This activity also strengthens their understanding of word relationships.

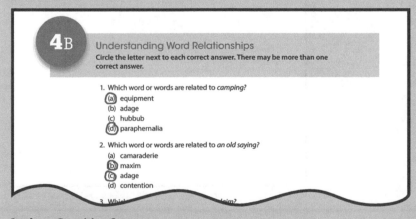

Students Requiring Support

This activity supports students with limited vocabulary, as they relate new academic vocabulary words with words they may use in everyday spoken language. To provide more intensive support for English learners, pair these students with partners who share a home language and direct them to complete this activity collaboratively.

Learning Objectives

Students will . . .

- recall meanings of words.
- read fill-in-the-blank sentences to determine whether context clues confirm and support the meanings of words.
- use words to correctly complete sentences.

Guidance

Tell students that word meaning is highly contextual; the other words in a sentence provide information about meaning and even shape a word's meaning. Explain that their task is to determine whether the given vocabulary word fits within a specific sentence. Complete one item with the class, explaining that if a word does not fit into a sentence, the space provided should be left blank.

Practice

When students have completed the activity, review the correct answers as a class.

. . . .

Learning Objectives

Students will . . .

- consider word relationships.
- connect new words with familiar words to enhance understanding of word relationships.

Guidance

Complete the first item with students. Stress the importance of selecting words that have the strongest and most obvious connections. Some students may be able to creatively connect words that don't have a readily apparent relationship. Student focus should be directed instead on selecting words with clear connections.

Practice

After students have completed the activity, call on volunteers to share their thinking and explain why they selected the words they did.

Practice Activities continued

Word Study

The Word Study activities extend and deepen vocabulary knowledge in a variety of ways. Students may identify synonyms and antonyms, explore how prefixes and suffixes change word meanings and parts of speech, learn about Latin and Greek roots, or complete analogies.

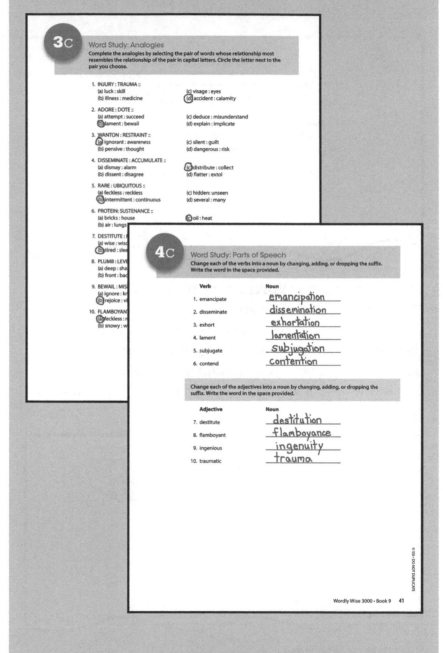

Learning Objectives

Students will . . .

- explore grammar concepts, meaningful word parts, Greek and Latin roots, and analogies.

- complete activities that deepen and extend word knowledge.

Guidance

Explain to students that Word Study activities vary. Each time students encounter a new and different type of Word Study activity, complete one item with the class to model the activity, and then have students complete the rest of the items independently.

Practice

Once students have completed the activity, have them share their responses with a partner and explain their reasoning for each response.

Images of Words

This activity allows students to practice applying word meanings in a more sophisticated way. Students select any or all of the sentences that illustrate the meaning of a given vocabulary word.

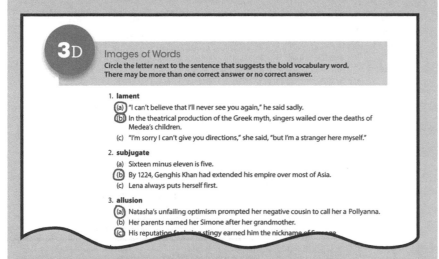

3D **Images of Words**
Circle the letter next to the sentence that suggests the bold vocabulary word. There may be more than one correct answer or no correct answer.

1. **lament**
   (a) "I can't believe that I'll never see you again," he said sadly.
   (b) In the theatrical production of the Greek myth, singers wailed over the deaths of Medea's children.
   (c) "I'm sorry I can't give you directions," she said, "but I'm a stranger here myself."

2. **subjugate**
   (a) Sixteen minus eleven is five.
   (b) By 1224, Genghis Khan had extended his empire over most of Asia.
   (c) Lena always puts herself first.

3. **allusion**
   (a) Natasha's unfailing optimism prompted her negative cousin to call her a Pollyanna.
   (b) Her parents named her Simone after her grandmother.
   (c) His reputation for being stingy earned him the nickname of Scrooge.

NEW ▶

Understanding Contextual Meanings

This activity exposes students to examples of words being used correctly in a variety of contexts and provides students with the opportunity to apply word knowledge by writing their own original sentences. Students read contextual sentences to determine whether a word is used correctly. If a word is used incorrectly, students write their own sentence, using the word correctly.

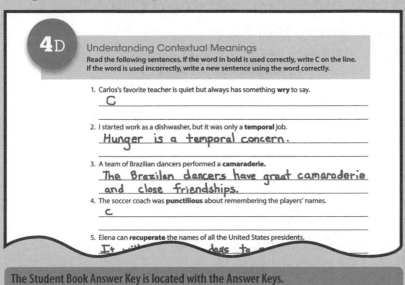

4D **Understanding Contextual Meanings**
Read the following sentences. If the word in bold is used correctly, write C on the line. If the word is used incorrectly, write a new sentence using the word correctly.

1. Carlos's favorite teacher is quiet but always has something **wry** to say.
   C

2. I started work as a dishwasher, but it was only a **temporal** job.
   Hunger is a temporal concern.

3. A team of Brazilian dancers performed a **camaraderie**.
   The Brazilan dancers have great camaraderie and close friendships.

4. The soccer coach was **punctilious** about remembering the players' names.
   C

5. Elena can **recuperate** the names of all the United States presidents.
   It will _____ days to _____

The Student Book Answer Key is located with the Answer Keys.

Learning Objectives
Students will . . .
- recall meanings of words.
- identify sentences that illustrate meanings of words.

Guidance
Model the activity by completing one item with the class, explaining why each sentence does or does not suggest the meaning of the given word. Tell students to read sentences carefully and to review the word list as needed while they complete the activity.

Practice
When students have completed the activity, call on volunteers to share their responses and explain how they eliminated incorrect answers.

· ·

Learning Objectives
Students will . . .
- identify correct and incorrect uses of words in sentences.
- apply word knowledge to create new, correct sentences using words.

Guidance
Tell students that in some sentences in the activity, the vocabulary word in bold is not used correctly. Their first task is to identify sentences that are incorrect. Then students will write new, correct sentences using the vocabulary words from those sentences. Explain that they may either create original sentences or model their new sentences on the ones they are replacing.

Practice
When students have completed the activity, call on volunteers to read aloud a sentence they have created.

Learning Objectives

Students will . . .

- read original passages that contain vocabulary words in context.
- answer open-response comprehension questions.
- demonstrate comprehension of the text and mastery of the words they have learned.

Guidance

Assign students either the primary passage in the Student Books, or the secondary passage in the Teacher's Resource Book. Depending on your students' needs, you may read the passage aloud or have a student read aloud as the class listens and follows along silently. Students will need to demonstrate their understanding of word meanings in context to answer the comprehension questions that follow. Remind students to follow directions and use complete sentences in their responses, including a vocabulary word if one is not used in the question.

Practice

Pair students with partners to discuss the passage and share their responses to the questions that follow.

. . . .

Learning Objectives

Students will . . .

- read about word families and learn about roots, prefixes, and suffixes.
- read about word origins to learn about the history of words.

Guidance

Tell students that reading the Fun & Fascinating Facts helps them expand and deepen their vocabulary knowledge beyond the words they are learning in the lessons.

Practice

Have students read the Fun & Fascinating Facts silently, and then share what they find most interesting with a partner.

Reading Vocabulary in Context

Vocabulary in Context

Students read an original passage that incorporates all of the vocabulary words from the lesson. The vocabulary words are integral to the understanding of the text and thus contribute to students' comprehension rather than distracting them from the content.

3E Vocabulary in Context
Read the passage.

Chile's First Lady of Letters

By order of the government, the country went into three days of mourning. All schools and official buildings were closed. Flags were lowered to half-mast. Was the nation **lamenting** the passing of a president or a famous general? No. The person whose death was being marked with such **pomp** was a poet. The country was Chile, the year was 1957, and the poet was Gabriela Mistral, born Lucila Godoy Alcayaga.

Lucila grew up in Chile's Valley of Elqui, a place she **alludes** to frequently in her poems as an earthly paradise of vineyards, fig orchards, and green hills. Her father **doted** on his child, making a garden for Lucila and listening with delight as she talked to the flowers, birds, and insects. But his **feckless** ways and frequent absences caused quarrels between Lucila's parents. When the little girl was three, her father disappeared from her life forever. Friends remembered her as a solitary child whose **pensive** ways cut her off from companionship. She compensated for this by creating a rich interior world for herself. By the age of eleven, she was writing her first poems.

| disseminate |
| dote |
| exhort |
| feckless |
| implicate |
| lament |
| monetary |
| pensive |
| pomp |
| stilted |
| subjugate |
| trauma |
| wanton |

▶ Answer each question with a sentence. If a question does not contain a word from the lesson, use one in your answer. Use each word only once.

1. What contradiction do you see in the way Mistral's father treated her?
   He doted on her, and then he abandoned her.

2. How did the **traumas** of Mistral's childhood and early adulthood influence the direction of her life?
   She consecrated her life to teaching and writing poetry.

3. Why did Mistral's poems seem revolutionary at the time she wrote them?
   Her tender, wistful writing contrasted with the stilted language that was common then.

Studying Word Parts and Origins

Fun & Fascinating Facts

At the end of each lesson, students read interesting facts related to word origins and word families.

Fun & Fascinating **FACTS**

- The Latin word *verus,* meaning "true," forms the root of several English words. To question the *veracity* of a statement is to question its truthfulness. When one speaks of "eternal *verities,*" one is referring to truths that continue to be true for all time. A *verdict* is a decision, especially one by a jury as to guilt or innocence, that is believed to be true. To *verify* something is to establish that it is true. Finally, to **aver** something is to declare it firmly, believing strongly in its truth.

- The Latin *vox* means "voice" and is combined with the Latin word *ferre,* "to carry," to form **vociferous.** Because a *vociferous* speech is one made in a loud voice, it carries for some distance.

NEW

Secondary Vocabulary in Context Passage

The Vocabulary in Context passage included in the Student Book is intended for on-level students who do not require reading support. A secondary passage is available in the Teacher's Resource Book as a differentiation resource for students who require support. It is written at a lower Lexile® than the passage in the Student Books.

While the Lexile measure differs, the content and topic of the passage does not. Students who use the secondary passage are able to answer the same open-response questions as peers.

3E Vocabulary in Context
Read the passage.

Chile's First Lady of Letters

Chile declared three days of mourning. Schools and official buildings closed. Flags were at half-mast. Was the nation **lamenting** a president's passing? No, the person whose death was being marked with such **pomp** was a poet. The year was 1957, and the poet was Gabriela Mistral, born Lucila Alcayaga.

Lucila grew up in Chile's Valley of Elqui, a place she **alludes** to in her poems as a paradise of vineyards, orchards, and hills. Her father **doted** on her, making a garden for Lucila and listening as she talked to flowers, birds, and insects.

Lesson Review Exercises

One option for students who require additional support in writing is assigning the Lesson Review exercises as an alternative to answering the open-response questions that follow the passage; these phrase cloze exercises are less writing-intensive, yet they assess the same understanding of words in context.

Name _____ Date _____

Lesson (3) Review Exercise

1. Gabriela Mistral grew up in Chile's fertile Valley of Elqui. In her poems she makes frequent **allusions** to its beautiful vineyards and orchards.

2. The loss of her father affected the young girl greatly. At the age of three, she went from being **doted** on by him to feeling abandoned.

3. Her first experience of love was not a happy one. She fell in love with a(n) **feckless** young man who was guilty of criminal behavior.

4. The man killed himself after a crime he committed was discovered. His death had a(n) **traumatic** effect on the young woman.

ting the pen name ... significant event f... arked a

Secondary passages and Lesson Review exercises are located with the Reproducible Masters.

Applying Vocabulary Knowledge

Learning Objectives

Students will . . .

- read more about one key word from the lesson.

- view an illustration that clarifies the word's meaning.

- use the word in discussion with peers.

- write notes or draw a symbol or picture representing the word.

- write about the word in response to a prompt.

Guidance

Depending on your class needs, you may want to read the information about the word aloud, and point out the illustration to discuss how it clarifies the word's meaning. Read the instructions and prompt aloud.

Practice

Pair students with partners or assign them to groups. Give students two minutes for discussion and then three minutes to write. When time is up, call on groups or pairs of students to share what they have written.

NEW ▶ Vocabulary Extension

Key words have been selected from each lesson that deserve extra attention. Newly developed activities have students apply their word knowledge using these key words. Students engage in collaborative discussion with peers and complete a brief writing activity. Students also write notes or draw pictures to clarify word meanings for themselves.

Most of the words chosen for Vocabulary Extension activities are high-frequency general academic words that are applicable across all content areas. Some words were chosen because they contained roots and/or affixes that are commonly found in academic texts.

Studying these words and their large word families extends students' vocabulary knowledge beyond the words and definitions in *Wordly Wise 3000*.

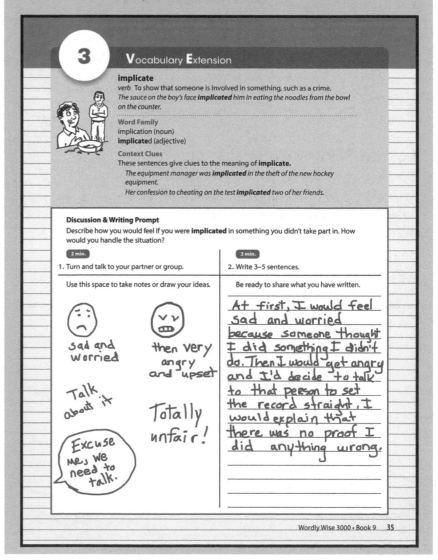

Supporting Diverse Learners

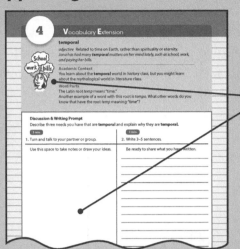

Visual Support
Each Vocabulary Extension word is illustrated to make its meaning more accessible to all students. English learners will especially benefit from visual support to reinforce meaning.

Students also have space to draw their own visual representations of words.

Guidance for Differentiating Instruction

The Vocabulary Extension activities provide students with the opportunity to write, draw, respond to questions, discuss words and meanings, and interact with their peers.

Each Vocabulary Extension activity comes with a page of suggestions to guide you in differentiating these activities to diverse learners so that every student can benefit, including English learners, students who require reading support, students who require writing support, and students who thrive on additional academic challenge.

LESSON 3: implicate

Differentiation Options for the Vocabulary Extension

The following suggestions are provided to help you differentiate instruction to student groups.

Support Strategies

1) Once students are in groups or pairs, ask them to use their own words to tell you what they think **implicate** means.

2) Have partners share stories about a time that they or someone they know was **implicated** in the breaking of a rule. Was the **implication** valid? Why or why not?

3) Read the prompt aloud and give students extra time to discuss before they write, if needed.

4) To provide extra scaffolding for students who struggle with writing, tell students to copy the following sentence starters in the writing space. Then have them complete each sentence in their own words.

• If I were implicated for something I didn't do, I would feel _____ .
(Sample response: *shocked and angry*)

• I would handle the situation by _____ .
(Sample response: *defending myself with evidence*)

EL Strategies

Use any of the activities from Support Strategies or those below to help English learners understand and practice the new vocabulary word.

1) Review the context sentence under the definition on the Vocabulary Extension page. Then have students look at the image of a boy being **implicated** on the Vocabulary Extension page. Ask students to use available language (single words, phrases, or si_____ _____ ribe the image. P_____ _____ions,

---

Guidance for differentiating Vocabulary Extension activities is located in the Vocabulary Extensions section.

Reviewing the Lesson

Review Puzzle and Lesson Review Exercises

A crossword or hidden-message puzzle following every fourth lesson provides an entertaining and challenging review. The Lesson Review exercises give students further practice with utilizing context clues to select words that correctly complete each fill-in-the-blank sentence.

Learning Objectives

Students will . . .

- retrieve words from memory.
- complete activities that help them review words and meanings.

Guidance

Tell students that the crossword and hidden-message puzzles are a fun way for them to review words and meanings. Assign Lesson Review exercises to help students review words and give them extra practice with using context clues.

Practice

Have students do the puzzle and/or the Lesson Review exercises individually or in groups. Discuss the answers as a group.

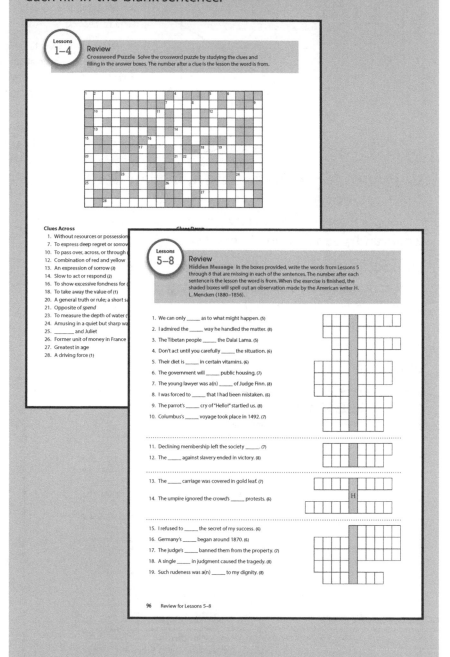

The answer keys for the Review Puzzles and Lesson Review exercises are located with the Answer Keys.

Assessing Word Knowledge

Lesson, Midterm, and Final Tests

Lesson Tests are designed to assess students' comprehensive understanding of every vocabulary word, including every word form and meaning listed in the word list. The Lesson, Midterm, and Final Tests present words from the lessons in original passages and include questions that refer to the specific meanings of these words in context. Not only does this provide yet another exposure to words in different contexts, building incremental word knowledge, but it also prepares students for similar passage-based questions in standardized state and national assessments.

Learning Objectives

Students will . . .

- reinforce their long-term retention of words as they retrieve words and meanings from memory.

- build awareness of growing word knowledge.

Guidance

Administer the Lesson Test after each week's lesson. When students have completed the test, you may choose to review answers as a class or provide feedback individually by marking the tests and returning them to students. Administer the Midterm Test after Lesson 10 and the Final Test after Lesson 20.

Multiple versions of the Midterm and Final Tests are provided. The multiple versions are all comparable and assess similar content.

NEW **Passage-based Questions**

The Lesson Tests now include updated standardized test preview/practice items that place vocabulary words in context and ask students to determine meaning based on that context.

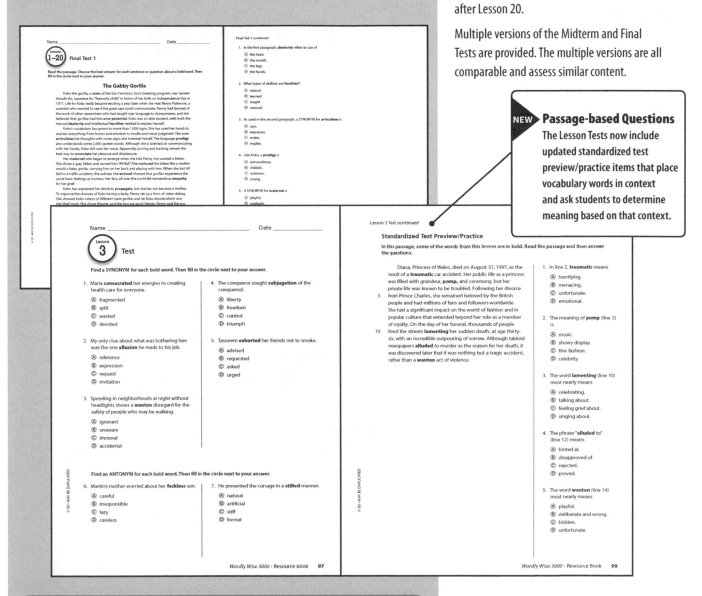

Lesson, Midterm, and Final Tests are located with the Reproducible Masters. Test answer keys are located in the Answer Keys section.

Learning Objectives

Students will . . .

- use *Wordly Wise 3000* study sets to practice learning words and definitions in an ad-free environment.
- test themselves on their knowledge.
- play motivating games to reinforce long-term retention of words.

Guidance

Encourage students to participate in a minimum of two sessions of Quizlet flashcard study, game play, or practice testing per week, either in class or at home. Explain that research shows that the more frequently students revisit words from a lesson and practice retrieving the words from memory, the longer they will retain word knowledge.

Practice

Students can choose from seven available study and game modes (Flashcards, Learn, Spell, Test, Match, Gravity, and Live) to practice and master *Wordly Wise 3000* vocabulary. Quizlet provides an entertaining twist on practice testing, an incredibly effective learning strategy.

Wordly Wise 3000 Partners with Quizlet!

Quizlet is a fun and engaging learning application that can be used anytime, providing additional value for both teachers and students. On the Quizlet platform, students can practice and master their vocabulary with interactive games and study activities. All official *Wordly Wise 3000* study sets are pre-loaded into Quizlet, saving valuable prep time for teachers.

Quizlet's games and study activities increase students' exposure to words and meanings, build long-term retention, and encourage interactive play with *Wordly Wise 3000* words.

Quizlet

Practice Tests on Quizlet.com

Students may practice for lesson, cumulative, midterm, or final tests by using any of the *Wordly Wise 3000* resources and games on Quizlet.com. Research shows that students benefit most when they practice testing on at least two separate occasions, rather than all at once. To maximize the benefits of using Quizlet, assign students two or more sessions of game play and study, spaced apart.

Students Requiring Support

Emphasize the educational goal of playing vocabulary games. Ensure students understand that it is word knowledge that matters, not speed. Explain that students may choose to use Quizlet's flashcards, learn, spell, or test modes to remove time pressure entirely. Students can customize the difficulty of their gaming sessions by slowing down or speeding up the pace of the game. The audio option to hear words and definitions read aloud may also be slowed down.

Student Access to official *Wordly Wise 3000* content on Quizlet

Each Student Book includes a 12-month subscription for students to access *Wordly Wise 3000* study sets on Quizlet. Your students will find unique Quizlet access codes and directions on how to use Quizlet on the inside front covers of their *Wordly Wise 3000* Student Books. These directions are also provided to the right.

1. Go to: www.quizlet.com/p/wordlywise3000.
2. Click the title of your workbook and then click the lesson you are studying.
3. Create a username and password.
4. Enter the access code located on the inside front cover of your workbook.
5. Study with Quizlet's fun learning activities and games, compete for high scores, and track your own progress.

Teacher Access to official *Wordly Wise 3000* content on Quizlet

Each Teacher Classroom Set includes an upgraded 12-month Quizlet Teacher subscription providing access to pre-loaded, official *Wordly Wise 3000* study sets and analytics. The Quizlet Teacher subscription allows you to view at-a-glance all student activity within Quizlet and can be sorted by day, week, or year. This information can be used to determine which words or meanings students are struggling with and to help use class time wisely to reinforce those words. The upgraded subscription also includes Quizlet Live, where students can play collaborative team games to enhance communication, focus, and learning.

How to activate your Quizlet Teacher upgrade and access official *Wordly Wise 3000* content:

1. Locate your Teacher subscription card and enter the unique URL.
2. Sign up for a Quizlet account (or log into your existing Quizlet account).
3. While signing up, specify that you are a teacher.
4. On the next page, click "Activate Quizlet Teacher" to add your upgrade to your account.
5. Follow the student instructions above to access the *Wordly Wise 3000* content, but use the unique teacher access code located on the Teacher subscription card.

Get the most out of your Quizlet Teacher upgrade:

1. Create a Quizlet class and add the *Wordly Wise 3000* study sets to it; invite your students to the class to give them easy access to this material.
2. As students study, view their activity and progress with Quizlet's Class Progress feature.
3. For more detailed instructions and information about your new upgrade, go here: www.quizlet.com/help/how-teachers-can-use-quizlet.

WORDLY WISE i3000™

NEW! Engaging, Direct Academic Vocabulary Instruction

Grades 2–12

Wordly Wise i3000 is a subscription-based web application that provides engaging, direct academic vocabulary instruction to develop the critical link between vocabulary and reading comprehension. The robust activities, social sharing and interaction, and differentiated instruction within our cutting-edge digital application allow the flexibility to meet the needs of today's varying student populations— empowering students to have successful encounters with grade-level vocabulary and practice.

Wordly Wise i3000 Benefits:

- Practice activities and assessments are automatically scored and reported in real-time.

- Teachers have immediate insight into student learning and progress throughout the program.

- Access is provided to Quizlet online study tools and games.

- All program resources are located in one convenient place.

More Activities and More Engagement to Reach More Students:

More Activities – New engaging, research-based activities align with current state and national standards and assessments. All practice activities are self-paced, provide instant feedback, and are automatically scored, providing value to both students and teachers.

More Engagement – Social sharing and interaction allows students to apply and extend their learning while also providing motivation, engagement, and additional support.

Reach More Students – Differentiated reading passages allow teachers to work with below-grade-level students to practice on-grade-level vocabulary. For each lesson, teachers seamlessly assign the appropriate on-grade- or below-grade-level reading passage to each student.

Wordly Wise 3000
Partners with Quizlet

Students can practice and master their vocabulary with Quizlet, a fun and engaging learning application that can be used anywhere at any time, adding value for both teachers and students. These study and game activities offer additional reinforcement of vocabulary words.

To learn more, visit
epsbooks.com/WW3000

Vocabulary Extensions

Directions

1) Introduce the activity:

- Introduce the activity by explaining to your students that this page helps them learn even more about one of the *Wordly Wise 3000* words.

- You may choose to read aloud the top part of the page and to point out the illustration, or direct students to read it silently.

2) Explain the prompt/assignment:

- Tell students they will read and discuss the prompt with one another (in groups or in pairs) before independently writing a response to it.

3) Assign students to groups or partners:

- Assign students to groups or partners, depending on your class needs and your plans to differentiate the activity. Once students are in groups or pairs, have them begin discussion.

4) Keep track of time:

- This is a short activity, so it is important to keep track of time. When discussion time is over, have students work independently to respond to the prompt. After writing time is over, call on a few students to share their responses.

Vocabulary Extensions

Differentiation Options for the Vocabulary Extension

The following suggestions are provided to help you differentiate instruction to student groups.

Support Strategies

1) Once students are in groups or pairs, ask them to use their own words to tell you what they think **reiterate** means.

2) Read the definition on the Vocabulary Extension page. Then read the sentence under Academic Context. Have students rephrase the sentence without using the word **reiterate.** Clear up any misconceptions students may have.

3) Read the prompt aloud and give students extra time to discuss before they write, if needed.

4) To provide extra scaffolding for students who struggle with writing, tell students to copy the following sentence starters in the writing space. Then have them complete each sentence in their own words.

   • I once had to reiterate something when _____ .
   (Sample response: *I was giving directions to my house*)

   • It was important that my meaning was clear because _____ .
   (Sample response: *I didn't want my friends to get lost*)

EL Strategies

Use any of the activities from Support Strategies or those below to help English learners understand and practice the new vocabulary word.

1) Use a combination of gestures and simple language to illustrate the meaning of the word **reiterate.**

2) Once students are in groups or pairs, ask them to use available language (single words, phrases, or simple sentences) to describe the meaning of **reiterate** to a partner. If necessary to help students develop oral language, model and prompt sentences, such as:

   • To **reiterate** means "to repeat."

3) If it applies to students in your group, point out the Spanish cognate for **reiterate:** *reiterar.* Allow EL students to use their native language to discuss the meaning of the word with one another.

4) Read the prompt aloud and give students extra time to discuss before they write, if needed.

5) To provide extra scaffolding for students who struggle with writing, tell students to copy the following sentence starters in the writing space. Then have them complete each sentence in their own words.

- I reiterated something when _____ .
  (Sample response: *I was giving directions to my house*)

- It was important to be clear because _____ .
  (Sample response: *I didn't want my friends to get lost*)

Enrichment Strategies

Challenge students to write a poem using many words that have the prefix *re-*, meaning "again." Tell students to be mindful that *re-* can also mean "back." Invite volunteers to share their poems with the group.

LESSON 2: utilitarian

Differentiation Options for the Vocabulary Extension

The following suggestions are provided to help you differentiate instruction to student groups.

Support Strategies

1) Once students are in groups or pairs, ask them to use their own words to tell you what they think **utilitarian** means.

2) Review the contextual sentence under the definition on the Vocabulary Extension page. Then have students look at the image of **utilitarian** boots on the Vocabulary Extension page. Ask partners to discuss the image and how the illustrated item could be considered **utilitarian.**

3) Read the Word Parts section on the Vocabulary Extension page. Have students give other examples of words with the root *util*. If they need help, offer suggestions such as *utilize*. Then help students connect the meaning of the word with the meaning of its root, "useful."

4) Read the prompt aloud and give students extra time to discuss before they write, if needed.

5) To provide extra scaffolding for students who struggle with writing, tell students to copy the following sentence starter in the writing space. Then have them complete the sentence in their own words.

- One example of a utilitarian item is _____ .
  (Sample response: *a stepstool*)

EL Strategies

Use any of the activities from Support Strategies or those below to help English learners understand and practice the new vocabulary word.

1) Review the contextual sentence under the definition on the Vocabulary Extension page. Then have students look at the image of **utilitarian** boots on the Vocabulary Extension page. Ask questions about the image. Is the illustrated item useful? Does it look beautiful? Use their responses to introduce the meaning of **utilitarian.**

2) Have students use available language (single words, phrases, or simple sentences) to define **utilitarian.** If necessary to help students develop oral language, model and prompt sentences, such as:

• **Utilitarian** means "practical."
• Duct tape is a **utilitarian** tool.

3) Read the prompt aloud and give students extra time to discuss before they write, if needed.

4) To provide extra scaffolding for students who struggle with writing, tell students to copy the following sentence starter in the writing space. Then have them complete the sentence in their own words.

• One example of a utilitarian item is _____ .
(Sample response: *a stepstool*)

Enrichment Strategies

Have students identify two more words with the root *util,* define them, and use them in a contextual sentence.

LESSON 3: inestimable

Differentiation Options for the Vocabulary Extension

The following suggestions are provided to help you differentiate instruction to student groups.

Support Strategies

1) Once students are in groups or pairs, ask them to use their own words to tell you what they think **inestimable** means. If necessary, break down the word into parts and have students define each part. For example: **inestimable** = *in* + *estimate* + *able* ("cannot be estimated").

2) Review the contextual sentence under the definition on the Vocabulary Extension page. Then have students look at the image of an **inestimable** amount of sand grains on the Vocabulary Extension page. Ask students to discuss why the image is a good example of **inestimable.**

3) Have students brainstorm examples of things that are **inestimable**. If they need ideas, suggest the number of stars in the universe.

4) Read the prompt aloud and give students extra time to discuss before they write, if needed.

5) To provide extra scaffolding for students who struggle with writing, tell students to copy the following sentence starter in the writing space. Then have them complete the sentence in their own words.

• A person who has made inestimable contributions to the country is
_____ . (Sample response: *Rosa Parks*)

EL Strategies

Use any of the activities from Support Strategies or those below to help English learners understand and practice the new vocabulary word.

1) Review the contextual sentence under the definition on the Vocabulary Extension page. Then have students look at the image of an **inestimable** number of sand grains on the Vocabulary Extension page. Ask questions about the image. Can we ever know how many grains of sand there are on a beach? Use their responses to introduce the meaning of **inestimable.** Offer help with pronunciation; point out the number of syllables (five) and which syllable is emphasized (the second syllable). Practice the word chorally and individually until pronunciations are firm.

2) Once students are in groups or pairs, ask them to use their own words to define **inestimable** to a partner.

3) If it applies to students in your group, point out the Spanish cognates for **inestimable** (*inestimable*) and the words in the Word Family: **estimate** (*estimar* [verb] and *la estimación* [noun]) and **underestimate** (*subestimar*). Allow EL students to use their native language to describe the meanings of the words to one another.

4) Read the prompt aloud and give students extra time to discuss before they write, if needed.

5) To provide extra scaffolding for students who struggle with writing, tell students to copy the following sentence starter in the writing space. Then have them complete the sentence in their own words.

   • _____ has made inestimable contributions in our community.
   (Sample response: *Rosa Parks*)

Enrichment Strategies

Challenge students to use one or more words from the Word Family on the Vocabulary Extension page when responding to the prompt.

LESSON 4: autonomy

Differentiation Options for the Vocabulary Extension

The following suggestions are provided to help you differentiate instruction to student groups.

Support Strategies

1) Once students are in groups or pairs, ask them to use their own words to tell you what they think **autonomy** means.

2) Read the Word Parts section on the Vocabulary Extension page. Have students give other examples of words with the prefix *auto-*. Then help students connect the meaning of the word with the meaning of its prefix, "self."

3) Discuss with students times they wish they had more **autonomy.** Why did they feel this way?

4) Read the prompt aloud and give students extra time to discuss before they write, if needed.

5) To provide extra scaffolding for students who struggle with writing, tell students to copy the following sentence starter in the writing space. Then have them complete the sentence in their own words.

• Having autonomy as an adult makes me _____ because _____ . (Sample response: *nervous; there will be a lot of things that I will be responsible for, such as paying bills*)

EL Strategies

Use any of the activities from Support Strategies or those below to help English learners understand and practice the new vocabulary word.

1) Offer help with the pronunciation of **autonomy.** Point out the number of syllables (four) and which syllable is emphasized (the second syllable). Practice the word chorally and individually until pronunciations are firm.

2) Have students use available language (single words, phrases, or simple sentences) to describe what they think **autonomy** means.

3) If it applies to students in your group, point out the Spanish cognate for **autonomy:** *la autonomía.* Allow EL students to use their native language to describe the meaning of the word to one another.

4) Tell students words or phrases that express a similar idea:

If you have **autonomy,** you have . . .
• freedom
• independence

5) Read the prompt aloud and give students extra time to discuss before they write, if needed.

6) To provide extra scaffolding for students who struggle with writing, tell students to copy the following sentence starter in the writing space. Then have them complete the sentence in their own words.

• Having autonomy as an adult makes me _____ because _____ . (Sample response: *nervous; I will be responsible for a lot of things*)

Enrichment Strategies

Discuss the meaning of **autonomous** and **autonomously** with students. Extend the prompt by asking students to predict the types of decisions that will be easy to make **autonomously** and those that they will need help from others to make.

LESSON 5: explicit

Differentiation Options for the Vocabulary Extension

The following suggestions are provided to help you differentiate instruction to student groups.

Support Strategies

1) Once students are in groups or pairs, ask them to use their own words to tell you what they think **explicit** means.

2) Review the contextual sentence under the definition on the Vocabulary Extension page. Then have students look at the image of an **explicit** sign on the Vocabulary Extension page. Ask students to describe how the sign's message is **explicit.**

3) Have partners write a set of directions to a local gathering place, such as a restaurant or a park. Challenge them to be as **explicit** as possible, citing street names and landmarks, for example. Then read each pair's directions to the group and have all students determine whose directions are the most **explicit.**

4) Read the prompt aloud and give students extra time to discuss before they write, if needed.

5) To provide extra scaffolding for students who struggle with writing, tell students to copy the following sentence starter in the writing space. Then have them complete the sentence in their own words.

• It is important to be explicit when _____ .
(Sample response: *explaining to someone how to drive a car*)

EL Strategies

Use any of the activities from Support Strategies or those below to help English learners understand and practice the new vocabulary word.

1) Once students are in groups or pairs, ask them to use available language (single words, phrases, or simple sentences) to describe to a partner what **explicit** means.

2) Tell students that it is important to be **explicit** about something when trying to prevent injury or to make sure something is done correctly.

3) If it applies to students in your group, point out the Spanish cognates for **explicit** (*explícito*) and the words from the Word Family: **explicitly** (*explícitamente*) and **implicit** (*implícito*). Allow EL students to use their native language to describe the meanings of the words to one another.

4) Read the prompt aloud and give students extra time to discuss before they write, if needed.

5) To provide extra scaffolding for students who struggle with writing, tell students to copy the following sentence starter in the writing space. Then have them complete the sentence in their own words.

• It is important to be explicit when _____ .
(Sample response: *explaining to someone how to drive a car*)

Enrichment Strategies

Challenge students to use at least one word from the Word Family on the Vocabulary Extension page in their response to the prompt.

LESSON 6: expound

Differentiation Options for the Vocabulary Extension

The following suggestions are provided to help you differentiate instruction to student groups.

Support Strategies

1) Once students are in groups or pairs, ask them to use their own words to tell you what they think **expound** means.

2) Have partners brainstorm a list of people who **expound** frequently, such as a teacher, a lawyer, or a parent.

3) Call on individual students and ask when they **expound** their views, what subjects they like to talk about.

4) Read the prompt aloud and give students extra time to discuss before they write, if needed.

5) To provide extra scaffolding for students who struggle with writing, tell students to copy the following sentence starter in the writing space. Then have them complete the sentence in their own words.

   • After high school, I plan to _____. (Sample response: *attend community college before transferring to a four-year university*)

EL Strategies

Use any of the activities from Support Strategies or those below to help English learners understand and practice the new vocabulary word.

1) Once students are in groups or pairs, ask them to use available language (single words, phrases, or simple sentences) to describe the meaning of **expound** to a partner.

2) Tell students words or phrases that express a similar idea to **expound**:

   If you **expound,** you . . .
   • talk about
   • give details
   • explain

3) Read the prompt aloud and give students extra time to discuss before they write, if needed.

4) To provide extra scaffolding for students who struggle with writing, tell students to copy the following sentence starter in the writing space. Then have them complete the sentence in their own words.

   • After high school, I plan to _____. (Sample response: *go to college*)

Enrichment Strategies

As students **expound** their plans for the future in their response to the prompt, have them include an approximate timetable for their plans.

LESSON 7: correlate

Differentiation Options for the Vocabulary Extension

The following suggestions are provided to help you differentiate instruction to student groups.

Support Strategies

1) Once students are in groups or pairs, ask them to use their own words to tell you what they think **correlate** means.

2) Read the Word Parts section on the Vocabulary Extension page. Tell students that, in addition to *com-* changing to *cor-* before an *r* for ease of pronunciation, there are other variations: *com-* before words that start with *b, p, m; col-* before words that start with *l;* and *con-* before words that start with other letters. Have students give other examples of words with the prefix *com-* or one of its variations *col-, con-,* or *cor-.* If they need help, suggest *colloquial, correct,* or *concurrent.*

3) Read the prompt aloud and give students extra time to discuss before they write, if needed.

4) To provide extra scaffolding for students who struggle with writing, tell students to copy the following sentence starter in the writing space. Then have them complete the sentence in their own words.

   • I think having good grades and a successful career (are/are not) correlated because _____ . (Sample response: *are; if someone is diligent with their studies, he or she will work hard at a job, too*)

EL Strategies

Use any of the activities from Support Strategies or those below to help English learners understand and practice the new vocabulary word.

1) Once students are in groups or pairs, ask them to use available language (single words, phrases, or simple sentences) to describe the meaning of **correlate** to a partner.

2) Use a simple illustration to demonstrate the word **correlate.** For example, you could draw a simple graph showing how a savings-account balance is **correlated** to the deposits to the account.

3) If it applies to students in your group, point out the Spanish cognate for **correlate:** *corelacionar.* Allow EL students to use their native language to describe the meaning of the word to one another.

4) Read the prompt aloud and give students extra time to discuss before they write, if needed.

5) To provide extra scaffolding for students who struggle with writing, tell students to copy the following sentence starter in the writing space. Then have them complete the sentence in their own words.

   • I think having good grades and a successful career (are/are not) correlated because _____ . (Sample response: *are; if someone studies hard, he or she will probably work hard at a job, too*)

Enrichment Strategies

Have students identify three more words with the prefix *com-* (or derivatives *con-, col-,* or *cor-*), define them, and use them in a contextual sentence.

LESSON 8: soliloquy

Differentiation Options for the Vocabulary Extension

The following suggestions are provided to help you differentiate instruction to student groups.

Support Strategies

1) Once students are in groups or pairs, ask them to use their own words to tell you what they think **soliloquy** means.

2) Ask students if they have every heard a **soliloquy,** and where.

3) Read the Word Parts section on the Vocabulary Extension page. Have students give other examples of words with the Latin roots *sol* or *loq.* If they need help, offer suggestions, such as *solitary, desolation, loquacious,* or *eloquent.* Then help students connect the meaning of each word with the meaning of its root.

4) Read the prompt aloud and give students extra time to discuss before they write, if needed.

5) To provide extra scaffolding for students who struggle with writing, tell students to copy the following sentence starter in the writing space. Then have them complete the sentence in their own words.

    • One purpose of a soliloquy is _____ . (Sample response: *to let only the audience know what the character is thinking*)

EL Strategies

Use any of the activities from Support Strategies or those below to help English learners understand and practice the new vocabulary word.

1) Have students use available language (single words, phrases, or simple sentences) to tell what they think **soliloquy** means. Use their responses to help you introduce the meaning of **soliloquy.** Make sure students understand that only the audience knows what the character is thinking when the character speaks in **soliloquy.**

2) If it applies to students in your group, point out the Spanish cognate for **soliloquy:** *el soliloquio.* Allow EL students to use their native language to describe the meaning of the word to one another.

3) Read the prompt aloud and give students extra time to discuss before they write, if needed.

4) To provide extra scaffolding for students who struggle with writing, tell students to copy the following sentence starter in the writing space. Then have them complete the sentence in their own words.

    • One purpose of a soliloquy is _____ . (Sample response: *to tell the audience what the character thinks*)

Enrichment Strategies

Challenge partners to write a few sentences to compare and contrast a **soliloquy** and a *monologue* in a play. Encourage them to use their knowledge of word parts, as well as the information in the Word Parts section on the Vocabulary Extension page, in their comparison (for example, the prefix *mono-* means "one," and the Greek root *log* means "to speak"). Students should realize that the word meanings are very similar. If necessary, share with students that only the audience can hear a **soliloquy,** while a *monologue* is a long speech by one character in the presence of other characters.

LESSON 9: disparate

Differentiation Options for the Vocabulary Extension

The following suggestions are provided to help you differentiate instruction to student groups.

Support Strategies

1) Once students are in groups or pairs, ask them to use their own words to tell you what they think **disparate** means.

2) Review the contextual sentence under the definition on the Vocabulary Extension page. Then have students look at the image of two friends with **disparate** opinions on the Vocabulary Extension page. Ask partners to discuss how the image is an example of the word **disparate.**

3) Read the Word Parts section on the Vocabulary Extension page. Have students give other examples of words with the Latin root *par.* If they need help, suggest *compare* or *parity.* Then help students connect the meaning of each word with the meaning of its root.

4) Read the prompt aloud and give students extra time to discuss before they write, if needed.

5) To provide extra scaffolding for students who struggle with writing, tell students to copy the following sentence starter in the writing space. Then have them complete the sentence in their own words.

   • If a friend and I had disparate opinions about the same issue, I would
   _____ . (Sample response: *talk with my friend about it so that we could understand each other's viewpoint*)

EL Strategies

Use any of the activities from Support Strategies or those below to help English learners understand and practice the new vocabulary word.

1) Have students use available language (single words, phrases, or simple sentences) to describe the meaning of **disparate.**

2) Tell students words or phrases that express a similar idea:

   If two things are **disparate,** they are . . .
   • different
   • not equal

3) If it applies to students in your group, point out the Spanish cognate for **disparate:** *dispar.* Allow EL students to use their native language to describe the meaning of the word to one another.

4) Read the prompt aloud and give students extra time to discuss before they write, if needed.

5) To provide extra scaffolding for students who struggle with writing, tell students to copy the following sentence starter in the writing space. Then have them complete the sentence in their own words.

   • If a friend and I had disparate opinions about the same issue, I would
   _____ . (Sample response: *talk to my friend about it to understand the other side of the issue*)

Enrichment Strategies

Have students write a dialogue between themselves and a friend using the issue they wrote about in the response to the prompt. Use synonyms or antonyms from the Vocabulary Extension page, if possible. If time allows, have students write a resolution to the disagreement.

LESSON 10: expunge

Differentiation Options for the Vocabulary Extension

The following suggestions are provided to help you differentiate instruction to student groups.

Support Strategies

1) Once students are in groups or pairs, ask them to use their own words to tell you what they think **expunge** means.

2) Review the contextual sentence under the definition on the Vocabulary Extension page. Ask students to restate the sentence without using the word **expunge.**

3) Ask students to think of possible reasons someone would want to **expunge** something from the following: an answer on a test, an e-mail to a friend, a political candidate's history, a memory.

4) Read the prompt aloud and give students extra time to discuss before they write, if needed.

5) To provide extra scaffolding for students who struggle with writing, tell students to copy the following sentence starter in the writing space. Then have them complete the sentence in their own words.

   • Someone might want to expunge something from the school record because
   _____ . (Sample response: *if one or two bad grades are removed, the person's GPA might rise*)

EL Strategies

Use any of the activities from Support Strategies or those below to help English learners understand and practice the new vocabulary word.

1) Use gestures or illustrations to demonstrate the meaning of **expunge.** For example, write 2 + 2 = 5; then erase the 5 to show that you **expunged** the incorrect answer.

2) Once students are in groups or pairs, ask students to use available language (single words, phrases, or simple sentences) to describe the meaning of **expunge** to a partner.

3) Review the synonyms and antonyms on the Vocabulary Extension page. Ask students to explain how these words are connected to **expunge.**

4) Read the prompt aloud and give students extra time to discuss before they write, if needed.

5) To provide extra scaffolding for students who struggle with writing, tell students to copy the following sentence starter in the writing space. Then have them complete the sentence in their own words.

   • Someone might want to expunge something from the school record because _____ . (Sample response: *if one or two bad grades are removed, the person's GPA might rise*)

Enrichment Strategies

Have students write a short narrative about an embarrassing experience they would like **expunged** from their memories. Tell them to include dialogue, if applicable.

LESSON 11: postulate

Differentiation Options for the Vocabulary Extension

The following suggestions are provided to help you differentiate instruction to student groups.

Support Strategies

1) Once students are in groups or pairs, ask them to use their own words to tell you what they think **postulate** means.

2) Read the definitions on the Vocabulary Extension page. Then read the sentence under Academic Context. Have students use the context of the sentence to determine which meaning of **postulate** is indicated.

3) As a group, compare and contrast the verbs **postulate** and *prove.*

4) Read the prompt aloud and give students extra time to discuss before they write, if needed.

5) To provide extra scaffolding for students who struggle with writing, tell students to copy the following sentence starter in the writing space. Then have them complete the sentence in their own words.

   • Scientists have postulated the existence of life on other planets, and I think _____ . (Sample response: *they could be right*)

EL Strategies

Use any of the activities from Support Strategies or those below to help English learners understand and practice the new vocabulary word.

1) Use gestures and verbal clues to demonstrate the meaning of **postulate.**

2) Once students are in groups or pairs, ask them to use available language (single words, phrases, or simple sentences) to describe the meaning of **postulate** to a partner.

3) If it applies to students in your group, point out the Spanish cognate for **postulate:** *postular.* Allow EL students to use their native language to describe the meanings of the word to one another.

4) Read the prompt aloud and give students extra time to discuss before they write, if needed.

5) To provide extra scaffolding for students who struggle with writing, tell students to copy the following sentence starter in the writing space. Then have them complete the sentence in their own words.

   • Scientists have postulated the existence of life on other planets, and I think
   _____ . (Sample response: *they could be right*)

Enrichment Strategies

Challenge partners to each choose a side to the question of life on other planets. Have them outline their position and prepare notes as though they will formally debate the issue.

LESSON 12: antithetical

Differentiation Options for the Vocabulary Extension

The following suggestions are provided to help you differentiate instruction to student groups.

Support Strategies

1) Once students are in groups or pairs, ask them to use their own words to tell you what they think **antithetical** means.

2) Review the contextual sentence under the definition on the Vocabulary Extension page. Then have students look at the image on the Vocabulary Extension page. Ask partners to discuss how the image is an example of the word **antithetical.**

3) Read the Word Parts section on the Vocabulary Extension page. Have students give other examples of words with the prefix *anti-* and then define those words, if possible.

4) Read the prompt aloud and give students extra time to discuss before they write, if needed.

5) To provide extra scaffolding for students who struggle with writing, tell students to copy the following sentence starter in the writing space. Then have them complete the sentence in their own words.

   • One example of two ideas that are antithetical are _____ .
   (Sample response: a *vegetarian lifestyle and a meat-eating lifestyle*)

EL Strategies

Use any of the activities from Support Strategies or those below to help English learners understand and practice the new vocabulary word.

1) Use illustrations and simple verbal clues to demonstrate the meaning of **antithetical.**

2) Review the contextual sentence under the definition on the Vocabulary Extension page. Then have students look at the image on the Vocabulary Extension page. Have them use available language (single words, phrases, or simple sentences) to describe the image. Then challenge students to define **antithetical** in their own words.

3) If it applies to students in your group, point out the Spanish cognate for **antithetical:** *antitético.* Allow EL students to use their native language to describe the meaning of the word to one another.

4) Read the prompt aloud and give students extra time to discuss before they write, if needed.

5) To provide extra scaffolding for students who struggle with writing, tell students to copy the following sentence starter in the writing space. Then have them complete the sentence in their own words.

   • One example of two ideas that are antithetical are _____ . (Sample response: *love and hate*)

Enrichment Strategies

Have students identify two more words with the prefix *anti-,* define them, and use them in a contextual sentence.

LESSON 13: context

Differentiation Options for the Vocabulary Extension

The following suggestions are provided to help you differentiate instruction to student groups.

Support Strategies

1) Once students are in groups or pairs, ask them to use their own words to tell you what they think **context** means.

2) Read the definitions on the Vocabulary Extension page. Then read the sentences under Academic Context. Have students use the **context** of each sentence to determine which meaning of **context** is used in each sentence.

3) Read the prompt aloud and give students extra time to discuss before they write, if needed.

4) To provide extra scaffolding for students who struggle with writing, tell students to copy the following sentence starter in the writing space. Then have them complete the sentence in their own words.

   • It is important to know the context of a conversation because _____ . (Sample response: *it helps you understand the situation so you can contribute appropriate thoughts about it*)

EL Strategies

Use any of the activities from Support Strategies or those below to help English learners understand and practice the new vocabulary word.

1) Use simple verbal clues to convey the meanings of **context.**

2) Once students are in groups or pairs, ask them to use available language (single words, phrases, or simple sentences) to describe the meanings of **context** to a partner.

3) If it applies to students in your group, point out the Spanish cognates for **context** (*el context*) and the words from the Word Family: **contextual** (*contextual*) and **contextualize** (*contextualizar*). Allow EL students to use their native language to describe the meanings of the words to one another.

4) Read the prompt aloud and give students extra time to discuss before they write, if needed.

5) To provide extra scaffolding for students who struggle with writing, tell students to copy the following sentence starter in the writing space. Then have them complete the sentence in their own words.

   • It is important to know the context of a conversation because _____ .
   (Sample response: *it helps you understand the situation so you can respond appropriately*)

Enrichment Strategies

Tell students that if something is taken **out of context,** this means you don't know the particular circumstances to help you understand what happened. Conversely, if a situation has been thoroughly explained, it has been **put into context.** Have students use one of these phrases in their response to the prompt.

LESSON 14: transcend

Differentiation Options for the Vocabulary Extension

The following suggestions are provided to help you differentiate instruction to student groups.

Support Strategies

1) Once students are in groups or pairs, ask them to use their own words to tell you what they think **transcend** means.

2) Review the contextual sentence under the definition on the Vocabulary Extension page. Then have students look at the image of a jet **transcending** the sound barrier on the Vocabulary Extension page. Ask partners to discuss what is happening in the image. If necessary, tell them that the image shows a jet airplane that has just broken the sound barrier, which means the plane is now traveling faster than the speed of sound. Have students use this information to explain why the picture is an example of the word **transcend.**

3) Read the Word Parts section on the Vocabulary Extension page. Have students give other examples of words with the root *scend*. If necessary, offer suggestions,

such as *ascend*. Then help students connect the meaning of each word with the meaning of its root, "to climb."

4) Read the prompt aloud and give students extra time to discuss before they write, if needed.

5) To provide extra scaffolding for students who struggle with writing, tell students to copy the following sentence starter in the writing space. Then have them complete the sentence in their own words.

   • The sentence means _____ . (Sample response: *there are no limits to what art can mean to people*)

EL Strategies

Use any of the activities from Support Strategies or those below to help English learners understand and practice the new vocabulary word.

1) Use illustrations and simple language to describe the meaning of **transcend** to students. Help students understand that the *sc* spelling in **transcend** makes the sound /s/.

2) Write **transcend** on the board. Underline the prefix *trans-*. Ask students what this prefix means ("across"), and then challenge them to think of other words with this prefix. If necessary, suggest *transmit, transfer,* or *transport*. Have students define the words, if possible.

3) Read the prompt aloud and give students extra time to discuss before they write, if needed.

4) To provide extra scaffolding for students who struggle with writing, tell students to copy the following sentence starter in the writing space. Then have them complete the sentence in their own words.

   • The sentence means _____ . (Sample response: *art is very important to people*)

Enrichment Strategies

Have students extend their response to the prompt by describing things other than art that are so profound that they **transcend** culture, politics, technology, or time.

LESSON 15: graphic

Differentiation Options for the Vocabulary Extension

The following suggestions are provided to help you differentiate instruction to student groups.

Support Strategies

1) Once students are in groups or pairs, ask them to use their own words to tell you what they think **graphic** means.

2) Have students look at the image of a woman creating **graphic** art on the Vocabulary Extension page. Ask students to describe examples of **graphic** art she might be creating.

3) Read the definitions on the Vocabulary Extension page. Then read the sentences under Academic Context. Have students use the context of each sentence to determine which meaning of **graphic** is used in each sentence.

4) Read the prompt aloud and give students extra time to discuss before they write, if needed.

5) To provide extra scaffolding for students who struggle with writing, tell students to copy the following sentence starters in the writing space. Then have them complete each sentence in their own words.

   • The graphic (arts/design) class I took was _____ . (Sample response: *arts; interesting because we learned art techniques that have been used for centuries*)

   • I have not taken a graphic arts or graphic design class, because _____ . (Sample response: *I'm more interested in science and math*)

EL Strategies

Use any of the activities from Support Strategies or those below to help English learners understand and practice the new vocabulary word.

1) Discuss the image of a woman creating **graphic** art on the Vocabulary Extension page. Have students use available language (single words, phrases, or simple sentences) to describe examples of **graphic** art she might be creating. Use students' responses to help you introduce the meaning of **graphic.** Point out that the *ph* in **graphic** makes the sound /f/.

2) Show students a few examples of **graphic** art from books or the Internet.

3) If it applies to students in your group, point out the Spanish cognate for **graphic:** *gráfico.* Allow EL students to use their native language to describe the meaning of the word to one another.

4) Read the prompt aloud and give students extra time to discuss before they write, if needed.

5) To provide extra scaffolding for students who struggle with writing, tell students to copy the following sentence starters in the writing space. Then have them complete each sentence in their own words.

   • The graphic (arts/design) class I took was _____ . (Sample response: *arts; interesting because we learned art techniques that have been used for centuries*)

   • I have not taken a graphic arts or graphic design class, because _____ . (Sample response: *I'm more interested in science and math*)

Enrichment Strategies

Help students use **graphic** language to write a few sentences to describe what it's like to eat their favorite food.

Differentiation Options for the Vocabulary Extension

The following suggestions are provided to help you differentiate instruction to student groups.

Support Strategies

1) Once students are in groups or pairs, ask them to use their own words to tell you what they think **terminus** means.

2) Read the Word Parts section on the Vocabulary Extension page. Have students give other examples of words with the root *term*. If necessary, offer suggestions, such as *exterminator.*

3) Read the prompt aloud and give students extra time to discuss before they write, if needed.

4) To provide extra scaffolding for students who struggle with writing, tell students to copy the following sentence starter in the writing space. Then have them complete the sentence in their own words.

   • One example of something that has a terminus is _____ .
   (Sample response: *a mail carrier's route*)

EL Strategies

Use any of the activities from Support Strategies or those below to help English learners understand and practice the new vocabulary word.

1) Have students look at the image of a mapped route's **terminus** on the Vocabulary Extension page. Ask them to point to the end of the route. Use students' responses to introduce the meaning of **terminus.**

2) Once students are in groups or pairs, ask them to use available language (single words, phrases, or simple sentences) to describe what a **terminus** is.

3) Tell students words or phrases that express a similar idea:

   A **terminus** is like . . .
   • an end
   • the last stop

4) Read the prompt aloud and give students extra time to discuss before they write, if needed.

5) To provide extra scaffolding for students who struggle with writing, tell students to copy the following sentence starter in the writing space. Then have them complete the sentence in their own words.

   • _____ has a terminus. (Sample response: *A mail carrier's route*)

Enrichment Strategies

Have partners come up with three synonyms for **terminus.** Challenge them to use all three words in their response to the prompt.

Differentiation Options for the Vocabulary Extension

The following suggestions are provided to help you differentiate instruction to student groups.

Support Strategies

1) Once students are in groups or pairs, ask them to use their own words to tell you what they think **autocratic** means.

2) Have students show they know the meaning of **autocratic** by acting out the word or by verbally describing it.

3) Read the Word Parts section on the Vocabulary Extension page. Have students give other examples of words with the Greek root *crat*. If they need help, offer suggestions such as *democratic* or *aristocrat*. Then help students connect the meanings of the words with the meaning of their root, "rule."

4) Read the prompt aloud and give students extra time to discuss before they write, if needed.

5) To provide extra scaffolding for students who struggle with writing, tell students to copy the following sentence starter in the writing space. Then have them complete the sentence in their own words.

• I think living under an autocratic government _____ . (Sample response: *would mean not having many civil rights or opportunities to succeed*)

EL Strategies

Use any of the activities from Support Strategies or those below to help English learners understand and practice the new vocabulary word.

1) Review the contextual sentence under the definition on the Vocabulary Extension page. Then have students look at the image of an **autocratic** leader on the Vocabulary Extension page. Prompt students with questions about the image. Use their responses to introduce the word **autocratic.**

2) Write **autocratic** on the board. Underline the prefix *auto-*. Ask students what it means ("self"), and challenge them to think of other words with this prefix. If necessary, suggest *automobile* or *autograph*. Have students define the words, if possible.

3) If it applies to students in your group, point out the Spanish cognate for **autocratic:** *autocrático/a*. Allow EL students to use their native language to describe the meaning of the word to one another.

4) Read the prompt aloud and give students extra time to discuss before they write, if needed.

5) To provide extra scaffolding for students who struggle with writing, tell students to copy the following sentence starter in the writing space. Then have them complete the sentence in their own words.

• I think living under an autocratic government _____ . (Sample response: *would mean not having many civil rights or opportunities to succeed*)

Enrichment Strategies

Write *autocrat,* **autocratic,** and *autocracy* on the board. Describe the nuances in meaning among the related words. Have students extend this knowledge to define *democrat, democratic,* and *democracy* (in which the Greek root *dem* means "people").

LESSON 18: criterion

Differentiation Options for the Vocabulary Extension

The following suggestions are provided to help you differentiate instruction to student groups.

Support Strategies

1) Once students are in groups or pairs, ask them to use their own words to tell you what they think **criterion** means.

2) Have students discuss the **criteria** for joining a club at school, for obtaining a driver's license, or for getting a part-time job.

3) Ask students what **criteria** they require when choosing a movie to see or a book to read.

4) Read the prompt aloud and give students extra time to discuss before they write, if needed.

5) To provide extra scaffolding for students who struggle with writing, tell students to copy the following sentence starter in the writing space. Then have them complete the sentence in their own words.

   • One of the criteria for a recent project was _____ . (Sample response: *to write an essay with a clear thesis and three cited sources*)

EL Strategies

Use any of the activities from Support Strategies or those below to help English learners understand and practice the new vocabulary word.

1) Have students look at the image of a writing rubric's assessment **criteria** on the Vocabulary Extension page. Ask students to use available language (single words, phrases, or simple sentences) to explain what **criteria** might be used to assess writing. Use students' responses to help them understand what **criterion** means, and help them understand that **criterion** is singular and has an irregular plural form: **criteria.**

2) Give extra practice with the pronunciation of **criterion** and **criteria.** In particular, point out that the *i* in the first syllable is a long *i* (not a short-*i* or long-*e* sound). Offer choral and then individual practice saying the word.

3) If it applies to students in your group, point out the Spanish cognate for **criterion:** *el criterio.* Allow EL students to use their native language to describe the meaning of the word to one another.

4) Read the prompt aloud and give students extra time to discuss before they write, if needed.

5) To provide extra scaffolding for students who struggle with writing, tell students to copy the following sentence starter in the writing space. Then have them complete the sentence in their own words.

• One of the criteria for a recent project was _____ .
(Sample response: *to write an essay with a clear thesis and three cited sources*)

Enrichment Strategies

Have students think about an activity they are involved in, such as 4-H or student council. Ask them to make a list of the **criteria** that must be followed to perform successfully in their chosen activity. If there is time, have them tell why each **criterion** is important.

LESSON 19: unilateral

Differentiation Options for the Vocabulary Extension

The following suggestions are provided to help you differentiate instruction to student groups.

Support Strategies

1) Once students are in groups or pairs, ask them to use their own words to tell you what they think **unilateral** means.

2) Read the Word Parts section on the Vocabulary Extension page. Have students give other examples of words with the prefix *uni-*. If they need help, offer suggestions such as *uniformity*. Tell students that the prefix *bi-* means "two," and then challenge them to define *bilateral*.

3) Ask students why it might sometimes be important to make a **unilateral** decision.

4) Read the prompt aloud and give students extra time to discuss before they write, if needed.

5) To provide extra scaffolding for students who struggle with writing, tell students to copy the following sentence starter in the writing space. Then have them complete the sentence in their own words.

• When planning for my future, I will _____ because _____ .
(Sample response: *include my family; I make better decisions with advice from my parents*)

EL Strategies

Use any of the activities from Support Strategies or those below to help English learners understand and practice the new vocabulary word.

1) Use simple language to describe the meaning of **unilateral** to students.

2) Write **unilateral** on the board. Underline the prefix *uni-*. Ask students what other words they know with this prefix, such as *uniform*. Help them relate the meaning of each word they suggest to the meaning of the prefix ("one").

3) If it applies to students in your group, point out the Spanish cognate for **unilateral:** *unilateral*. Allow EL students to use their native language to describe the meaning of the word to one another.

4) Read the prompt aloud and give students extra time to discuss before they write, if needed.

5) To provide extra scaffolding for students who struggle with writing, tell students to copy the following sentence starter in the writing space. Then have them complete the sentence in their own words.

- When I plan for my future, I will _____ because _____ .
  (Sample response: *ask my family for advice; I can make better decisions*)

Enrichment Strategies

Have students identify two more words with the prefix *uni-*, define them, and use them in a contextual sentence.

LESSON 20: extrapolate

Differentiation Options for the Vocabulary Extension

The following suggestions are provided to help you differentiate instruction to student groups.

Support Strategies

1) Once students are in groups or pairs, ask them to use their own words to tell you what they think **extrapolate** means.

2) Read aloud the Academic Context sentence on the Vocabulary Extension page. Ask students to restate the sentence without using the word **extrapolate.**

3) Write **extrapolate** on the board. Underline the prefix *extra-*. Ask students what other words they know with this prefix, such as *extraordinary*. Help them relate the meaning of the word to the meaning of the prefix ("outside").

4) Read the prompt aloud and give students extra time to discuss before they write, if needed.

5) To provide extra scaffolding for students who struggle with writing, tell students to copy the following sentence starters in the writing space. Then have them complete each sentence in their own words.

- A question I might ask a small group of students is _____ .
  (Sample response: *Do you think summer vacation should be longer?*)

- The answer to this question will likely be: _____ .
  (Sample response: *Yes*)

- I can extrapolate that most students would answer this way because _____ . (Sample response: *everyone I know would rather be on vacation than in school*)

EL Strategies

Use any of the activities from Support Strategies or those below to help English learners understand and practice the new vocabulary word.

1) Once students are in groups or pairs, ask them to use available language (single words, phrases, or simple sentences) to describe the meaning of **extrapolate** to a partner.

2) Ask students if they can name any synonyms for **extrapolate.** If necessary, suggest *hypothesize, guess,* or *predict.*

3) If it applies to students in your group, point out the Spanish cognate for **extrapolate:** *extrapolar.* Allow EL students to use their native language to describe the meaning of the word to one another.

4) Read the prompt aloud and give students extra time to discuss before they write, if needed.

5) To provide extra scaffolding for students who struggle with writing, tell students to copy the following sentence starters in the writing space. Then have them complete each sentence in their own words.

• A question I might ask a small group of students is _____ .
(Sample response: *Do you think summer vacation should be longer?*)

• The answer to this question will likely be: _____ .
(Sample response: *Yes*)

• I can extrapolate that most students would answer this way because
_____ . (Sample response: *everyone I know would rather be on vacation than in school*)

Enrichment Strategies

Have students identify two more words with the prefix *extra-,* define them, and use them in a contextual sentence.

Reproducible Masters

Name _____ Date _____

Rate Your Word Knowledge

Write the words from Lesson _____ in the spaces provided.
Fill in the circle to rate your knowledge of each word.

1. _____
   - O I've never seen this word before.
   - O I've seen this word before, but I don't know what it means.
   - O I think I know what this word means.
   - O I know what this word means and can use it in a sentence.

2. _____
   - O I've never seen this word before.
   - O I've seen this word before, but I don't know what it means.
   - O I think I know what this word means.
   - O I know what this word means and can use it in a sentence.

3. _____
   - O I've never seen this word before.
   - O I've seen this word before, but I don't know what it means.
   - O I think I know what this word means.
   - O I know what this word means and can use it in a sentence.

4. _____
   - O I've never seen this word before.
   - O I've seen this word before, but I don't know what it means.
   - O I think I know what this word means.
   - O I know what this word means and can use it in a sentence.

5. _____
   - O I've never seen this word before.
   - O I've seen this word before, but I don't know what it means.
   - O I think I know what this word means.
   - O I know what this word means and can use it in a sentence.

6. _____
   - O I've never seen this word before.
   - O I've seen this word before, but I don't know what it means.
   - O I think I know what this word means.
   - O I know what this word means and can use it in a sentence.

7. _____
   - O I've never seen this word before.
   - O I've seen this word before, but I don't know what it means.
   - O I think I know what this word means.
   - O I know what this word means and can use it in a sentence.

© SSI • MAY BE DUPLICATED

8. _____
- ○ I've never seen this word before.
- ○ I've seen this word before, but I don't know what it means.
- ○ I think I know what this word means.
- ○ I know what this word means and can use it in a sentence.

9. _____
- ○ I've never seen this word before.
- ○ I've seen this word before, but I don't know what it means.
- ○ I think I know what this word means.
- ○ I know what this word means and can use it in a sentence.

10. _____
- ○ I've never seen this word before.
- ○ I've seen this word before, but I don't know what it means.
- ○ I think I know what this word means.
- ○ I know what this word means and can use it in a sentence.

11. _____
- ○ I've never seen this word before.
- ○ I've seen this word before, but I don't know what it means.
- ○ I think I know what this word means.
- ○ I know what this word means and can use it in a sentence.

12. _____
- ○ I've never seen this word before.
- ○ I've seen this word before, but I don't know what it means.
- ○ I think I know what this word means.
- ○ I know what this word means and can use it in a sentence.

13. _____
- ○ I've never seen this word before.
- ○ I've seen this word before, but I don't know what it means.
- ○ I think I know what this word means.
- ○ I know what this word means and can use it in a sentence.

14. _____
- ○ I've never seen this word before.
- ○ I've seen this word before, but I don't know what it means.
- ○ I think I know what this word means.
- ○ I know what this word means and can use it in a sentence.

15. _____
- ○ I've never seen this word before.
- ○ I've seen this word before, but I don't know what it means.
- ○ I think I know what this word means.
- ○ I know what this word means and can use it in a sentence.

© SSI • MAY BE DUPLICATED

Going, Going, Gone!

A man attending an auction scratches his ear and is **mortified** to learn that with this movement he has bought a stuffed, mounted moose head with antlers. The story, though **apocryphal,** is a staple of auction folklore and expresses the fear people have of being drawn unwittingly into the bidding fray. The fear is unjustified. Bidding in public auctions is done by **gesticulating** in the auctioneer's direction while holding a numbered card aloft. The possibility of anyone making an unintended offer is slight.

In the **arcane** world of private, fine art auction houses, events are conducted with restraint. People attending are known to the auctioneer and each other because many are dealers buying for their business or clients. As the **imperturbable** auctioneer presides over sale of an item whose price may reach tens of millions of dollars, a person may bid by doing nothing more than catching the auctioneer's eye. Tugging an ear or looking at the ceiling may be signals arranged beforehand with the auctioneer to indicate a desire to withdraw from bidding.

The success of any auction, public or private, depends on the skill of the person conducting the auction. A good auctioneer must be a **raconteur,** with amusing stories to tell and the wit to keep them brief. By using **levity,** he or she can relax the crowd and help bids flow freely.

Various **subterfuges** are employed to create interest and maintain alertness. The auctioneer may cry "Sold!" just as bidding is getting underway. One lucky person gets a valuable item for a song, and the rest learn that if they **vacillate,** a bargain may slip away. Auctioneers have been known to drop a (not valuable) vase as an **expedient** to get the attention of a crowd drifting into boredom.

Given the large number of auctions in the United States each year, there is an increasing demand for people to conduct them. This demand is met in part by schools for auctioneers. The oldest and largest is the Missouri Auction School in Kansas City, founded in 1905. It **convenes** four times a year for nine-day courses attended by up to one thousand people hoping to become professional auctioneers.

Doing their best to **exude** the confidence auctioneers must demonstrate, students conduct mock auctions while the class acts as potential bidders. They develop their **peripheral** vision so as not to miss bids from the side of the hall, and they practice the American style of conducting auctions in a singsong chant. An uninterrupted flow of words is punctuated by **reiterated** reminders of the last bid, followed by the bid the auctioneer wants to get from the audience. His or her chant might go like this:

© SSI • MAY BE DUPLICATED

". . . . *thirty* dollar bid an' now forty, now forty . . . *thirty* dollar bid and *willya* gimme forty . . . *thirty* dollar bid an' now five . . . *thirty-five* dollar bid and *willya* gimme forty . . ."

Why the chant? It places less strain on the auctioneer's voice than saying the same words for long periods of time. In addition, the rhythmical pattern of speech draws and maintains the attention of the audience. Finally, as one student explained, "Chanting makes less obvious the sometimes long, quiet intervals between bids, thus obscuring the fact that the bidding is anything but lively."

Auctions are popular entertainment in the United States. Whether the bidding increases in **increments** of five dollars or in hundreds of thousands of dollars, they offer excitement, suspense, and, occasionally, high drama. Perhaps this explains why millions of Americans attend auctions each year.

© SSI • MAY BE DUPLICATED

Looking at Llamas

The llama, a member of the camel family, is not listed among the **fauna** of North America. Since the early 1900s, when they were introduced from South America, llamas have made themselves at home so that there are now many thousands living in the United States. Though the first llamas were imported as exotic pets, llamas outgrew this limited role as symbols of **opulence.** Their intelligence, affability, enjoyment of human company, and ability to perform many **utilitarian** tasks placed them in demand.

Today, sheep ranchers use llamas to guard their flocks from coyotes and **marauding** dogs, which account for more than half of all sheep losses. When all other measures failed to prevent these predators, sheep ranchers used llamas to defend their flocks. Llamas are extremely protective of their charges. The llama will **interpose** itself between the flock and a coyote or dog; its aggressive posture usually **disconcerts** the attacker, and it backs off. If it doesn't, the llama charges. While this usually drives the predator away, occasionally the llama becomes the victim.

Other supporters of llamas are the United States Forest Service and the National Park Service. Rangers take advantage of the fact that llamas are independent animals. With a **modicum** of training, they make excellent pack animals. Rangers use them to transport supplies in areas wheeled vehicles cannot go. Because of their two-toed padded feet, llamas are less destructive of fragile trails than horses or mules, which have hard hooves. Their **phlegmatic** nature makes llamas easy to manage. This is important for volunteers, who need extensive training with horses and mules but require minimal instruction in handling llamas.

Once shown a task, llamas will do it. One occupation they are employed in makes use of this intelligence. Llamas are found in increasing numbers on golf courses, acting as caddies. Loaded with golfing **accoutrements,** llamas plod along between holes, wait patiently at greens, and have a calming effect on golfers who may become **choleric** after missing a putt. Llamas are fastidious and easily trained, so each hole has a toilet area for their use.

Even as these accommodating creatures enter more occupations, their traditional role as pets continues. Llamas establish a rapport with owners and are gentle with children. A healthy llama sells for less than a thousand dollars, but the **patricians** of the llama world, those used for breeding, sell for more than fifteen thousand dollars.

© SSI • MAY BE DUPLICATED

One myth about the llama is that it has a **propensity** to spit in people's faces. This does not **comport** with the facts. It is true that if it is frightened, it may respond in this way, or if its forbearance is severely tested, an **aggrieved** llama may show displeasure by spitting. Owners are quick to point out that this behavior is rare and is usually directed at another llama invading its space. So well disposed are llamas toward people that they play a **therapeutic** role in helping people with mental illnesses. In one program, patients are assigned a llama to serve as a companion and pack animal on wilderness treks. Human and llama establish a bond, offering the patient an opportunity to relate to another creature in a nonthreatening situation. The practice is effective, the program's director says, because "llamas accept you just the way you are."

© SSI • MAY BE DUPLICATED

No Excuses

When Wilma Rudolph was born on June 23, 1940, she weighed only four and a half pounds and had an **incipient** form of polio, a once-common disease that causes paralysis and even death. As an infant, she was frequently ill. Her mother cared for her at home because there was only one doctor in their segregated town of Clarksville, Tennessee, who would treat African American patients. By age four, Wilma had contracted both double pneumonia and scarlet fever, exacerbating her condition. In her weakened state, she was vulnerable to the polio virus, which caused the muscles in her leg to **atrophy.** It seemed unlikely she would ever walk as she had used to.

On the advice of her doctor, Rudolph began a weekly **regimen** of heat and water therapy at a Nashville hospital. Mrs. Rudolph saw to it that her daughter exercised and received leg massages at home four times daily, and Wilma practiced her exercises **zealously,** despite constant pain. The treatments proved **efficacious;** at age five Wilma was fitted with a steel leg brace and took her first steps. With effort, she learned to walk, all the while despising the brace. Wilma was **stoic** about her hardships; she exuded confidence and was determined that someday she would walk without the brace.

As she worked toward this goal, the constant encouragement she received from her parents was of **inestimable** value. She also had a remarkable fourth-grade teacher, Mrs. Hoskins. Although something of a **martinet,** this woman was fair, treating everybody equally. She **inculcated** in her students the idea that they should think positively about their lives and their goals. "Do it, don't daydream about it," she would exhort. "No excuses!" Rudolph drew strength from this strong-minded teacher, and at age nine, she appeared in public without her brace for the first time. "From that day on," she later wrote, "people were going to . . . start thinking about me differently, start saying Wilma is a healthy kid." By the time she was eleven, she no longer needed to wear the brace.

Wilma demonstrated how healthy she was in the seventh grade as a member of the school basketball team. Her speed and her long arms and legs reminded her coach of a mosquito, and he nicknamed her Skeeter, saying, "You're little, you're fast, and you always get in my way." She joined the school track team, where her gift for running became apparent. In an Amateur Athletic Union meet in Philadelphia, Rudolph won all of her nine races. Her **stellar** accomplishments on the track soon attracted national attention. At age sixteen, Wilma Rudolph became the youngest

© SSI • MAY BE DUPLICATED

member of the United States Olympic track team, competing in the 1956 Melbourne Games. She gave what she considered a **lackluster** performance, winning a bronze medal in the 400-meter relay. She resolved to do better in the 1960 Olympics in Rome.

At the Olympic trials for the 1960 Games, Rudolph set a world record in the 200-meter dash and also qualified for the 100-meter dash and the 400-meter relay. Only a few years after discarding the leg brace, she had become a tall, **vibrant** woman on the verge of her greatest triumph. But shortly after arriving in Rome, she stepped in a hole and twisted her ankle, which became swollen and discolored. It was at this point that the **prodigious** willpower that had served her so well in the past was called into service. Despite the injury, Wilma competed, winning gold medals in all three of her events. She became the first woman to do so in the history of Olympic track and field.

In 1962, she retired from the track and became a teacher and a coach. She said she quit because "I couldn't top what I did, so I'll be remembered for when I was at my best." In the early 1960s, few big corporations offered the **emoluments** that now make sports heroes millionaires. Wilma Rudolph never became affluent, but her achievements on and off the track, as a pioneer in the civil rights and women's rights movements, established her as an **icon** to other athletes, to women, to African Americans, and to people with physical differences. Everyone can draw strength from her example and find inspiration in her story.

© SSI • MAY BE DUPLICATED

Tibet's God-King?

The thirteenth Dalai Lama was not simply the head of the government of Tibet. Like his predecessors, he was revered as a god-king—as the reincarnation of the Buddha of Compassion—by the Buddhist people of that land. When he died in 1933, they believed his soul would enter the body of a child, who would become the next Dalai Lama. In accordance with Tibetan tradition, a Buddhist monk was appointed to rule Tibet as regent during this **interim** period. One day, the regent fell into a **reverie,** during which he saw where the new Dalai Lama would be found. He described in detail the house and its **environs.** Search parties looked for the place and the child, the first step in a time-honored procedure for seeking, locating, and training the new leader of Tibet.

In summer 1937, after officials had covered over a thousand miles and interviewed several candidates, they received promising details about a two-year-old boy living in the province of Amdo in northeastern Tibet. Government officials traveled **incognito** to his house. The place the boy lived precisely matched the regent's vision. As a test, officials showed the boy several pairs of objects. One item of each pair had belonged to the former Dalai Lama; the other was a copy. When asked to choose between them, the boy invariably rejected the copies. The officials were convinced that the search for the new incarnation of their leader was over.

Tibet is bounded by the Himalaya Mountains to the south and west and by desert to the north and east, and it is not easily accessible to the outside world. Lhasa, its capital, was long known as the "Forbidden City." An imposing **edifice,** Potala Palace, is built into a towering rock face overlooking Lhasa. A quarter of a mile long, filled with thousands of rooms, halls, and chapels connected by narrow corridors, this huge building is dark and gloomy, and in the bitter cold of winter, it can seem more like a **mausoleum** than a residence. The little boy was **ensconced** in an apartment in the palace and began the training program that would prepare him to be the country's spiritual leader. After three years he was installed as the fourteenth Dalai Lama in an elaborate ceremony. Those who witnessed the events remarked on the five-year-old's grave manner and perfect **composure.**

To the north and east of Tibet is China. Over the centuries, Tibet has learned to be **circumspect** in dealing with its powerful neighbor. China had long claimed Tibet as a Chinese province but had allowed it to maintain **autonomy,** but in 1949, China came under Communist rule, and one year later the Chinese army invaded

© SSI • MAY BE DUPLICATED

Tibet on eight fronts. The **hapless** Tibetan army was swept aside; its soldiers were outnumbered, ill trained, poorly armed, and, as devout Buddhists, opposed the taking of all life. The Dalai Lama was forced to agree that Tibet was a Chinese province. In return, he was promised there would be no change in his status or powers. That promise was soon broken.

Communist leaders in Beijing outlawed religion in China and would not tolerate a province where almost a third of the men were monks and where Buddhism dominated every aspect of the people's lives. Chairman Mao promised to "liberate" the Tibetan people from the **thralldom** of religion. The Tibetan people were never asked if they wanted such "liberation."

Chinese soldiers initiated the systematic destruction of the religious and cultural institutions of Tibet. They **pillaged** the monasteries, stripping them of all treasures, which were sent to China to be sold. Thousands of monks who resisted were shot. Only a few of Tibet's six thousand monasteries, temples, and libraries survived intact. Tibetan youths were sent to China for Communist **indoctrination,** while the rest of the population was organized into forced labor groups. Chinese settlers entered the country and took up residence.

In March of 1959, when it appeared that Chinese officials were planning to arrest the Dalai Lama, he fled to northern India, where he established a government-in-exile. By the end of the year, nearly eight thousand Tibetan refugees joined him. Since then, he has worked tirelessly to return Tibet to its earlier state of independence. He travels the world, lecturing about the **heinous** crimes committed against his people and advocating peaceful means of resolving conflicts. He was awarded the 1989 Nobel Peace Prize in recognition of his nonviolent campaign to end Chinese domination of Tibet. Whether he and his followers will ever return to their homeland is difficult to foresee, yet the Dalai Lama remains a powerful symbol of Tibet's lost independence. If in the end he cannot return, the fourteenth Dalai Lama may well be the last.

The Quiz-Show Scandal

Sponsors who pay to advertise products on television are not permitted to dictate the content of the shows during which their commercials run. Their role is limited to deciding which shows they will advertise on. This was not always the case. A change in the relationship between sponsors and programs was triggered in the 1950s by one of television's most **unsavory** episodes—the quiz-show scandal. Its **repercussions** are felt today.

Early television producers looked to radio for ideas for their shows. *The $64 Question*, popular on radio, became a television program renamed *The $64,000 Question*. Contestants were asked simple questions at the start, which became more **abstruse** as the dollar amount for a correct answer increased. Successful contestants returned each week, with their winnings **accruing** until they reached $64,000, the top prize and an enormous sum at the time.

The program became the most popular show on television. Soon there was a **surfeit** of big-money quiz shows. Because competition for viewers was intense, many shows were not the simple tests of knowledge they **purported** to be.

Producers came under pressure from sponsors and networks to make shows as dramatic and entertaining as possible to draw more viewers and gain higher ratings. Viewers were **inveigled** into thinking that contestants were hearing questions for the first time. In fact, contestants were coached on questions beforehand. Their furrowed brows and anguished looks as they thought of the correct answers were rehearsed **histrionics.**

A lecturer from Columbia University named Charles Van Doren was a contestant on a quiz show called *Twenty One*. Van Doren, from a distinguished family that included a Pulitzer Prize–winning poet, was impressed that the show glorified knowledge rather than athletics or show business. There were no **improprieties** when Van Doren first discussed appearing on the show, but soon he was drawn into a web of deception as producers' hints about questions and answers became more **explicit.** When they dropped all pretense and offered him a chance to see the questions before shows, he at first indignantly rejected the proposal but in the end **acquiesced.** Van Doren was persuaded that if he won, he would help make this show about knowledge as exciting as those showing crime and violence.

Too many people knew the show was fixed for it to remain a secret for long. The suspicions of the New York district attorney were aroused, and he began an

© SSI • MAY BE DUPLICATED

investigation. A former contestant came to him with a devastating **revelation.** The contestant was given the answers to questions that would be asked on *Twenty One*. At first, Van Doren and others involved in the show denied the charges. They claimed their reputations were being **besmirched** by a former loser on the show. The problem with the district attorney's case was that it was not illegal to feed contestants the answers. Congress got into the act. If there were no laws against rigging TV quiz shows, maybe there should be.

Congressional hearings were held, and those involved in *Twenty One* and similar shows were forced to testify under oath in the glare of the national spotlight. A **penitent** Van Doren expressed regret at deceiving the public, friends, and family. He was fired from his job as a television consultant and resigned his position at Columbia University.

Along with twenty others, Van Doren was charged with perjury for lying before the district attorney's grand jury. All received suspended sentences. As a result of the scandal, laws were passed to regulate television, but the public's faith in the **probity** of those who ran television received a blow from which it never completely recovered.

© SSI • MAY BE DUPLICATED

The Dorothy and Herbert Vogel Collection

The National Gallery of Art in Washington, D.C., was a gift to the nation from banking and industry **mogul** Andrew W. Mellon. Although some wealthy people are uncompromising **philistines,** such acts of **munificence** are common among those who can afford them. When visitors to the National Gallery see works from "The Dorothy and Herbert Vogel Collection," they are excused for thinking the Vogels were wealthy. In fact, nothing could be further from the truth.

Herbert Vogel, an **avuncular** man with a twinkle in his eye, was a postal clerk in New York City. His wife, Dorothy, was a reference librarian at the Brooklyn Public Library. They married in 1962 and honeymooned in Washington, D.C. Visits to the National Gallery during their stay inspired them to try painting, an effort they soon abandoned. Instead they became **inveterate** collectors of other people's work. To do so, they lived frugally, using Dorothy's salary to pay expenses, while everything Herbert earned was spent acquiring art. Though neither came from a wealthy family, they had in common a love of art and considerable **perspicacity** in selecting works from talented artists at the beginning of their careers. Many later became famous, which increased the value of their work.

New York in the sixties was an exciting place for artists. Op art, pop art, minimalism, and conceptualism were some of the **nascent** movements that took the art world by storm. Painters and sculptors met in Greenwich Village to **expound** their theories and argue. Herbert Vogel, who worked irregular hours, took the subway to Manhattan to participate in these **convivial** gatherings. After sitting quietly and absorbing the ideas of the artists, some of whom had not sold a single work, he returned home to share his experiences with his wife.

The Vogels became acquainted with artists and began making purchases. It was a **propitious** time to start a collection; works that would later sell for tens of thousands of dollars could be bought for mere hundreds or even less. The Vogels never disclosed what they paid for a piece—to put a cash value on art was **anathema** to them. They appreciated pieces for their **intrinsic** worth, not for what they would bring on the open market. The Vogels never tried to cash in on their art collection by selling any of their pieces.

The Vogels' taste in art was **eclectic;** they bought what they loved, could afford, and had room for. This last consideration is important, for by 1992, their tiny apartment was crammed with two thousand paintings, drawings, and sculptures.

© SSI • MAY BE DUPLICATED

It was then that the Vogels decided to donate their treasures to the nation, and they chose the National Gallery of Art for their collection because it does not charge for admission and never sells any of its works of art. Five vans transported the treasured objects to their new home. The Vogels **assuaged** whatever sadness they felt by reflecting on the living space they had gained and on the fact that they would continue to collect art.

In 2009, the couple divided another 2,500 pieces of art among art institutions across the United States. They called this project *The Dorothy and Herbert Vogel Collection: 50 Works for 50 States.* People in every part of the nation will benefit from the Vogels' collecting expertise and generosity.

In his play *Lady Windemere's Fan,* Oscar Wilde defines a cynic as someone "who knows the price of everything and the value of nothing." The Vogels reversed this **epigram,** for it can truly be said that, where art is concerned, they knew the value of everything and the price of nothing.

© SSI • MAY BE DUPLICATED

Tsunami: The Big Wave

Geologists know the Earth's crust is not solid rock but is instead made of interlocking "plates" riding on a molten mantle. These plates move slowly. When they slide or grind against one another, an earthquake may be triggered. If this **upheaval** occurs on the ocean floor, the result can be more catastrophic; it may **presage** a tsunami, ocean waves of such force that they sweep away whole villages and **pulverize** buildings.

When an undersea section of the Earth's crust shifts, it displaces a huge volume of water, releasing **kinetic** energy. Because this energy is distributed over the depth of the water, its effects are not immediately apparent. All that is seen are slight waves on the surface, even though they are traveling at over six hundred miles an hour. It is not until these undersea waves reach shallower waters that they unleash their power. The energy that was diffused over a depth of several miles is now concentrated in water just hundreds of feet deep and getting shallower. A wave's velocity decreases, but its compressed energy forces it to grow. What began thousands of miles away as a surface **undulation** two or three feet high becomes a wall of water thirty to one hundred feet high, smashing everything in its path.

The regions most in danger from tsunamis are those **contiguous** to the Pacific Ocean, where undersea geological events are frequent. A tsunami powerful enough to cause serious damage occurs in the Pacific every ten to fifteen years. Japan is prone to tsunamis; an area of intense **seismic** activity lies close to its eastern shore. The **etymology** of the name *tsunami* reflects Japan's familiarity with this phenomenon; it comes from two Japanese words, *tsu* (harbor) and *nami* (wave). Because Japanese tsunamis have a short distance to travel, coastal dwellers receive almost no warning of them. In the most vulnerable areas, seawalls were built to **repulse** the tsunami, but a fifty-foot wall is of little value against a hundred-foot wall of water.

The Hawaiian **archipelago,** located in the mid-Pacific with no large land masses nearby, is vulnerable to tsunamis. In 1946, an earthquake measuring 7.8 on the Richter scale and centered near Alaska's Aleutian Islands set off a tsunami over one hundred feet high when it reached the Alaskan coast. It struck Hawaii about five hours later, traveling at 490 miles per hour; waves fifty feet high flooded the coast, killing 173 people.

As a result, the United States established the Pacific Tsunami Warning Center, located outside Honolulu. There, seismologists (scientists who study earthquakes) practice the **recondite** science of tsunami prediction by monitoring plate activity over the Pacific. Quiet spells are punctuated by periods of **frenetic** action when needles on instruments start jumping, indicating an earthquake. The seismologists **correlate** data to pinpoint the location of the earthquake and estimate the likelihood of a tsunami and its magnitude.

On the morning of December 26, 2004, an earthquake, measuring 9.0 on the Richter scale, struck beneath the sea off the coast of Sumatra, Indonesia. The earthquake—the fourth largest since 1900—sent a wall of water **careening** across the Indian Ocean, and waves over one hundred feet high crashed without warning on the shores of South Asian countries. The hardest hit were Indonesia, Sri Lanka, India, and Thailand. More than 280,000 people lost their lives, and millions more were missing or injured. The force of the tsunami was so intense that entire villages were washed away.

Many wondered why there had been no warning. While countries of the Pacific Rim have a system that gives them three to fourteen hours' warning of a tsunami, there is no such system in the Indian Ocean countries. A mixture of circumstances such as poverty and remoteness of islands—not a **cavalier** attitude toward these giant waves—is responsible for this situation. Anyone who has witnessed a tsunami understands the importance of providing this warning and will never forget this most fearsome of natural disasters.

© SSI • MAY BE DUPLICATED

The Gift of Tragedy

What do movies, sitcoms, plays, and opera have in common? All trace their origin back twenty-five centuries to a Greek named Aeschylus, who lived from c. 525 to c. 456 BCE. He is one of the **triumvirate** of Greek writers, with Sophocles and Euripides, who refined tragedy as a literary form and helped make Athens the cradle of Western civilization in the fifth century BCE.

As a young man in Athens, Aeschylus joined thousands of **votaries** of Dionysus who attended festivals honoring the god. Citizens competed to have work performed at these events, which combined music, dance, and choral recitations. These performances included an interlude in which the leader of the chorus and an actor known as the "answerer" delivered **soliloquies.**

In 499 BCE, Aeschylus competed in this event and for the next forty years. His accomplishment was to refuse to be bound by the **strictures** of the past. He introduced a second actor so the two could address each other in stage dialogue. In this sense, Aeschylus invented character and plot, the twin essentials of drama. He broadened his subject matter to include themes from history and ancient myth. He also elevated the language of the drama; his stately **cadences** gave it a nobility appropriate to his tragic themes. The Aeschylean **canon** consists of ninety plays, of which seven have survived whole; we know of the remainder only through fragments or contemporary references.

The characters in Aeschylus's plays are not ones audiences identify with easily. In *Prometheus*, with one exception, they are deities. Prometheus is regarded as a **renegade** by the other gods for stealing the secret of fire and giving it to humans. The play's action is minimal, consisting of a sequence of visitors to Prometheus, who is chained to a rock as punishment.

The second great playwright of this era, Sophocles (c. 496–406 BCE), wrote one hundred plays, of which seven survive. He is probably the first to use a third actor, thereby increasing the scope of the drama. He also introduced painted scenery, giving his plays a more realistic touch. His characters are on an all-too-human scale, and audiences from ancient times to the present identified with them.

Antigone, in the play of the same name, is a great Sophoclean tragic heroine. Her brother Polyneices is killed in an unsuccessful attempt to **usurp** the throne of Creon, ruler of Thebes. Creon denies him proper burial. When Antigone defies his **edict** by performing the burial ceremonies, he orders her put to death even though

© SSI • MAY BE DUPLICATED

she is **betrothed** to his son Haemon. In a fit of rage, Haemon berates his father, but Creon is adamant. Warned by the prophet Tiresias that he has committed **blasphemy** against the gods, Creon has a change of heart, but too late: Antigone has hanged herself. In despair, Haemon also commits suicide, as does Creon's wife. Creon, whose offense was to keep a corpse among the living, himself becomes "a living corpse," as he acknowledges in the final moments of the play.

Sophocles said of his younger rival Euripides (c. 480–406 BCE) that while he, Sophocles, represented people as they ought to be, Euripides represented them as they are. Nineteen of Euripides's ninety-two plays have survived, and they contain strong-willed characters whose violent passions lead to the drama's tragic **denouement.** His characters, including women, are drawn with such complexity that the audience's sympathies are divided or shift during the play. Medea, in the play of that name, first arouses our pity as a woman of powerful emotions whose husband, Jason, brings her to a land where she feels like a stranger. When he becomes **enamored** of another woman, her **insensate** rage leads her to murder their two children. In modern translations, the play continues to enjoy widespread popularity, almost twenty-five centuries after it was written.

Euripides died in 406 BCE. In tribute to his friend and rival of fifty years, the ninety-year-old Sophocles modified the **vestments** of the performers as a show of mourning. A few months later, Sophocles, too, was dead, and the golden age of Greek tragedy came to an end.

© SSI • MAY BE DUPLICATED

Reaching the Heights

Fear of heights is a common **phobia.** In mild cases, this fear is the **queasy** feeling people get when looking from a tall building at the **lilliputian** people below. In extreme cases, it can trigger an acute attack of **vertigo.** This fear lessens when people lose contact with the ground, even if they are very high up. Think of how **blasé** people are boarding an airplane.

Because few people want to risk their lives working hundreds of feet in the air on tall structures, builders pay high wages to those who will. The Dominion Bridge Steel Company proposed building a bridge over the Saint Lawrence River, near Quebec City, in the 1880s. One end of the bridge would be on Mohawk land. Tribal leaders gave permission to build, provided that the company **reciprocate** by hiring Mohawks to work on the project. The new workers had no experience with construction and were **relegated** to positions as unskilled laborers.

As the bridge progressed, skilled riveters, perched precariously above the river, were astonished to see these laborers walking nonchalantly along high, narrow girders (beams) to watch them work. Some riveters attributed the Mohawks' actions to **bravado;** others believed they simply felt no fear of heights.

One of the project managers, seeing their curiosity, wondered if the Mohawks wanted to learn riveting and other skilled jobs. Given the **disparity** in wages for laborers and skilled ironworkers, the Mohawks readily said yes. Soon, Mohawk riveting crews were at work. The first member would heat rivets in a bucket of hot coals resting on a plank. When one was red-hot, he would remove it with tongs and toss the glowing **projectile** to the second crew member, who caught it in a bucket and placed it in a hole through two steel beams. The third member, using a tool called a dollar bar, held it in place, while the fourth flattened the end with a rivet gun. In this way, the steel girders were fastened together. When the bridge was completed, the Mohawk crews moved to other projects. They were joined by other Mohawks who shared their **proclivity** for moving nimbly on narrow walkways far above ground.

The twenty-one-story Flatiron Building, completed in 1902, marked the **advent** of the Manhattan skyscraper-building boom, which peaked in the 1920s. Tall buildings created an enormous demand for ironworkers, which Mohawk crews satisfied. They helped **fabricate** the steel skeleton of the 1,250-foot Empire State Building in 1930, for years the tallest building on Earth, and twenty years later helped erect a 204-foot television antenna atop it.

© SSI • MAY BE DUPLICATED

The first Mohawks began arriving in New York in the early 1920s and found **domiciles** in Brooklyn. Previously living as **itinerant** workers, they now led settled lives with their families and had only to travel across the East River to reach the Manhattan work sites. During the 1960s and 1970s when there were many construction jobs in New York, the Mohawk community grew to some one thousand people. The Cuyler Presbyterian Church offered services conducted in Mohawk, and local restaurants served Mohawk dishes. The section around Brooklyn's Pacific Street became another tiny piece in the ethnic mosaic of New York. When the building boom finally declined in the last decades of the century, families returned to Canada and New York.

© SSI • MAY BE DUPLICATED

The Wall

The Vietnam War had devastating repercussions for Americans and others. It began in 1956 when American military advisers went to South Vietnam to aid its government against communist opposition. This opposition was supported by North Vietnam, which was already governed by a communist regime. By the late 1960s, the United States was deeply involved in what became a war of **attrition,** measured by daily "body counts" as each side hoped to exhaust the other into giving up. Fifty-eight thousand Americans died, and a third of a million were wounded. Two million Vietnamese lives were lost, including many thousands of civilians. The country was devastated by intensive bombing and by toxic chemical **defoliation** to eliminate the cover of trees and vegetation. The war cost U.S. taxpayers two hundred billion dollars. It ended in 1975 with a North Vietnamese victory.

A total of 2.7 million American men and women served in Vietnam. As they returned home, many were not given the hero's welcome that Americans returning from previous wars had received. Instead, they were met by a public divided over the war. Many Americans found it difficult to show support for those who had fought in a war they believed was wrong, although most veterans had been compelled to serve. Soldiers were **upbraided** as war criminals and murderers by extreme opponents of the war. Veterans were hurt and confused by the **opprobrium** they encountered.

Some retreated into silence but could not **expunge** the horrific war experiences from their memories. In contrast, a public **amnesia** regarding the war developed. Many were unwilling to confront the war's issues: its human and material costs, the animosity between opponents and supporters, and the fact that America was defeated.

In the late 1970s, veterans of the Vietnam War started a fund to build a memorial to those who had died. They raised nine million dollars and held a competition to select a design, with the **proviso** that the memorial express no political view.

Maya Lin was an architecture student at Yale University when a professor required that his students submit a design for the memorial. The popular conception of a memorial was something like the **equestrian** statues of Civil War generals. In Lin's opinion, such **hackneyed** representations were a simplification of war. Her design called for walls of polished black granite to be built into the earth, set in the shape of a shallow V. Carved into the stone would be the names of all killed or missing, in chronological order by the date of death or disappearance. The wall would increase in height as one descended until, at its **vertex,** where the trench is deepest, it

© SSI • MAY BE DUPLICATED

would be ten feet high. Visitors could run their fingers over the names. This **tactile** quality was to become an important aspect of Lin's work.

Congress chose **verdant** ground between the Lincoln Memorial and the Capitol as the site of the memorial. In spring 1981, the judges of the competition, after evaluating the 1,421 entries, declared Maya Lin's proposal the winner. The vote was unanimous, but the public's reaction to the design, reflecting ambivalence about the war, was divided. Those opposing it called it "a degrading ditch" and "a wall of shame" that **sullied** the memory of the dead. They wanted a memorial that would honor the dead. To **appease** critics, they placed a statue of three soldiers near the entrance, and later added a second statue of three servicewomen.

Despite the initial criticism, Lin's wall, dedicated in 1982, has been a focal point for discussion of the war. The memorial draws over a million visitors a year, more than any other site in the nation's capital. It is a powerful tribute to the fallen, from Harry C. Cramer, an army captain killed in 1957, to Richard Van de Geer, killed on May 15, 1975, during the **debacle** of the war's final days. Many are moved to tears by their visit. Lin has said that the wall "was not meant to be cheerful or happy, but to bring out in people the realization of loss and a cathartic healing process." She succeeded in her aim.

© SSI • MAY BE DUPLICATED

Dwarf Mammoths

Before the 1990s, references asserted **unequivocally** that the ancestral elephants known as mammoths became extinct ten thousand years ago at the end of the Ice Age. The Ice Age was a period when the polar ice sheet advanced and retreated for one and a half million years.

Scientists think mammoths grew gradually to great size as a means of defense. A **multifarious** array of predators—wolves, saber-toothed tigers, and lions—had adapted to the climate **prevailing** along the ice sheet. But preying on this **behemoth** of an animal would have been difficult. Because there was a **plenitude** of smaller animals sharing the land, whose meat was just as **succulent,** mammoths were ignored.

The warming trend that caused the retreat of the ice sheet resulted in rising sea levels and a changed climate less **salubrious** for animals, including the mammoth with its four-inch-thick layer of fat and shaggy coat. Temperatures rose, and rainfall increased. Rich, dry grasslands became soggy **tundra** with few plants. The mammoth found less vegetation to eat. This was not the first climatic change this creature had lived through. The polar ice cap had advanced and retreated four or five times during the Ice Age, and the mammoth had survived these **vicissitudes.** The difference this time was the arrival of a predator more intelligent than any before.

The end of the Ice Age made it possible for humans to extend the range of their activity. They began **impinging** on the mammoth's northern habitat. This animal provided hunters with food, clothing, and shelter. Its curving twelve-foot tusks could be formed into a frame that became a hut when covered with skins. The mammoth population, thinned by the decrease in its food supply, ill adapted to the warmer climate, and hunted by humans, gradually lost the battle for survival. The population became **attenuated** until, ten thousand years ago, the species became extinct.

Or so it was believed. Then in March 1993, a Russian research team announced that fragments of mammoth bone and tusk and a number of teeth had been dug up on an island one hundred miles off the coast of northeastern Siberia. That in itself was unremarkable. Entire mammoth carcasses have been **disinterred** from the frigid wilderness of Alaska and Siberia. Deep-frozen for ten thousand years, the meat had escaped the **putrefying** effects of air and water and was still edible, though perhaps not tasty. What startled the scientific community now was the age and size of the mammoths to which the teeth belonged. Some of the teeth belonged to normal-sized mammoths ten to fourteen feet tall and thirteen to twenty thousand years old. But other teeth belonged to adult mammoths six feet tall and only four to seven thousand years old. Was it possible there was a dwarf of the species?

The term "dwarf mammoth" is an **oxymoron,** but evidence that such a creature existed was certain, and the explanation was intriguing. Wrangel Island, where the fragments were found, was formed when the sea level rose at the end of the Ice Age, isolating the island mammoths from those on the mainland. The porous rock on Wrangel allowed for good drainage. Fertile soil produced abundant vegetation. Scientists **postulate** that with no predators and a limited grazing area, there was no survival value to be gained from great size. The evidence indicates that over six thousand years, each generation of island mammoth became smaller until their height was less than half that of their ancestors. We don't know what happened to the last generation of dwarf mammoths four thousand years ago. What scientists do know is that humans visited Wrangel Island at one point. They think the dwarf mammoths, like their mainland relatives, were hunted to extinction.

© SSI • MAY BE DUPLICATED

A Child of the Sixties

Some entertainers stay popular by avoiding controversy. They keep quiet on divisive issues; to express opinions may offend those with **antithetical** views. Throughout her career, folk singer Joan Baez has risked her reputation, profession, and life fighting for peace and social justice.

Her first album, released in 1960, came at the beginning of a tumultuous decade. The United States was in the **throes** of a civil-rights revolution while fighting an unpopular war in Vietnam. Dr. Martin Luther King Jr. was leading marches and addressing rallies; students were burning draft cards and going to jail for refusing to serve in the armed forces, acts considered courageous by supporters and **craven** by critics.

In 1963, when Dr. King delivered the "I Have a Dream" speech in Washington, D.C., Baez led the crowd of several hundred thousand singing the civil-rights anthem "We Shall Overcome." When Dr. King led protests against injustice, she marched with him. She was active in the antiwar movement. Like many who protested the Vietnam War, Baez was arrested and sent to jail.

This desire for justice and change was embodied by Woodstock, a three-day music festival held at a **bucolic** New York farm in 1969. Young people from across America came to Woodstock in a spirit of **amity** and love to celebrate the ideals of the decade. Baez was there, voicing her convictions in song. If anyone deserves the **sobriquet** "Child of the Sixties," it is Joan Baez.

In December 1972, Baez and others visited North Vietnam just as the United States grew more **bellicose,** increasing bombing attacks. During their stay, the visitors shared the **privations** of the Vietnamese people in makeshift shelters as bombs fell—a gesture regarded by Baez's critics as **tantamount** to treason.

Baez was born in 1941 to a Scottish American mother and a Mexican American father. Joan went to school in a middle-class California community with a substantial Hispanic population. Because she spoke only English, the Hispanic children at school avoided her, while the white children would have nothing to do with her because they considered her Hispanic. This isolation made her **introspective** but also gave her the strength to be self-reliant, a quality her parents encouraged.

Music provided a way for her to reach out. Baez has what one critic has called "an achingly pure soprano" voice. She bought her first guitar at age fifteen and began singing at school gatherings. Audiences responded enthusiastically; she had found her

© SSI • MAY BE DUPLICATED

métier. The family moved to Boston following Joan's high school graduation, and Baez began singing in coffeehouses. Within three years her concerts were sold out, her albums were best sellers, and her picture was on the cover of *Time* magazine. She had joined the **exalted** ranks of elite musicians but did not abandon her ideals.

Baez used her fame to draw attention to the causes she championed and gave them financial and personal support. Critics were quick to **impugn** her sincerity, perhaps in the belief that people should be **penurious** themselves when speaking out on behalf of the poor. She ignored their **animadversions** and carried on doing what she had always done—singing and campaigning for social-justice causes. In a 1998 interview, Baez looked back on a career of four decades that had produced forty albums. She was also looking ahead, she said, anticipating the day when she would stop singing professionally and devote her time to social activism, prose writing, or just catching her breath. Happily for her fans, she keeps postponing that day.

Kwanzaa

Beginning ten years after Columbus's 1492 voyage and continuing for 350 years, Africans were taken by force and brought to the Americas as enslaved people. Those who traded and owned enslaved people not only deprived Africans of their freedom but also stripped away their identity, for when people were carried off in chains, ties to their cultures were **sundered.** Africans in the New World struggled to maintain their customs and beliefs, in spite of the **travails** of slavery, yet much was lost. They had to create a new cultural identity in the **context** of the American society that enslaved them.

In 1965, African American professor Maulana Karenga was disturbed by riots in Watts, an African American section of Los Angeles. The riots showed frustration over injustices, including poverty, unemployment, poor housing, inadequate health care, and lack of hope. Karenga believed the **malaise** that afflicted urban African Americans was caused not just by physical poverty but also by spiritual and cultural deprivation. His resolve to address these issues was the **genesis** of a unique holiday that would draw upon the cultural heritage of people of African ancestry.

"There is nothing so powerful as an idea whose time has come" sounds like a **platitude,** but it applies to Karenga's idea. The holiday he proposed, which he named Kwanzaa, is today celebrated by millions of people, not only African Americans, but also people of African descent around the world. The name comes from the Swahili phrase *matunda ya kwanza,* meaning "first fruits." It is celebrated **concurrently** with the Christmas–New Year season, although it has no religious significance.

Karenga based Kwanzaa on *Nguzo Saba,* or "seven principles" he drew from African thought. The first is *Umoja* (unity). African Americans **reconcile** their differences and strive for unity in family, community, nation, and race. Next is *Kujichagulia* (self-determination). To be controlled by others is **debasing** to the human spirit. Real power comes from defining, naming, creating, and speaking for oneself and one's people. *Ujima* (collective work and responsibility) fosters the spirit of **altruism** by encouraging individuals to take responsibility for the well-being of others and to solve problems and build community. The next principle, *Ujamaa* (cooperative economics), stresses African American ownership of businesses and **enjoins** the community to support them. The fifth principle is *Nia* (purpose). Its goal is to make community building the vocation of African American people. *Kuumba* (creativity) stresses the importance of seeking new ways for individuals to make their

© SSI • MAY BE DUPLICATED

communities more beautiful and beneficial. The final principle, *Imani* (faith), stresses the cultivation of a belief in the African American people, in parents and leaders, and in the rightness and victory of their struggle.

African Americans celebrate Kwanzaa by laying out a woven mat with fruits and vegetables symbolizing the rewards of collective labor and ears of corn representing children. These items reflect the traditions of harvest celebrations that Kwanzaa stems from. A candelabra, called a *kinara*, holds seven candles: a black one in the center, three red ones to the left, and three green ones to the right. The three colors represent the people, their struggle, and the future and hope, respectively, and individual candles represent the Nguzo Saba. The black candle is lit on the first day of Kwanzaa, and another each day afterward, alternating from left to right. After each candle is lit, people discuss the principle of the day and how they strive to embody it in daily life.

On the evening of the sixth day, usually December 31, a feast called the *Karamu* is held; participants bring dishes of African American **cuisine.** A cup is filled, and **libations** are offered. The cup is passed to all present. Then celebrants, beginning with the eldest, speak **extemporaneously** about their life experiences, their pleasure at being present, and their hopes. On the last day, presents may be exchanged, but the **crass** giving of expensive store-bought gifts is discouraged. They prefer books and handmade gifts reflecting African heritage.

© SSI • MAY BE DUPLICATED

Washington National Cathedral

When delegates from Israel and Arab states arrived in the United States for Middle East peace talks in 1991, it seemed appropriate that they and their American hosts participate in an **ecumenical** religious service. A **venue** for this gathering, Washington National Cathedral, was completed one year before. There, under its vaulted 120-foot ceiling, followers of the Christian, Muslim, and Jewish faiths were able to **transcend** their differences and join in worship.

When the nation's capital was laid out, the idea for a national cathedral was **mooted** by French architect Pierre L'Enfant, who was selected by George Washington to plan it. L'Enfant proposed "a great church for national purposes . . . equally open to all." The idea fell into **abeyance** because such an institution might violate a **tenet** of the constitution forbidding the establishment of a state-approved religion.

In 1893—one hundred years after Washington laid the cornerstone of the Capitol building—Congress granted a charter to the Protestant Episcopal Cathedral Foundation to build the cathedral. It is variously known as Washington National Cathedral and the National Cathedral, but its official name is the Cathedral Church of Saint Peter and Saint Paul. Because no government money was used to build this **edifice**, the **sacrosanct** separation of church and state was preserved. The cathedral was to have no local congregation. It would serve as an interreligious house of worship.

Fifty-seven acres on Mount St. Alban, the highest point in the city, were chosen as the site. President Theodore Roosevelt laid the cornerstone for the new building in 1907. Work proceeded slowly, at a pace **commensurate** with the magnitude and complexity of the project. The first section, Bethlehem Chapel, opened in 1912. Seventy-eight more years passed before the final stone was set in place to complete the **pinnacle** on the South Tower of the sixth largest cathedral in the world. If this time span suggests a **dilatory** pace, consider this: England's Canterbury Cathedral took five hundred years to complete!

The cathedral was built in the fourteenth-century English Gothic style: **Buttresses** supported exterior walls, and **gargoyles** looked out over the city. Sculptors, stone masons, and artists working in stained glass, metal, and needlepoint devoted countless hours to its embellishment. One of the cathedral's two hundred stained-glass windows commemorates the 1969 lunar landing; embedded in one window is a sliver of moon rock presented by the *Apollo 11* crew.

On the west **facade** is a sculptural relief twenty-one feet across entitled *The Creation*, originally called *Ex Nihilo* ("Out of Nothing"). It is a **sensuous** composition of figures emerging from the void. The artist was Frederick Hart, who sculpted the seven-foot bronze statue *The Three Servicemen* at Washington's Vietnam Veterans Memorial.

The National Cathedral is in its infancy, especially when compared with the cathedrals of Europe. But it has begun to gather historical associations. The **requiem** service for President Eisenhower was held there in 1969. Helen Keller, with her teacher and companion Anne Sullivan, is buried there, as are President and Mrs. Woodrow Wilson. And Dr. Martin Luther King Jr. preached his last Sunday sermon there before his tragic assassination.

© SSI • MAY BE DUPLICATED

Birds of a Feather

The late nineteenth century in America is called the "Age of Elegance" because privileged citizens **flaunted** their status by purchasing beautiful and elaborate homes, clothing, art, and other luxuries. Women competed to display their beauty, refinement, and culture. They spent an **inordinate** amount of time on appearance, a preoccupation apparent in the hats they wore.

To produce striking creations, hat designers made extravagant use of birds. They employed birds' feathers, wings, heads, and entire birds, sometimes as many as six birds on one hat. All kinds were used, including robins, scarlet tanagers, blue jays, woodpeckers, owls, and shore birds. White egret plumes, known as aigrettes, atop a woman's head were believed to give her an **enticing** air. She might have a fan of dyed ostrich feathers. There was nothing new in this. Feathers as articles of adornment or symbols of power had been prized for thousands of years, but during America's "Gilded Age," as this period is also known, things got out of hand. Five million birds were killed annually in the United States to meet the demands of fashion.

Harriet Lawrence Hemenway was born into the **genteel** world of Boston high society in 1858. Her parents and grandparents were merchants and public benefactors, and she married into a family of equal wealth. Her position in society, reinforced by her strong personality, provided her with a **coterie** of admirers who welcomed her guidance on fashion at teas, drawing-room gatherings, or grand balls. Exquisite clothing and elaborate aigrettes were part of this world.

Change was in the air, however. Articles appeared describing the cost of feathers: Whole colonies of birds were being killed, leaving their young alone and without care. In 1895, Hemenway read an account of the slaughter of a heron colony. The **graphic** description made the use of feathers for embellishment **repugnant** to her. She banished them from her wardrobe and called upon friends, who regarded her as an **arbiter** of fashion, to do the same. Women who **demurred** were excluded from social gatherings, prompting them to change their minds. This boycott had little effect on the feather trade nationally. Hemenway carried the battle further by organizing a **conclave** of the city's scientific and social elite to form the Massachusetts Audubon Society. Its stated purpose was "to discourage buying and wearing for ornamental purposes the feathers of any wild bird . . . and to otherwise further the protection of our native birds."

© SSI • MAY BE DUPLICATED

Hemenway demonstrated she was a **redoubtable** foe of the feather industry. Within a year, the society's membership approached one thousand. With names like Cabot, Lowell, Saltonstall, and Adams, it read like a roster of Boston's **oligarchy.** One hundred chapters were established throughout the state, nearly all headed by women. By the turn of the century there were Audubon Societies in seventeen states, and in 1905 the National Association of Audubon Societies was formed.

A movement to ban the use of feathers for personal decoration was **inimical** to the feather industry. Companies argued that ending the trade would cost many jobs. But the opposition remained adamant. In 1910, a bill passed in New York that prohibited the sale of almost all North American nongame birds, either whole or parts. In 1913, Congress passed a bill that forbade the importation of any wild-bird plumage. A senator from Missouri, arguing against it, made the **ludicrous** claim that herons existed "so that we could get aigrettes for the bonnets of our beautiful ladies." Further regulations to protect birds were enacted later.

The end of the feather trade and its **concomitant** reduction in the slaughter of birds was caused by something more powerful than laws. Public opinion, led in Boston by Harriet Hemenway, had turned against it. Knowledge and determination combined to start a movement for the protection of wildlife that thrives to this day.

© SSI • MAY BE DUPLICATED

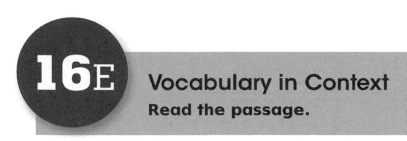

Gateway to the Promised Land

Trace your **lineage** three or four generations, and you may find you are one of the hundred million Americans descended from immigrants who came to the United States by way of Ellis Island. This small plot of land in New York harbor was the **terminus** of an ocean journey for millions of people from around the world. Once immigrants moved past inspection on Ellis Island, they continued to their destinations. One-third of them would go no farther than New York, the great **metropolis** a mile to the north, while the other two-thirds went to every part of the country.

The federal government assumed responsibility for immigration from the states in 1891. The following year, it began using Ellis Island to process would-be residents. This was a logical choice because New York City was the destination for many arriving from Europe, and the deep harbor allowed steamships to dock.

Between 1892 and 1924, twelve million people passed through Ellis Island— often more than five thousand a day. It was therefore miraculous that the **conflagration** of 1897, which destroyed the original buildings, took no lives.

In the Baggage Room inside the entrance, arrivals deposited their few **chattels** in tied-up bundles and battered suitcases. They proceeded to the Registry Room. This room was a **commodious** hall on the second floor where officials decided who would be admitted to the country.

Candidates for residence had to be mentally competent, able to support themselves, and in reasonably good health. Only one in fifty was denied entry, usually for medical reasons or because inspectors considered them politically **subversive.** Atop the stairs in the Registry Room, doctors studied people as they ascended, looking for signs of **listlessness** or shortness of breath that might indicate heart or lung disease. Those about whom there were legal or medical doubts were **sequestered** on the third floor. They remained there in **limbo** for weeks or months until their cases were decided. Most passed through in three to five hours and went on their way. The **perfunctory** medical examinations seldom took more than sixty seconds to complete. People suffering from illnesses such as trachoma, a particularly **virulent** eye disease that spreads rapidly and can cause blindness, were automatically denied entry.

By 1954, immigration had slowed considerably, and steamships were giving way to airliners. Immigration through Ellis Island was closed. In 1965, the island was incorporated into the nearby Statue of Liberty National Monument but was not

© SSI • MAY BE DUPLICATED

maintained. Ten years later, concerned over the buildings' **ramshackle** condition, the Ellis Island Restoration Project began. Donations allowed the main brick and limestone building to be restored to its former **pristine** condition, and for construction within it of a museum honoring America's immigrant tradition.

It opened in 1990 as the Ellis Island Museum of Immigration, boasting exhibits, artifacts, films, **archives,** and a research library. One feature is the Ellis Island Oral History Project, which has conducted interviews since 1973 and has amassed two thousand firsthand accounts of the immigrant experience. These are accessible via computer terminals; users can see the faces and hear the stories of people who passed through Ellis Island on their way to what, for many, was the promised land.

Machiavelli

When someone is shrewd or **duplicitous,** or acts in bad faith, we describe that person as *Machiavellian.* The word comes from Niccoló Machiavelli, an Italian diplomat who lived from 1460 to 1527. In addition to his duties in the city-state of Florence, he was a prolific author, and his **felicitous** style places him in the forefront of Italian writers. Machiavelli's works include histories, plays, and treatises on war, politics, and diplomacy. But he is famous, or perhaps **notorious,** because of one book—his handbook for rulers called *The Prince.*

Machiavelli was born in Florence, when Italian city-states were almost continuously at war. Florence was a republic where citizens participated in government. In 1469 when Machiavelli was born, Florence was controlled by Lorenzo de' Medici, known as Lorenzo the Magnificent. He was a cruel yet cultivated man under whose **autocratic** rule the arts flourished. France invaded northern Italy in 1494, helping Florentines **oust** the Medici family, and for two decades the city was again a republic.

After the Medici departed, Machiavelli served in Florence's government. Though born into a distinguished family, he was in **impecunious** circumstances because his father had incurred debts he could not repay. Machiavelli found employment as a clerk and quickly proved his worth. He was elected to the chancery, the ruling body of Florence, and served as its **emissary** on missions to France, Germany, and Rome. He helped form a citizen army to replace the fickle **mercenary** bands Florence had previously relied on for defense.

In 1512, a Spanish army loyal to the pope, with whom the Medici had ties, conquered the city and ended French influence. Florence had fallen, despite Machiavelli's efforts to improve its defenses. The Medici were restored to power, and Machiavelli's career ended abruptly. After being tortured and incarcerated as a traitor, he was allowed to retire to his property outside the city, where he devoted himself to writing.

Deeply affected by the fall of Florence and disturbed by the disunited state of Italy, Machiavelli sought in *The Prince* (1513) to answer this question: What were the qualities of a strong leader, one who could defend his territory, secure his power, and achieve his goals? The book contains many **precepts** that deal with the holding and wielding of power, and it advises rulers to be ruthless in exercising power. Ideally, a ruler should be both loved and feared. As Machiavelli states in his **forthright** manner, this is seldom possible, in which case it is better that the ruler be feared.

Perhaps reacting to Lorenzo's extravagances, he also advises the wise ruler to be **parsimonious** in public spending and allow people to prosper, with one exception: A ruler can be generous in granting the spoils of victory to his successful army, but only when the proceeds come from the defeated enemy. While earlier philosophers judged rulers by the morality of their actions, Machiavelli argued that morality and religion were tools to be used as the ruler saw fit. Though a religious man, he believed that Christianity applied to warfare had a **debilitating** effect on military virtues. Scholars believe this **jaundiced** view of human nature came from his observations of the diplomatic and political intrigues of his day.

These views shocked the Catholic hierarchy and the faithful. Machiavelli's outspoken, often **caustic,** opinions made him unpopular, especially with those who did not realize he wanted to shock his readers by appearing wicked. The French coined the word *Machiavellianism* as a **pejorative** term, influenced by their animosity toward Italy. Ultimately, whether *The Prince* reflects Machiavelli's own morality or is simply a candid discussion of the qualities a ruler needs in turbulent times is a question historians and readers must answer for themselves.

© 331 • MAY BE DUPLICATED

Prisoners of Conscience

When the United Nations **promulgated** its Universal Declaration of Human Rights in 1948, it was a significant event. No longer could a government say that the treatment of citizens within its borders was an "internal matter" and not the world's business. This historic document calls for minimum standards of decent treatment for citizens; for example, Article 5 **proscribes** torture, while Article 9 states that no one shall be subject to arbitrary arrest, detention, or exile. Nevertheless, some governments pay lip service to human rights while abusing their citizens. This **hypocrisy** exists because the United Nations lacks the power to enforce the Declaration.

In 1961, the autocratic Antonio Salazár ruled Portugal. He denied the Portuguese the right to express political opinions. When two students had the **effrontery** to raise their glasses publicly in a toast "to freedom," **retribution** followed. The two were arrested and sentenced to seven years' imprisonment. A London lawyer named Peter Benenson was **incensed** when he heard of their plight. He organized a letter-writing campaign that bombarded the Salazár government with demands for the students' release. Because of the embarrassing publicity, and to put the affair behind him, Salazár released the pair.

Benenson's success inspired him to expand his efforts. The world's jails were filled with people **bereft** of hope who had committed no crimes but who had run afoul of the **regimes** in their countries. The idea that those responsible would heed letters from people outside their borders was **derided** by critics as futile, but Benenson was not deterred. His appeals received an outpouring of support. In 1961 he formed the human-rights advocacy group Amnesty International.

In 2011, Amnesty International (AI) marked its fiftieth year. Now AI has seven million members and operates in 150 countries. Since its founding, AI has worked on behalf of many thousands of prisoners of conscience. Before "adopting" someone as a prisoner of conscience, AI ensures that the person meets certain **criteria.** Those eligible for adoption are persons who have not **espoused** violence and who have been detained because of religious or political views, racial or ethnic origin, or gender, in violation of the Universal Declaration of Human Rights.

AI employs teams of investigators to gather information **pertinent** to each case and to **substantiate** allegations of abuse. This is a difficult task, given that governments practicing human-rights abuses are uncooperative. In cases where the

© SSI • MAY BE DUPLICATED

government wishes to avoid public castigation, the **impending** arrival of an AI team can result in the release of prisoners, though the government might not admit the connection between AI and the release.

Once adopted, a prisoner of conscience has his or her case assigned to local chapters. Members send letters and telegrams to officials, perhaps including a country's president, minister of justice, chief judge, or prison warden, asking them firmly and politely to **redress** the wrong. In many cases, this approach has worked. Amnesty International was awarded the 1977 Nobel Peace Prize in recognition of its efforts to bring freedom, justice, and peace to the world.

© SSI • MAY BE DUPLICATED

Elephant Memories

When American Cynthia Moss arrived in Africa as a tourist in 1967, she experienced an **epiphany** that changed her life. It was her first visit to the continent, but she recalled having "this overwhelming sense that I had come home." Africa's hold on Moss was **consolidated** when she visited Tanzania and encountered elephants. Studying these mammals was to become her life's work.

She returned to Africa in 1968 and has lived there since. First she worked as a journalist and editor of *Wildlife News*, a publication of the African Wildlife Foundation (AWF). Then, in 1972, under the **aegis** of the AWF, she and another researcher began a study of the elephants from Kenya's Amboseli National Park. They lived among elephants and noted their behavior, which has taught us about the social life of these complex, highly intelligent creatures.

Elephants travel in family groups of immature calves and generations of cows. Herds are led by the oldest (and often wisest) of the females, the matriarch. Bull calves are driven from the herd when they reach maturity and travel alone or with other males to find mates. Moss noted the bonds between individuals. In her book *Elephant Memories*, she describes two herds meeting at a water hole. Individuals greeted each other by intertwining their **pendulous** trunks and clicking their tusks together as their **stentorian,** joyful trumpeting filled the air. Elephants also experience grief over the death of a comrade. Moss observed herd members trying to "bury" a dead elephant by covering its body with branches and dirt. They maintain vigils for hours over the corpse of a relative.

Moss's **tenure** as director of the Amboseli Elephant Research Project coincided with a mounting worldwide demand for ivory carvings, causing the price of ivory to increase over twenty years. These carvings were not mere **baubles** but intricately crafted objects tempting to dealers and collectors. This demand **portended** the extinction of the African elephant, the chief source of ivory, unless action was taken. Marauding poachers with powerful weapons rampaged through central and east Africa. They slaughtered two thousand elephants per week during the 1980s for their tusks. By bribing **complaisant** officials to turn a blind eye, the poachers operated with impunity. Africa's elephant population declined from 1.3 million to about six hundred thousand in the decade prior to 1989.

Moss, her associate Joyce Poole, and others began a campaign to save the African elephant. The Kenyan government adopted the **pragmatic** view that

© SSI • MAY BE DUPLICATED

live elephants were more valuable than the tusks of dead ones because tourists, drawn by East Africa's wildlife, provided much of the country's income. With the backing of international conservation organizations, Kenya began to enforce laws against poaching.

Other African countries followed Kenya's lead, and the Convention on International Trade in Endangered Species, to which over 180 countries belong, declared a **moratorium** on the trading of ivory. The price of ivory plummeted, and poaching became a less **viable** occupation, though some illegal trading continues. Whether the African elephant has been saved from extinction or merely given a temporary **reprieve** is still unknown. Moss is cautiously optimistic. "If the ban stays in place . . . things will improve," she says. But she points out that it will take several decades before the herds recover from the **depredations** of the 1970s and 1980s. The illegal ivory trade still threatens wild elephants with extinction, as some thirty thousand elephants are poached each year. In response to the illegal trade, Kenya held massive bonfires of confiscated ivory. The first in 1989 was a symbolic act to dramatize Kenya's **unilateral** ban on ivory trading. The most recent, in 2016, destroyed more ivory at one time than ever before, representing six thousand to seven thousand dead elephants, with an estimated value of $105 million.

© SSI • MAY BE DUPLICATED

It's a Right-Handed World!

Left-handers make up about ten to fifteen percent of the population, but they have received more than their share of hostility. The Bible reflects this longstanding **antipathy:** It contains more than one hundred favorable references to the right hand and about twenty-five unfavorable references to the left hand. Throughout history, character flaws have been **imputed** to lefties, and well-known British psychologist Sir Cyril Burt **excoriated** them this way in 1937: "They squint, they stammer, they shuffle and shamble, they flounder about like seals out of water."

Burt promulgated the view that left-handedness in children is an **idiosyncrasy** to be corrected early—a view that was widely accepted among British and American **pedagogues.** One justification was that left-handed children are often **maladroit,** which is true when they are required to use tools, such as scissors, designed for the right hand. We now know that forcing lefties to use their right hand can have a **deleterious** effect; compelled to do something that does not come naturally, they fare poorly at many tasks, and their self-esteem suffers.

Left-handers had something else to worry about in 1991 when psychologists Stanley Coren and Diane Halpern **propounded** the theory that left-handers die earlier than right-handed people do. The two studied the death certificates of one thousand individuals, noting the ages people had died and determining whether they were right- or left-handed. The average left-hander died at sixty-six, while the right-handers lived on average to be seventy-five. Other scientists felt that **extrapolating** from such a small sample of the population was suspect. They believed that a study with more subjects might **negate** Coren and Halpern's findings. Many similar studies have not replicated their results.

The debate that followed brought the question of human handedness to the forefront, and it raised questions without answers. Truly **ambidextrous** persons are rare, but hands are mirror images of each other, so what causes one to be dominant? Why is there a **preponderance** of right-handers? Has this always been the case? Most scientists agree that apes and other nonhuman primates do not favor one hand, while human babies exhibit a propensity to do so at age two or later. Handedness may not be genetic, because one identical twin can be right-handed and the other left-handed, but this issue is not resolved.

The question of whether right-handedness has always been prevalent is difficult, but the answer seems to be in the affirmative. Five-thousand-year-old tools such

© SSI • MAY BE DUPLICATED

as bronze sickles were made for right-handers, and stone tools from earlier periods fit the right hand better. More **grisly** evidence, hundreds of thousands of years old, points to the same conclusion. Ancient skulls were found showing injuries caused by frontal blows to the head. These blows occurred more frequently on the left side, indicating that assailants were generally right-handed.

The view that left-handedness is a defect is **passé;** lefties can buy specially designed scissors and tools, though cars and other heavy equipment are still built only for right-handers. That may explain why, according to Coren and Halpern's study at least, left-handers are five times more likely to die in accidents. Perhaps these statistics affected the outcome of Coren and Halpern's study; certainly, they point to the need for greater understanding and accommodation of left-handedness.

One well-documented advantage lefties have is in sports, particularly baseball. A southpaw (another word for a lefty) pitches with the body facing toward first base and can more easily pick off base stealers, while a left-handed batter's **stance** allows for a quicker start when running to first base. About thirty percent of major league pitchers are left-handed. The list of lefties, from Leonardo da Vinci and Ludwig van Beethoven to Bill Gates and Ruth Bader Ginsburg, shows that even in a right-handed world, left-handers thrive.

© 331 • MAY BE DUPLICATED

Name _____ Date _____

Lesson (1) Review Exercise

1. People naturally get a little nervous when attending their first auction, but what at first seems _____ soon becomes familiar and enjoyable.

2. Those attending auctions must decide quickly whether to stay in or drop out of the bidding. One who _____ has lost.

3. An auctioneer must be a good judge of what is appropriate. Humor is good for warming up the crowd, but it's important that the _____ not get out of hand.

4. Auctioneers must keep tight control of the proceedings. They are _____ when they lose track of the bidding, and those who made the bids get upset.

5. A good auctioneer's view includes every person in the room. Excellent _____ vision is a great help.

6. Not all storytellers are auctioneers, but all auctioneers are storytellers. Conducting an auction seems to bring out the _____ in the person holding the gavel.

7. There is a rhythm to the words chanted by auctioneers. They _____ the last bid made while repeatedly suggesting what the next offer should be.

8. The asking price of a lot may be set low early in the bidding to encourage plenty of bids. The _____ come fast at first and then slow down as bidders drop out.

9. Accepting a very low bid early or dropping an inexpensive vase to wake up a crowd are some of the _____ practiced by auctioneers.

10. Auctioneers have an unlimited number of stories with which to entertain the crowd. Most of them are _____ , but that doesn't matter as long as they're funny.

11. Classes in auctioneering are held in Kansas City four times a year. Up to a thousand would-be auctioneers _____ for one of the nine-day courses.

12. Some wealthy collectors are too well known to show up at an art auction. They find it _____ to have an agent there to do the actual bidding.

13. A number of signals may be arranged between the auctioneer and secret bidders. Each discreet _____ means something different.

14. Tensions run high when the bidding is in the tens of millions. At such times the auctioneer must avoid getting excited and _____ an air of calmness.

15. Excitement mounts when two avid collectors are pursuing the same art object. The higher the bidding goes, the more _____ the auctioneer tries to appear.

Name _____ Date _____

Lesson ② Review Exercise

1. Llamas were first brought into the United States a hundred years ago. Although not among the native _____ , they have established themselves here.

2. Llamas are a fast-growing species in the United States. Americans have a(n) _____ for owning unusual pets, and llamas certainly qualify.

3. Camels and llamas are closely related. Both have haughty, almost _____ expressions that make them seem to think they are better than humans.

4. More and more people are discovering that llamas make wonderful pets. They require a(n) _____ of attention and are less demanding than dogs.

5. Llamas are easygoing creatures, but they don't like to be crowded. They are easily _____ if their space is invaded by a person or another llama.

6. Their patience makes them ideal companions for people suffering from a variety of problems. The llama's _____ nature seems to have a calming effect.

7. In one program in South Carolina, children with special needs go on wilderness treks with their assigned llamas. All the _____ needed for camping are carried by llamas.

8. A number of studies have been done on these relationships. The _____ value of associating with llamas is now well established.

9. On more and more golf courses, llamas act as caddies. They have a calming effect on golfers, who tend to become _____ when missing an easy putt.

10. A llama carrying a set of clubs is becoming a familiar sight. These four-legged caddies _____ themselves with dignity as they make their way around the course.

11. Golfers who score poorly may blame the llama for putting them off their game. It's true that golfers who are used to human caddies may find them _____ at first.

12. Coyotes are a serious problem for sheep farmers because _____ packs of these fierce creatures will attack an unprotected flock, causing losses for the farmer.

13. Farmers use llamas to protect their sheep. Should coyotes or other predators approach, the llama will _____ itself between the flock and the threatening animal.

14. Llamas fit in everywhere they are needed. They are equally at home in _____ surroundings or on a forest trail in the wilderness somewhere.

15. Llamas protect sheep, act as caddies, and make excellent companions for people. These are some of the _____ purposes for which llamas are used.

© SSI MAI BE DUPLICATED

Name _____ Date _____

Lesson ③ Review Exercise

1. Access to medical treatment in Tennessee in the 1940s was limited. Poor African American patients received mostly _____ treatment at that time.

2. As a small child plagued by illnesses, Wilma Rudolph's prospects did not look good. She could have had no idea of the _____ future that lay ahead.

3. Polio affected Rudolph's ability to walk. Muscles that aren't used _____ , and this makes a bad situation worse.

4. Rudolph had heat and water therapy as well as regular leg massages. The _____ required routine fifty-mile trips to Nashville.

5. Improvement was slow at first. The _____ of the treatment was eventually proved when the five-year-old learned to walk using leg braces.

6. At age nine, Rudolph was able to throw away her leg braces. Being able to walk like the other children was a gift of _____ value.

7. Determination, courage, strength, and athletic ability are a rare combination. Rudolph possessed all these qualities, and this made her a(n) _____ in the sports world.

8. The source of these attributes remains a mystery. Some are innate, but others can be _____ by those like Rudolph's fourth-grade teacher, Mrs. Hoskins.

9. Mrs. Hoskins was a powerful influence on young Rudolph. She was a(n) _____ because she needed to be, and she was a role model because of who she was.

10. She demanded a lot of her students, and they appreciated this. Rudolph became a(n) _____ admirer of Mrs. Hoskins.

11. Rudolph's best year was 1960. In the Rome Olympics that year she gave a(n) _____ performance, limping away with the gold medals.

12. Running in three Olympic events with a swollen ankle wasn't easy. Rudolph's _____ attitude helped her endure the pain while winning the medals.

13. For a sports prodigy today, the opportunities to get rich are enormous. Corporations offer athletes _____ sums of money just for wearing their logos.

14. Today's stars of track and field become like minor corporations themselves. The _____ offered by corporate sponsors take many forms.

15. Rudolph's active years as a runner were mostly in the 1950s. Corporate interest in athletics was in its _____ stage and sponsorships then were scarce.

© SSI • MAY BE DUPLICATED

Name _____ Date _____

Lesson (4) Review Exercise

1. Following the death of the thirteenth Dalai Lama, the regent had to make the next move. During

   a(n) _____ , he had a vision of the future Dalai Lama's home.

2. Officials who searched the country for the future Dalai Lama could not afford to make mistakes.

   They were extremely _____ in conducting the search.

3. It was important that the officials conducting the search not be recognized. For this reason they

   traveled _____ as they went from place to place.

4. The search for the new Dalai Lama ended at the home of a two-year-old boy. The house and its

   _____ matched the description given by the regent.

5. The two-year-old future Dalai Lama was removed from his parents' home and taken to Lhasa. He

   was _____ within the Potala Palace, which became his new home.

6. The Potala Palace is more than a quarter of a mile long. This monumental

   _____ is built into a towering rock face overlooking Lhasa.

7. The Dalai Lama is deeply steeped in Buddhism. His _____ and rigorous

   training ended when he was five years old.

8. The Dalai Lama is living proof of the efficacy of Buddhism. The fact that he never loses his

   _____ despite provocation is due to his Buddhist training and beliefs.

9. Chairman Mao was the ruler of China and was zealously obeyed. The entire nation was in

   _____ to his every whim.

10. The Chinese dictator promised to respect Tibet's independence. Yet it soon lost its

    _____ status when Mao decided to "liberate" the country.

11. For thousands of years Tibet had lived at peace with itself and the world. Its present

    _____ condition is due to China's aggressive policy toward the country.

12. China's treatment of Tibet has been called "wanton aggression." Its most _____

    crime is attempting to force a deeply religious people to abandon their beliefs.

13. On Mao's orders, Chinese soldiers descended on Tibet like a horde of locusts. They

    _____ the Buddhist temples and shipped their valuable contents to China.

14. The Dalai Lama now lives in exile and undoubtedly has fond memories of the Potala Palace.

    Visitors to Lhasa may think, the palace looks like a(n) _____ .

15. No one knows what will happen when the fourteenth Dalai Lama dies. Will he be the last, or will a

    fifteenth holder of the office be found after the usual _____ ?

Name _____ Date _____

Lesson ⑤ Review Exercise

1. The 1950s quiz-show scandal left its mark on television. It is one of the more _____ episodes in the industry's history.

2. One justification for the quiz shows at the time was that they encouraged interest in education. Presumably, the more _____ the questions, the more educational the program.

3. Prior to the quiz-show scandal, viewers had no idea they were being deceived. The scandal _____ television's reputation and made viewers more cynical.

4. The idea that the quiz shows were fixed may not have occurred to viewers. When the truth came out, it was a(n) _____ to the viewing public.

5. Subtle hints given to Charles Van Doren soon became more obvious. The process was gradual, and the exact moment of his _____ to deliberate deception is hard to pinpoint.

6. At some point the line was crossed. What had once been vague now became _____ and left no room for doubt that the show was fixed.

7. At first, Van Doren rejected being given the chance to see questions before the show. But eventually he promised to overlook the _____ of what he was doing.

8. Viewers did not suspect that Van Doren had been fed the answers. They thought the vast knowledge he displayed had _____ from years of study.

9. The deception made unusual demands on the contestants. They were required to put on a(n) _____ display that would have challenged a trained actor.

10. The television network rewarded Van Doren with a consulting job and other perks. He may have felt he was _____ into wrongdoing by such corporate largesse.

11. When he was first questioned about the scandal, Van Doren stuck to his story that he was innocent. He expressed indignation that his _____ was being attacked.

12. The fallout from the scandal began almost immediately. One of the _____ was that Congress became involved.

13. By the time Congressional hearings were under way, Van Doren had changed his story. He no longer _____ to be innocent of any acts of wrongdoing.

14. Van Doren was not a man who sought the spotlight. He probably felt that with the Congressional hearings, there was a(n) _____ of publicity.

15. Along with Van Doren, twenty defendants were charged with perjury, and all apologized for their wrongdoing. By expressing _____ , each defendant received a suspended sentence.

© SSI • MAY BE DUPLICATED

Name _____ Date _____

Lesson ⑥ Review Exercise

1. Visit the Herbert and Dorothy Vogel rooms at the National Gallery of Art in Washington. The collection on display is the _____ gift of two New Yorkers.

2. The Vogels were ordinary middle-class New Yorkers. What set them apart was that they _____ their hunger for fine art by becoming collectors.

3. It was their love of art that brought Herbert and Dorothy together. Each recognized something _____ in the other person that drew them to each other.

4. Herbert Vogel lived an ordinary life except for one extraordinary thing. His motto might have been "Collect art like a(n) _____ on a mail carrier's salary."

5. The Vogels bought most of their works from artists who were exploring and inventing new paths in art. Art on the cutting edge is _____ to most people.

6. There's a reason experimental art appeals to few people. Most have a(n) _____ suspicion of the new and unfamiliar.

7. The author of the passage describes Herbert as stocky, with a twinkle in his eye. He is also described as _____ , which may mean he had nieces and nephews.

8. Herbert frequented the cafes in Greenwich Village where artists hung out. The _____ atmosphere there stimulated discussion.

9. "Do we love it, and can we afford it, and do we have room for it?" These are the three criteria the Vogels used, and this led to the _____ nature of their collection.

10. The Vogels followed this simple philosophy religiously. They had no fancy theories to _____ on the nature of art or why people feel the urge to collect it.

11. The Vogels were lucky in one respect. They started collecting at a(n) _____ time when works could be bought for a tenth or a hundredth of their subsequent worth.

12. The sixties was an exciting decade in American art. A number of _____ movements like op and pop art were beginning to make it into the mainstream.

13. Oscar Wilde defined a cynic as someone "who knows the price of everything and the value of nothing." This quote is known as a(n) _____ .

14. The Vogels donated 2,500 pieces of art from their collection to art institutions across the United States. With their love of art and intellect, one could never call them _____ .

15. The Vogels proved one thing when building up such a valuable collection. You don't have to be rich, but you do have to be _____ .

© 3300 • MAY BE DUPLICATED

Name _____ Date _____

Lesson (7) Review Exercise

1. Earthquakes, tsunamis, and hurricanes have two things in common. They pack inestimable amounts of _____ energy, and they are destructive of life and property.

2. For many, tsunamis are the most terrifying of natural disasters. A wall of water tens of feet high _____ everything in its path, leaving terrible destruction in its wake.

3. The strength of a tsunami can be truly and literally awesome. Hundred-foot boats are torn from their moorings and come _____ down streets.

4. A shift in Earth's tectonic plates transfers energy to the water. The surface starts to _____ as waves travel outward in the form of a tsunami.

5. The word *tsunami* has an interesting history. Its _____ derives from two Japanese words meaning "wave" and "harbor."

6. The so-called Pacific Rim circles the Pacific Ocean. The areas most at risk from tsunamis are those like Japan with coastlines _____ to the Pacific.

7. The Hawaiian islands are vulnerable to tsunamis. Recent history shows that the three thousand islands of the Indonesian _____ are not out of the danger zone.

8. Entire coastal villages have been washed away by tsunamis. People living in those areas understand the power of tsunamis and do not take a(n) _____ attitude toward them.

9. Some coastal defenses against tsunamis can be effective. But nothing can _____ a hundred-foot tsunami.

10. Predicting earthquakes is a relatively new branch of science. It's part _____ science and part intuition through the scientists' long familiarity with the subject.

11. High-speed computers are transforming the ability to predict earthquakes. They make it possible to _____ huge quantities of data in shorter and shorter time frames.

12. More accurate sensors are also making a difference. They measure _____ activity in real time and send it to the computers to sort out what it means.

13. Scientists must exercise caution before issuing warnings. Sudden movement of the needles, which register activity, may or may not _____ an earthquake.

14. Word of an approaching tsunami would set off an immediate panic. With no time to vacillate, those people in its path would begin a(n) _____ rush for safety.

15. A warning that turned out to be false would have dire consequences. The _____ caused in the lives of those thought to be at risk would be very great.

© SSI • MAY BE DUPLICATED

Name _____ Date _____

Lesson (8) Review Exercise

1. Aeschylus, Sophocles, and Euripides are the three great names in Greek tragedy. Aristophanes, who wrote comedies, can be added to this _____ .

2. The early Greek plays were tributes to the god Dionysus. Those taking part in the drama festivals considered themselves his _____ .

3. The plays were performed as acts of worship. The costumes worn by those performing were actually religious _____ .

4. To the ancient Greeks, the gods were all too real. To defy their laws was to commit _____ that would surely be punished.

5. The chorus plays an important part in Greek drama. It interrupts the action of the play to comment, in stately _____ , on what is happening to the characters.

6. When the actor addresses the audience directly, the action stops. This is known as a _____ , and it lets the audience know what the character is thinking.

7. Why did Polyneices attempt to overthrow Creon? His justification was the belief that Creon himself had _____ the Theban throne when he became king.

8. After Polyneices dies, a series of tragedies follows. These are some of the events leading to the _____ of the play.

9. Creon feels justified in denying Polyneices a decent burial. He believes that Antigone's brother was a(n) _____ for whom death was insufficient punishment.

10. Creon incurs the anger of the gods, who inflict terrible punishment on him. He had broken the _____ that required respectful burial of the dead.

11. Creon is one of the great tyrants of world literature. He is someone so _____ with power that in a fit of pique he makes a deadly decision.

12. This decision occurs after Creon learns that it was his future daughter-in-law who has defied him. He is so _____ with rage that he orders her put to death.

13. Haemon berates his father for ordering Antigone put to death. Creon ignores his son's _____ and refuses to change his mind.

14. At last, warned by the prophet Tiresias, Creon does change his mind. But, too late, his _____ brings harm to him and his family.

15. The gods begin their revenge on Creon. When Haemon discovers his _____ has killed herself, he commits suicide also.

© JST • MAY BE DUPLICATED

Name _____ Date _____

Lesson (9) Review Exercise

1. In the 1880s, the Dominion Bridge Steel Company needed to use Mohawk land, while the Mohawks needed jobs; _____ between the two groups was achieved quickly.

2. The Mohawks hired by the bridge company had no experience in construction work. Because of this they were _____ to laboring jobs at first.

3. These Mohawks thought nothing of making their way along narrow beams high in the air. Unlike most people, they were quite _____ about heights.

4. They astonished their co-workers by doing their own version of a high-wire act. They were behaving naturally and were not engaging in acts of _____ .

5. Working far above the ground was something the Mohawk workers actually seemed to enjoy. This is a(n) _____ that not everyone shares.

6. Looking down from a great height at the world below isn't for everyone. It often induces the feeling of _____ .

7. The fear of heights is actually irrational. Even if you have made sure you're safe, many can't help getting that _____ feeling in the stomach.

8. Whatever the reason, the Mohawk workers had no fear of falling when working at a great height. They seemed to have no _____ regarding heights.

9. They were soon being trained as riveters. The _____ of the steel beams that form the framework is done by hammering red-hot rivets into place.

10. Steel rivets are first heated to soften the metal. The red-hot _____ are then tossed to a second member of the team, who catches them in a bucket and puts them in place.

11. Skyscrapers were built at an incredible rate in the 1920s. The _____ of the boom had occurred twenty years earlier with the construction of the Flatiron Building.

12. With the building boom centered in Manhattan, life changed for the Mohawks. They ceased being _____ and settled in increasing numbers in Brooklyn.

13. The Mohawk community in Brooklyn was largely self-contained. It was one of many _____ elements that made up the American mosaic at that time.

14. The section around Pacific Street had businesses that served the Mohawks. This area was where most of the Native American construction workers had their _____ .

15. The people who build skyscrapers see the world differently from the rest of us. We appear to them as _____ figures driving cars no bigger than ants.

© SSI • MAY BE DUPLICATED

Lesson ⑩ Review Exercise

1. President Lyndon B. Johnson pursued the Vietnam War by claiming to see "light at the end of the tunnel." He felt that to concede defeat would _____ the honor of the U. S.

2. Johnson wanted nothing less than victory. He was haunted by memories of the 1930s when attempts to _____ Hitler had failed and led to World War II.

3. Hopes for a quick victory over North Vietnam soon faded. The conflict settled into a war of _____ with the score kept by counting enemy soldiers killed.

4. The Vietnam War cost millions of lives, did inestimable damage, and accomplished none of its purposes. Many Americans wanted to _____ it from memory.

5. The war began with the 1957 death of army captain Henry Cramer. It ended with the _____ of 1975 when helicopters airlifted the last Americans to safety.

6. Much of Vietnam is forest, and this made it hard to spot enemy troop movements. The U.S. response was to _____ the trees with highly toxic chemicals.

7. After the war ended in 1975, it seemed that many Americans just wanted to forget about it. This collective _____ was their response to a wasteful and lost war.

8. Soldiers returning from the war in Vietnam were not always greeted as heroes. Some were more likely to be _____ as "war criminals" by opponents of the war.

9. War memorials are almost as old as war itself. Traditionally, they consist of _____ statues of victorious generals.

10. The design of the Vietnam Memorial could express no political viewpoint on the war. This _____ was necessary because of the strong feelings the war had aroused.

11. Maya Lin wanted to stay away from the typical image of generals on horseback. She rejected such a _____ approach in favor of a simple, partly buried wall of black granite.

12. Lin's design did not meet with universal approval. It aroused considerable _____ from opponents who likened it to a ditch or a "wall of shame."

13. Many memorials and public displays bear "Do Not Touch" signs. The _____ quality of the Vietnam Memorial is one of the things that make it different.

14. The memorial is situated between the Washington Monument and the Lincoln Memorial. The polished black granite wall contrasts with the _____ turf around it.

15. The wall is highest at its midpoint. At its _____ , where the names of Cramer and Richard Van de Geer are inscribed, it is ten feet high.

© SSI • MAY BE DUPLICATED

Name _____ Date _____

Lesson (11) Review Exercise

1. An animal fourteen feet high with curving twelve-foot tusks is hard to imagine. Such _____ were common until the end of the Ice Age, ten thousand years ago.

2. The hunters who first encountered mammoths must have been astonished at their size. The meat from just one provided a(n) _____ of food for a whole tribe.

3. The end of the last Ice Age was followed by the demise of many species. The northern grasslands became _____ . Both grazing animals and predators were affected.

4. The retreat of the ice sheet caused a rise in sea levels and temperature. This caused many fertile grasslands to become relatively barren _____ .

5. Sample cores removed from the Arctic ice sheet provide a record of Earth's history. The different levels record _____ of climate change over thousands of years.

6. The retreating Arctic ice cap extended the range of human exploration. It was only a matter of time before the first hunters _____ on mammoth territory.

7. Humans migrating north hunted mammoths in teams using spears. In the long run, the humans would _____ over the mammoths and drive them to extinction.

8. Scientists have found entire mammoth carcasses in Alaska and Siberia from ten thousand years ago. These carcasses had been deeply frozen all that time and were not _____ .

9. Scientists found the meat of the deeply frozen mammoth carcasses was actually still considered edible, but it wouldn't be very _____ to taste.

10. The notion of small mammoths once seemed farfetched. This changed when the existence of mammoth bones and teeth _____ on Wrangel Island became known.

11. A Russian research team made the find in 1993. Items among the _____ collection of mammoth teeth and bone fragments were four thousand years old.

12. So could mammoths have been alive just four thousand years ago? The answer from those who studied the bone and teeth fragments was _____ and affirmative.

13. Wrangel Island had a relatively mild climate, no predators, and plentiful vegetation. It was a(n) _____ spot for the herd of mammoths isolated on it.

14. The claim that mammoths lived four thousand years ago was first met with disbelief. It had been a(n) _____ of science that mammoths became extinct ten thousand years ago.

15. It also seemed absurd to speak of "very small" mammoths when the word itself means "huge." The _____ in this case, however, is precisely accurate.

© SSI • MAY BE DUPLICATED

Name _____ Date _____

Lesson (12) Review Exercise

1. The sixties was a turbulent decade in America. The country was in the _____ of the civil rights movement at home while fighting an unpopular war abroad.

2. It was also the decade of the three-day Woodstock music festival. The event took place in a _____ setting on a farm in upper New York State.

3. The message from Woodstock was "give peace a chance." If anyone attending the event held _____ views, they kept their thoughts to themselves.

4. Opponents of the Vietnam War claimed that it was unwinnable. Supporters of the war felt that for the U.S. to withdraw would be seen as a(n) _____ act.

5. Marching alongside Dr. Martin Luther King Jr. during protest marches was dangerous. He and his followers encountered increasingly _____ resistance from angry opponents.

6. Dr. King refused to retaliate when he was attacked. He _____ the spirit of nonviolence in his teachings and in his actions.

7. Folk singer Joan Baez offended many Americans when she visited North Vietnam in 1972 as part of a peace mission. "Traitor!" was one of the many _____ thrown at her.

8. Baez had a simple reason for visiting North Vietnam. She wanted to learn about the _____ of the North Vietnamese people during a time of war.

9. She was the first to admit that her opponents had the right to speak their minds. What upset Baez was when her patriotism was _____ .

10. Baez always spoke her mind on controversial issues. To take a strong stand against the majority view can be _____ to jeopardizing one's professional career.

11. She was born into a middle-class family and has had a lucrative career. Although she has never known _____ , she still identifies with the poor and downtrodden.

12. In high school, Baez was shunned by both Hispanic and white students. Perhaps this explains why she always strove for _____ among all groups of people.

13. Baez was fifteen before she took up the guitar. For a musician, she was a little late discovering her _____ , as many musicians discover their love of music early.

14. She is eclectic in her choices of music. Her recordings of spirituals have a brooding, _____ quality that draws deeply on her own feelings.

15. Baez is known as a "Child of the Sixties." This was a formative decade for her, and she is proud of her _____ .

Name _____ Date _____

Lesson (13) Review Exercise

1. For 350 years of its history, America was besmirched by the practice of slavery. Yet the _____ of African Americans did not end with its abolition.

2. Crime, unemployment, and poor housing created a spiritual poverty in the culture. Kwanzaa was one person's attempt to attack the _____ at its spiritual roots.

3. In 1965, Los Angeles was torn apart by riots. Dr. Maulana Karenga had his idea at the same time, and it is within this _____ that the origin of Kwanzaa must be understood.

4. The riots lasted for six days and had a profound effect on Karenga. The _____ of Kwanzaa can be traced to his state of mind as Los Angeles exploded.

5. Karenga was greatly disturbed by what was happening to his city. He saw a diverse community _____ by racial hatreds and misunderstandings.

6. The seven principles of Kwanzaa are not meant to be kept in separate boxes. All seven principles must come into play _____ to maximize their effect.

7. The first principle is *Umoja* or "unity." Followers of Kwanzaa who feel aggrieved for whatever reason are _____ to set aside their differences in a spirit of amity.

8. Self-determination, the second principle, emphasizes creating, defining, and speaking for oneself and one's people. It _____ the human spirit to be controlled by others.

9. The third principle is *Ujima*. It calls upon those who celebrate the festival to be more _____ in their outlook and deeds.

10. The sixth day is set aside for feasting and good fellowship. The speeches afterward begin with the oldest person present and are informal and _____ .

11. Africa is a huge continent with many diverse cultures. It is not surprising, therefore, that African American _____ takes multifarious forms.

12. Each speaker tries to express what is in her or his heart. A piercing insight or a tired _____ will receive equally respectful attention and genuine appreciation.

13. At the feast, a special cup is passed from person to person. The tradition of offering a(n) _____ at feasts has very ancient roots.

14. Presents are exchanged on the last day. These should preferably be inexpensive or handmade, as the giving of expensive store-bought gifts is considered _____ .

15. It's no accident that Kwanzaa is held during the holiday season, which is a time to celebrate joy and forgiveness and _____ any differences with others.

© SSI • MAY BE DUPLICATED

Name _____ Date _____

Lesson (14) Review Exercise

1. The idea of a national cathedral was first proposed by George Washington. It would
    _____ the religious differences that divide us and act as a national unifier.

2. He imagined a place of worship to act as a focal point for the nation. Its scale and grandeur would
    be _____ with that of a great power like the United States.

3. On Washington's instructions, Pierre L'Enfant drew up plans for the structure. The project fell into
    _____ until it was revived one hundred years later.

4. A century later, there remained a need for a national house of worship. It would provide a
    suitable _____ for occasions of great national solemnity.

5. One such occasion occurred following the death of former president Eisenhower. A(n)
    _____ service to honor him was held in the completed National Cathedral.

6. The National Cathedral took almost ninety years to complete. This is fast compared to the
    _____ pace when building Canterbury Cathedral, which took five hundred years.

7. The First Amendment to the U.S. Constitution declares the separation of church and state. It is
    considered _____ by most Americans.

8. There was concern that a national cathedral would violate the First Amendment. However,
    because only private funds were used in its construction, the issue was _____ .

9. The cathedral is operated by an Episcopalian foundation. Its purpose, however, is
    _____ , and it is not restricted to members of Protestant faiths.

10. Were use of the cathedral restricted in some way, it would violate the purpose of the cathedral. It
    is a(n) _____ of the foundation that it be available to all faiths.

11. Washington's National Cathedral is built in the Gothic style. Gothic architecture reached a(n)
    _____ of achievement in the 1200s with the cathedral at Chartres in France.

12. One of the true features of Gothic architecture can be found in the cathedral's foundation. Many
    _____ supported the exterior walls.

13. Frederick Hart's twenty-one-foot sculptural relief is one of the cathedral's great artworks. Its
    _____ shapes take the form of human figures emerging from the void.

14. Hart's sculptural relief is entitled *The Creation.* It is located above the door on the west
    _____ of the building.

15. The cathedral is decorated with grotesque figures carved in stone. These are
    _____ , a prominent feature in European cathedrals.

© SSI • MAY BE DUPLICATED

Name _____ Date _____

Lesson (15) Review Exercise

1. In the 1890s, ladies' feathered hats were regarded as the very pinnacle of fashion. Today, of course, when we look at pictures of them, they look merely _____ .

2. This period is sometimes called the "Age of Elegance." Purchasing elaborate homes, clothing, and other luxuries were some ways privileged citizens _____ their status.

3. Hat designers competed with each other to create ever more extravagant creations, and _____ amounts of money were spent on these hats.

4. The demand for feathers as articles of adornment increased dramatically. Naturally there was a(n) _____ rise in the number of birds being slaughtered.

5. The ladies wearing feathers on their heads thought of themselves as very proper. However, there was nothing _____ about the methods used to obtain the feathers.

6. Harriet Hemenway was shocked by a newspaper article. It gave a(n) _____ account of the slaughter of a flock of herons, and this led to her decision to act promptly.

7. Hemenway called a meeting of Boston's elite. The result of the _____ was the establishment of Audubon societies throughout the state.

8. The Boston society was made up of the city's wealthiest and most cultured citizens. To be allowed to join one of the _____ that formed around its members was an honor.

9. The Cabots and Lowells were two of Boston's most prominent families. Its members and others like them were the _____ of Boston's social and political affairs.

10. Boston was no different from other major American cities of that time. Most cities were ruled by a(n) _____ of one sort or another.

11. Within a year, Hemenway had organized a powerful group of one thousand members. No doubt many were _____ into joining by the presence of its distinguished founders.

12. Women who were less than enthusiastic found themselves excluded from many of Boston's social gatherings. This was _____ to their desire to be part of society.

13. There was wide support in Congress for ending the trade in exotic feathers. The senator from Missouri was one who _____ from the popular view.

14. The feather industry fought back when Hemenway took it on, claiming that many jobs would be lost. The industry was no match for such a(n) _____ foe.

15. Ending the trade in feathers changed public attitudes. What had once seemed beautiful now looked silly, and what had once been acceptable was now _____ .

© SSI • MAY BE DUPLICATED

Lesson (16) Review Exercise

1. Was one of your ancestors among the millions who passed through Ellis Island? You can probably find the answer in the _____ at the Ellis Island Museum.

2. The data on millions of immigrants is stored on computers. You can trace your _____ on one of several computer terminals within the museum.

3. The journey to Ellis Island was a long one. The few _____the newcomers brought with them comprised all their worldly possessions.

4. Most immigrants crossed the Atlantic in steerage class. Accommodations on board ships were crowded and far removed from the _____ first-class cabins.

5. The Statue of Liberty, completed in 1886, overlooks New York Harbor. It was a welcome sight to those heading for the _____ at Ellis Island.

6. Immigration officials decided who would and would not be admitted to the country. Any immigrants they were unsure about were _____ upstairs to await further action.

7. Most immigrants passed through Ellis Island in a matter of hours. Those who were detained for whatever reason remained in a kind of _____ for weeks or even months.

8. Medical teams studied the arriving immigrants. Those who appeared _____ received a thorough medical examination and faced expulsion if they failed.

9. Only one in fifty immigrants was denied entry, usually for medical or legal reasons. Immigrants with _____ diseases like trachoma were turned back.

10. Ninety-eight percent of immigrants were granted entry. If they seemed healthy, they were given a(n) _____ physical and sent on their way.

11. About a third of all immigrants stayed in the New York area. The rest fanned out and settled in other _____ centers.

12. The fire of 1897 completely destroyed the original wooden buildings on Ellis Island where immigrants were processed. Fortunately, no lives were lost in the _____ .

13. The fire had one positive effect. The _____ wooden buildings that were destroyed were replaced by an impressive brick and limestone edifice.

14. President McKinley was assassinated by an anarchist in 1901. As a result, officials became wary of giving entry into the United States to anyone who seemed politically _____ .

15. After Ellis Island was closed, the main building deteriorated. Private donations helped restore it, and it is now kept in _____ condition by the U.S. Parks Service.

© SSI • MAY BE DUPLICATED

Name _____   Date _____

Lesson (17) Review Exercise

1. Democracy was a somewhat rare form of government in Renaissance Italy. Most city-states at that time were _____ , but Florence was an exception.

2. Niccolò Machiavelli served the republic of Florence in several capacities. On several occasions he acted as a(n) _____ to various other states in Europe.

3. He was raised in unusual circumstances. Machiavelli's family was an aristocratic one but was too _____ to support a patrician lifestyle.

4. Machiavelli organized a volunteer army whose soldiers were patriotic citizens. He knew that a(n) _____ army owes its loyalty to whomever happens to be paying it.

5. In 1512, a Spanish army loyal to the pope invaded Italy. It _____ the ruling republican government and restored the Medici family to power.

6. Machiavelli's writings received close attention from the Catholic Church. It took a(n) _____ view of his opinions on the shortcomings of Christianity.

7. It was the content of Machiavelli's *The Prince* that aroused the ire of the church. The _____ tone in which he expressed his views was not the problem.

8. Machiavelli believed that Christianity applied to warfare was problematic. He felt it would _____ an army's ability to fight aggressively.

9. The views expressed by Machiavelli have always been controversial. The brutal realism of his advice, however, is mitigated by his _____ prose style.

10. He warns that an honest ruler cannot allow his good nature to be taken advantage of. If an opponent is being deceitful, the ruler must practice _____ .

11. A ruler who wishes to be loved will spend extravagantly on public projects. According to Machiavelli, a ruler who wishes to be feared will be much more _____ .

12. The problem Machiavelli ran into is a familiar one. People say they want to hear the truth, yet react negatively when it is given to them in a(n) _____ manner.

13. Some scholars believe that Machiavelli doesn't deserve the opprobrium attached to his name. In their view, "Machiavellian" should not be a(n) _____ description.

14. These scholars are probably in the minority. It may be unfair, but there will always be an element of _____ associated with the name Machiavelli.

15. Undoubtedly, Machiavelli's ideas have truth in today's world. One might find that the behavior of many world leaders is guided by one of Machiavelli's _____ .

© SSI • MAY BE DUPLICATED

Name _____ Date _____

Lesson (18) Review Exercise

1. Those who live under the rule of law take justice for granted. For those who live under a dictatorship, there is no _____ against injustice.

2. Dictatorship and democracy are two inimical systems of government. To speak one's mind freely without fear of _____ is the essence of democracy.

3. Antonio Salazár seized power of Portugal in 1932. His autocratic _____ lasted thirty-six years and was noted for its brutal suppression of freedom.

4. In 1961, two Portuguese students were jailed for toasting to "freedom." Under Salazár's iron rule, the Portuguese people were _____ of freedom, but hope was still alive.

5. Salazár wanted to send a message to those who thought like the two students. Do as they did, and you would be similarly punished for your _____ .

6. Salazár had pledged to follow the Universal Declaration of Human Rights. The document had been _____ by the United Nations in 1948.

7. But Salazár, like many leaders, did not follow the UN's declaration. They were _____ because their actions failed to follow the declaration they had pledged to obey.

8. Article 5 of the declaration forbids the use of torture on prisoners. Article 9 _____ arbitrary arrest and confinement.

9. People snickered when Peter Benenson told others of his idea for Amnesty International (AI). He ignored the _____ his idea had provoked and went ahead anyway.

10. Benenson succeeded in creating AI in 1961. Its aim was to help those who had committed no crime but were _____ of hope in jail.

11. The threat of an AI investigation often brings results. Even the _____ visit of an AI team can bring about a prisoner's release.

12. To safeguard its reputation for probity, AI is careful not to respond hastily. It does not act until it has made every effort to gather every _____ fact.

13. Governments being investigated by AI are often uncooperative. This can make it difficult to _____ accusations leveled against its ruling elite.

14. AI has clearly defined rules for its mission. Before "adopting" someone as a prisoner of conscience, that person must meet certain _____ .

15. For example, if you have been detained for your religious views, you are eligible. Those who have not _____ violence also meet the criteria.

© 331 • MAY BE DUPLICATED

Name _____ Date _____

Lesson (19) Review Exercise

1. Humans seem to have a love/hate relationship with planet Earth. The assault on the African elephant population is just one of the many _____ we commit.

2. Demand for ivory almost caused the extinction of the African elephant during the 1980s. Whether its _____ is merely a temporary one still remains to be seen.

3. Objects made of ivory have no real utilitarian value. While they may be no more than trinkets, the larger and intricately carved pieces can be very expensive _____ .

4. The Kenyan government realized the value of elephants to the country's income from tourism. This _____ view caused them to start enforcing laws against poaching.

5. In 1990, a complete ban on ivory trading was announced. The countries taking part come under the _____ of the Convention on International Trade in Endangered Species.

6. Bribery is the elephant poacher's secret weapon. When extra cash is offered to them, some poorly paid government officials are tempted to become more _____ .

7. After the ban, poaching activities became less profitable. The declared _____ on the ivory trade caused prices to plummet.

8. By acting together, the convention members increased their effectiveness. 180 countries _____ their efforts to combat the illegal ivory trade.

9. It may seem odd that so many different countries could agree on anything. That they did so may be a(n) _____ of better times for planet Earth.

10. Nations are more effective when they act in concert. A(n) _____ decision made by a single nation would break the trust of other nations.

11. Cynthia Moss can take some credit for the ban on the international ivory trade. It took place during her _____ as director of the Amboseli Elephant Research Project.

12. Many Kenyan farmers are concerned about elephants damaging their crops. It's crucial that a(n) _____ solution is found so that humans and elephants can coexist.

13. The African elephant is the largest land animal on the planet. Its _____ trumpeting also makes it one of the loudest.

14. The elephant's trunk is extremely versatile. This _____ organ is very sensitive to smells, can snap a branch or pick up a peanut, and can even suck water like a straw.

15. Imagine seeing elephants holding a silent vigil over a recently dead member of the herd. Such a sight might be a(n) _____ for the spellbound observer.

© SSI • MAY BE DUPLICATED

Name _____ Date _____

Lesson (20) Review Exercise

1. Most people are either left-handed or right-handed. If you happen to be
   _____ , you are one of a very small number.

2. Left-handed people make up only about ten to fifteen percent of the population. There have
   been numerous negative references _____ to "lefties" throughout history.

3. About thirty percent of major league pitchers are left-handed. This does not make up a(n)
   _____ of pitchers, but it's still three times greater than the national average.

4. The word *sinister* comes from the Latin for "left" or "left-handed." This shows how
   _____ toward lefties is embedded in the language.

5. A word to describe people who are awkward or clumsy is _____ . Its antonym,
   adroit, comes from the French phrase meaning "to the right."

6. It is not proven that left-handed people have more accidents because equipment is designed
   for right-handedness. There is nothing inherently _____ about being left-handed.

7. Sir Cyril Burt was a renowned British educational psychologist. In 1937, he unfortunately
   _____ left-handed people and shared this opinion often.

8. Burt promoted the view that left-handed children should be forced to use their right hand. He
   felt left-handedness was a(n) _____ that should be corrected early.

9. This view became widely accepted among many educators. However, the approach was
   _____ once educators realized the terrible effects it had on the children.

10. No instructor in a school of education would suggest forcing left-handed children to switch. This
    is another example of how _____ theory changes over time.

11. Stanley Coren and Diane Halpern studied the death certificates of a thousand people. As a result,
    they _____ the theory that lefties die earlier than right-handed people.

12. Other researchers have challenged this theory. They felt that the study sample was too small to
    _____ the data accurately and that more research was needed.

13. Scientists researching right-handedness in earlier times found _____ evidence: blows
    to ancient skulls occur more often on the left side, suggesting that the attacker was right handed.

14. Household tools catered solely to the right-handed. Manufacturers changed their
    _____ when they saw that the left-handed were a vital part of the market.

15. A greater understanding and accommodation of left-handedness continues to develop. Today, it
    is _____ to think of left-handedness as a defect in need of correction.

© 3S1 • MAY BE DUPLICATED

Name _____   Date _____

Lesson 1 Test

Find a SYNONYM for each bold word. Then fill in the circle next to your answer.

1. Although she is a novice, Rena **exudes** confidence in her abilities.

   Ⓐ disguises
   Ⓑ lacks
   Ⓒ exhibits
   Ⓓ suppresses

2. The president **convened** a cabinet meeting.

   Ⓐ summoned
   Ⓑ forgot
   Ⓒ dismissed
   Ⓓ remembered

3. Most urban legends are based on **apocryphal** stories.

   Ⓐ accurate
   Ⓑ spurious
   Ⓒ historical
   Ⓓ authentic

4. The river circled the **periphery** of the city.

   Ⓐ suburbs
   Ⓑ center
   Ⓒ edge
   Ⓓ harbor

5. The scale's needle **vacillated** between four and five grams before finally settling between the two.

   Ⓐ tended
   Ⓑ balanced
   Ⓒ wavered
   Ⓓ struggled

Find an ANTONYM for each bold word. Then fill in the circle next to your answer.

6. Paul was a valued party guest because of his skill as a **raconteur.**

   Ⓐ clown
   Ⓑ bore
   Ⓒ comic
   Ⓓ friend

7. Laura used **subterfuge** to escape punishment for cutting class.

   Ⓐ lies
   Ⓑ enemies
   Ⓒ skill
   Ⓓ honesty

© SSI • MAY BE DUPLICATED

8. Lorenzo was **mortified** by his fall in the lunchroom.

   Ⓐ pleased

   Ⓑ angered

   Ⓒ injured

   Ⓓ shamed

9. Yolanda's habit of studying with **expedient** memory devices, rather than taking the time to truly learn the material, proved a failure in the end.

   Ⓐ speedy

   Ⓑ inconvenient

   Ⓒ direct

   Ⓓ impersonal

10. High-level mathematics can be **arcane** to the layperson.

   Ⓐ mysterious

   Ⓑ useful

   Ⓒ unimportant

   Ⓓ simple

Choose the best way to complete each sentence or answer each question. Then fill in the circle next to your answer.

11. Which of the following would you most likely use to **gesticulate?**

   Ⓐ a lantern

   Ⓑ your hands

   Ⓒ flowers

   Ⓓ a pencil

12. **Incremental** change happens

   Ⓐ in huge leaps.

   Ⓑ a little at a time.

   Ⓒ in unknown amounts.

   Ⓓ without outside help.

13. In which of the following situations are you likely to find **levity?**

   Ⓐ at a funeral

   Ⓑ during a final exam

   Ⓒ at a party

   Ⓓ standing in a long line

14. Which of the following is most likely to be described as **imperturbable?**

   Ⓐ a rodeo bull

   Ⓑ a killer bee

   Ⓒ a wild bear

   Ⓓ a guide dog

15. **Peripheral** vision relates to things you can see

   Ⓐ to the side.

   Ⓑ straight ahead.

   Ⓒ in the dark.

   Ⓓ moving quickly.

© SSI • MAY BE DUPLICATED

Standardized Test Preview/Practice

In this passage, some of the words from this lesson are in bold. Read the passage and then answer the questions.

Tara usually knew the answer to any questions her teachers asked, but she **vacillated** over whether to raise her hand. She never liked speaking up in class. Her voice always sounded so nervous! It was strange how shy she felt in school.
5 She was a regular **raconteur** when she was at home with her family or spending time with friends, always telling stories and enjoying being the center of attention. She was very confident in those situations. But for some reason even the thought of speaking up in class made her start **exuding** sweat from every
10 pore.

So, she rarely raised her hand, and when she did say something, she played it safe—she usually just **reiterated** what someone else had already said. It was the **expedient** way to contribute in class so she could get credit for being part
15 of the discussion, but not risk expressing her own ideas and having them criticized or misunderstood.

1. The phrase "**vacillated** over" (line 2) most nearly means
   Ⓐ moved back and forth.
   Ⓑ skimmed over.
   Ⓒ had a hard time deciding.
   Ⓓ analyzed.

2. The meaning of **raconteur** (line 5) is
   Ⓐ skilled storyteller.
   Ⓑ speech maker.
   Ⓒ joker.
   Ⓓ confident person.

3. In line 9, **exuding** most nearly means
   Ⓐ wiping away.
   Ⓑ showing.
   Ⓒ projecting.
   Ⓓ oozing.

4. The meaning of **reiterated** (line 12) is
   Ⓐ listened to.
   Ⓑ repeated.
   Ⓒ paid attention to.
   Ⓓ denied.

5. In line 13, **expedient** means
   Ⓐ difficult.
   Ⓑ convenient.
   Ⓒ quickest.
   Ⓓ most effective.

© SSI • MAY BE DUPLICATED

Name _____ Date _____

Find a SYNONYM for each bold word. Then fill in the circle next to your answer.

1. Owning a vintage limited edition Rolls Royce is a display of great **opulence.**

    Ⓐ intelligence
    Ⓑ skill
    Ⓒ wealth
    Ⓓ rudeness

2. Reid was **disconcerted** by the stranger's barrage of personal questions.

    Ⓐ charmed
    Ⓑ flustered
    Ⓒ enlightened
    Ⓓ pleased

3. Some sports fans can get **choleric** when they think a referee makes a bad call.

    Ⓐ giddy
    Ⓑ self-righteous
    Ⓒ disappointed
    Ⓓ angry

4. The police are seeking a **marauder** whose reputation has made people all over Connecticut feel unsafe in their homes.

    Ⓐ thief
    Ⓑ shoplifter
    Ⓒ racketeer
    Ⓓ embezzler

5. Fresh air and sunshine can have a **therapeutic** effect on people.

    Ⓐ sickening
    Ⓑ healthful
    Ⓒ terrifying
    Ⓓ depressing

Find an ANTONYM for each bold word. Then fill in the circle next to your answer.

6. Grandmother wished she had a more **utilitarian** design.

    Ⓐ awkward
    Ⓑ impractical
    Ⓒ realistic
    Ⓓ overbearing

7. Melinda's clients valued her **patrician** style of interior design.

    Ⓐ unrefined
    Ⓑ elegant
    Ⓒ stingy
    Ⓓ inherited

© SSI • MAY BE DUPLICATED

8. Her father knew Lina was sick when she remained **phlegmatic** even when he offered to take her out for a pancake breakfast.

   Ⓐ calm
   Ⓑ excited
   Ⓒ belligerent
   Ⓓ practical

9. Sonya's **choleric** brother was always unpredictable in public.

   Ⓐ funny
   Ⓑ excitable
   Ⓒ calm
   Ⓓ nervous

10. As soon as they started hitting below the belt, the referee **interposed** himself between the boxers.

    Ⓐ intervened
    Ⓑ removed
    Ⓒ relaxed
    Ⓓ positioned

Choose the best way to complete each sentence or answer each question. Then fill in the circle next to your answer.

11. Which of the following would be considered **accoutrements** of a painter?

    Ⓐ museums
    Ⓑ lenses
    Ⓒ brushes
    Ⓓ visitors

12. Which of the following is most likely to be among Africa's **fauna?**

    Ⓐ an oasis
    Ⓑ a rhinoceros
    Ⓒ a palm tree
    Ⓓ a violet

13. Someone with a **propensity** for fighting has

    Ⓐ a largely peaceful personality.
    Ⓑ an ability to win most fights.
    Ⓒ a belief that fighting is wrong.
    Ⓓ a tendency to get into fights.

14. A gymnast with only a **modicum** of grace is likely to give what type of performance?

    Ⓐ a clumsy one
    Ⓑ a stellar one
    Ⓒ an agile one
    Ⓓ an expert one

15. Drew could only feel **aggrieved** when the scholarship committee treated him so

    Ⓐ kindly.
    Ⓑ generously.
    Ⓒ enthusiastically.
    Ⓓ unfairly.

© SSI • MAY BE DUPLICATED

Standardized Test Preview/Practice

In this passage, some of the words from this lesson are in bold. Read the passage and then answer the questions.

Sadaf liked watching spy movies with her mother, particularly the James Bond films. Both of them laughed at the way the villains in these films **comported** themselves. They acted like **marauding** pirates in one scene, completely
5 out of control and thirsty for money and power, and then turned around in the next scene and behaved in a much more **patrician** manner, delicately sipping from a cup of tea. The contrast was often hilarious.

One afternoon Sadaf watched a marathon of James Bond
10 movies with her mom, and they both noticed something equally amusing. Many of the villains seemed to share a predilection for keeping hungry sharks in tanks at their headquarters. They supposedly served a very **utilitarian** purpose: to kill the villain's enemies.
15 "They're very expensive pets," Sadaf's mother said, giggling. "Imagine spending all that money on special shark food and equipment in hopes that your enemy would fall into your private tank and be eaten."

This got Sadaf thinking about all the various **fauna** in
20 James Bond films. No matter what exotic location, there was always a threatening animal to be dealt with by the hero—scorpions, a giant squid, crocodiles, alligators, etc. How much did it cost the film companies to take care of and use these animals?

1. The phrase "**comported** themselves" (line 3) means
   - Ⓐ defeated themselves.
   - Ⓑ acted and behaved.
   - Ⓒ looked at themselves.
   - Ⓓ controlled themselves.

2. The word **marauding** (line 4) most nearly means
   - Ⓐ angry.
   - Ⓑ evil.
   - Ⓒ plundering.
   - Ⓓ greedy.

3. In line 6, **patrician** means
   - Ⓐ peaceful.
   - Ⓑ gentle.
   - Ⓒ wild.
   - Ⓓ civilized.

4. The meaning of **utilitarian** (line 13) is
   - Ⓐ practical.
   - Ⓑ decorative.
   - Ⓒ ridiculous.
   - Ⓓ perfect.

5. In line 19, **fauna** most nearly means
   - Ⓐ sea creatures.
   - Ⓑ weapons.
   - Ⓒ animals.
   - Ⓓ pets.

Lesson 3 Test

Find a SYNONYM for each bold word. Then fill in the circle next to your answer.

1. The class could feel the **vibrant** percussions of the drum corps rehearsing downstairs.

   Ⓐ vibrating
   Ⓑ pounding
   Ⓒ relentless
   Ⓓ distracting

2. Ashley was reluctant to admit it, but doing all the required reading for an assignment was an **efficacious** way to prepare for the test.

   Ⓐ easy
   Ⓑ speedy
   Ⓒ effective
   Ⓓ entertaining

3. The losing team seemed **stoic** in the face of defeat.

   Ⓐ reluctant
   Ⓑ devastated
   Ⓒ pathetic
   Ⓓ indifferent

4. Army training **inculcates** soldiers with values of teamwork and discipline.

   Ⓐ teaches
   Ⓑ rewards
   Ⓒ alienates
   Ⓓ requires

5. The painter's **stellar** representations of light in different seasons and at different times of day impressed even the normally jaded critics.

   Ⓐ unique
   Ⓑ ordinary
   Ⓒ outlandish
   Ⓓ outstanding

Find an ANTONYM for each bold word. Then fill in the circle next to your answer.

6. Gymnasts perform **prodigious** acts of flexibility and strength.

   Ⓐ repeated
   Ⓑ ordinary
   Ⓒ skillful
   Ⓓ wondrous

7. Ever since he received the telescope for his birthday, Travis has been preoccupied with **stellar** occurrences.

   Ⓐ arcane
   Ⓑ earthly
   Ⓒ repeated
   Ⓓ boring

© SSI • MAY BE DUPLICATED

8. Keri decorated her room with the **vibrant** colors that streaked the sky at sunset.

Ⓐ mixed
Ⓑ bright
Ⓒ dull
Ⓓ primary

9. The **efficacy** of many prescription drugs depends on the patient's proper usage.

Ⓐ value
Ⓑ content
Ⓒ failure
Ⓓ power

10. Dani's refusal to think, read, or write will cause her mind to **atrophy.**

Ⓐ develop
Ⓑ waste
Ⓒ remember
Ⓓ succeed

Choose the best way to complete each sentence or answer each question. Then fill in the circle next to your answer.

11. You are most likely to receive an **emolument** when you

Ⓐ commit a crime.
Ⓑ find change on the sidewalk.
Ⓒ finish a week of work.
Ⓓ need to be vaccinated.

12. Stanley prepared for the marathon with a daily workout **regimen. A regimen** is

Ⓐ a strategy.
Ⓑ a philosophy.
Ⓒ an obsession.
Ⓓ a routine.

13. Because of his refusal to bend any rule, Coach Brown was known to be a **martinet.** He is most likely

Ⓐ strict.
Ⓑ well-loved.
Ⓒ a performer.
Ⓓ successful.

14. While everyone else was hysterical, Lance, always the **stoic,** seemed

Ⓐ jovial.
Ⓑ unaffected.
Ⓒ angry.
Ⓓ spiritual.

15. If a painting is described as an **icon,** it is likely to be

Ⓐ popular.
Ⓑ religious.
Ⓒ controversial.
Ⓓ disturbing.

© SSI • MAY BE DUPLICATED

Standardized Test Preview/Practice

In this passage, some of the words from this lesson are in bold. Read the passage and then answer the questions.

While an **inestimable** number of people love acting and are passionate about it, relatively few are brave enough to pursue acting in films and television as a career. This is because even the most **zealous** and dedicated actors can
5 find themselves out of work for long periods of time. They can move to Hollywood, hire an agent, and go to several auditions a day, even get a few roles here and there in commercials, and still not be able to get work steadily enough to pay their rent.

Most actors are realistic about their careers. They know
10 only a few actors become successful, and very few become **icons** within the industry. They don't expect to become movie stars. They also know that even the stars with **prodigious** numbers of awards can go through times when they are unable to find work. It is not an easy industry to be successful
15 in for a lifetime. One **lackluster** performance onscreen, or one bad review, can seriously impact an actor's reputation.

1. The phrase "an **inestimable** number" (line 1) most nearly means
   Ⓐ a certain number.
   Ⓑ an exact number.
   Ⓒ a very large number.
   Ⓓ a very small number.

2. The meaning of **zealous** (line 4) is
   Ⓐ enthusiastic and passionate.
   Ⓑ crazy.
   Ⓒ realistic.
   Ⓓ organized and prepared.

3. The word **icons** (line 11) most nearly means
   Ⓐ wealthy.
   Ⓑ idolized.
   Ⓒ liked.
   Ⓓ misunderstood.

4. In line 12, **prodigious** means
   Ⓐ amazingly large.
   Ⓑ fewer.
   Ⓒ increasing.
   Ⓓ average.

5. The word **lackluster** (line 15) most nearly means
   Ⓐ horrible.
   Ⓑ uninspiring.
   Ⓒ interesting.
   Ⓓ worthwhile.

© SSI • MAY BE DUPLICATED

Name _____ Date _____

Lesson 4 **Test**

Find a SYNONYM for each bold word. Then fill in the circle next to your answer.

1. Viking marauders **pillaged** villages along the Atlantic coast.

Ⓐ inhabited
Ⓑ built
Ⓒ abandoned
Ⓓ plundered

2. Many fugitives try to travel **incognito.**

Ⓐ alone
Ⓑ together
Ⓒ unrecognized
Ⓓ frequently

3. Mark would not give up his **hapless** attempts at a writing career despite repeated failure.

Ⓐ addictive
Ⓑ unfortunate
Ⓒ successful
Ⓓ repeated

4. Premeditated murder is among the most **heinous** of crimes.

Ⓐ illegal
Ⓑ regrettable
Ⓒ savage
Ⓓ evil

5. Gross anatomy, a class taken in the first year of medical school, **indoctrinates** some students and convinces others to pursue a different career.

Ⓐ trains
Ⓑ changes
Ⓒ graduates
Ⓓ needs

Find an ANTONYM for each bold word. Then fill in the circle next to your answer.

6. The uninitiated should be **circumspect** about mountain biking.

Ⓐ excited
Ⓑ reckless
Ⓒ careful
Ⓓ fearful

7. Running for political office requires great **composure** under the constant attacks from opponents and scrutiny from the media.

Ⓐ money
Ⓑ calm
Ⓒ agitation
Ⓓ thievery

© SSI • MAY BE DUPLICATED

8. Ms. Diaz was appointed **interim** principal after Mr. Gresham's sudden departure.

   Ⓐ substitute
   Ⓑ permanent
   Ⓒ emergency
   Ⓓ temporary

9. By donning a blonde wig and dark glasses, Bridget was able to walk **incognito** through her neighborhood.

   Ⓐ disguised
   Ⓑ recognized
   Ⓒ quietly
   Ⓓ well-dressed

10. Religious cults provide more **indoctrination** than spiritual guidance.

    Ⓐ training
    Ⓑ commercials
    Ⓒ objectivity
    Ⓓ humor

Choose the best way to complete each sentence or answer each question. Then fill in the circle next to your answer.

11. Which of the following is most likely to be found in the **environs** of a major city?

    Ⓐ a neighboring state
    Ⓑ suburbs
    Ⓒ rural areas
    Ⓓ countries

12. Where is a robin's egg most likely to be **ensconced?**

    Ⓐ in a nest
    Ⓑ on a shelf
    Ⓒ in a cupboard
    Ⓓ in a pantry

13. Lost in a **reverie** about her upcoming vacation, when the teacher called on her, Annie was

    Ⓐ frightened.
    Ⓑ thrilled.
    Ⓒ unprepared.
    Ⓓ ready.

14. Which is most likely to build an **edifice?**

    Ⓐ a science class
    Ⓑ a bird in a tree
    Ⓒ a child on a beach
    Ⓓ generations of researchers

15. Carson craved being **autonomous** at work so he could be

    Ⓐ supervised.
    Ⓑ independent.
    Ⓒ realistic.
    Ⓓ important.

© SSI • MAY BE DUPLICATED

Standardized Test Preview/Practice

In this passage, some of the words from this lesson are in bold. Read the passage and then answer the questions.

Petra's mother thought cemeteries were peaceful and beautiful, and, as a result, so did Petra. She didn't think they were at all creepy or scary.

One day, Petra stopped at a cemetery she'd visited before.
5   She had a clear memory of a picnic there with her mother, right next to the **edifice** she was looking at now. It was an elaborate marble **mausoleum** with angels and roses carved into the door. She remembered that after they had eaten, her mother had fallen into a daydream while Petra watched an old
10 man walk very slowly toward a grave, pausing after each step to steady himself. Petra had to tap her mother's shoulder to jolt her out of her **reverie.**

"That's Mr. Goldstein," her mother told her. "He must be visiting his wife's grave. Poor guy. He's the most **hapless** person
15 I know. His wife passed away last year, right after his business went bankrupt and his boat was destroyed in a bad storm."

When Petra saw Mr. Goldstein stumble over a stone in his path, she jumped up to help him. "Be **circumspect** when you approach him so you don't scare him," her mother warned.
20 "On top of everything else, he's going deaf and won't hear you coming."

1. The word **edifice** (line 6) most nearly means
   (A) cemetery.
   (B) large, imposing structure.
   (C) system built over time.
   (D) door.

2. In line 7, **mausoleum** means
   (A) gravestone.
   (B) burial plot.
   (C) floral display.
   (D) large tomb.

3. The word **reverie** (line 12) most nearly means
   (A) place.
   (B) daydream.
   (C) imagination.
   (D) seat.

4. The meaning of **hapless** (line 14) is
   (A) hopeless.
   (B) friendly.
   (C) forgetful.
   (D) unlucky.

5. The meaning of **circumspect** (line 18) is
   (A) creepy.
   (B) cautious.
   (C) unstable.
   (D) quick.

© SSI • MAY NOT BE DUPLICATED

Name _____   Date _____

Find a SYNONYM for each bold word. Then fill in the circle next to your answer.

1. Her complicated teaching method makes simple subjects **abstruse.**

    Ⓐ easier
    Ⓑ intense
    Ⓒ difficult
    Ⓓ boring

2. If the club doubted Toby's **penitence** after he missed the fundraiser, his hard work at every subsequent event convinced them.

    Ⓐ regret
    Ⓑ embarrassment
    Ⓒ anger
    Ⓓ pride

3. The squad knew that practice was the key to winning, so their **acquiescence** to the intense rehearsal schedule came without a murmur of objection.

    Ⓐ support
    Ⓑ dissent
    Ⓒ acceptance
    Ⓓ commitment

4. The car salesperson's customers appreciated his **probity.**

    Ⓐ curiosity
    Ⓑ honesty
    Ⓒ fitness
    Ⓓ intelligence

5. After a heated debate, the manager **acquiesced** to Vance's demand for a raise.

    Ⓐ left
    Ⓑ complied
    Ⓒ disagreed
    Ⓓ shouted

Find an ANTONYM for each bold word. Then fill in the circle next to your answer.

6. The **surfeit** of ice cream varieties at the Dream Cream Ice Cream Parlor made it hard for Luz to decide which one she wanted in her sundae.

    Ⓐ abundance
    Ⓑ disrepair
    Ⓒ scarcity
    Ⓓ collection

7. Judging from that gory movie he took me to, Brian has **unsavory** tastes in film.

    Ⓐ wholesome
    Ⓑ laughable
    Ⓒ poor
    Ⓓ offensive

© SSI • MAY BE DUPLICATED

8. The bank would stand for no **improprieties** from the tellers when it came to the way they handled their cash.

Ⓐ mistakes

Ⓑ accidents

Ⓒ decorum

Ⓓ recommendations

9. Mark was **penitent** about forgetting to pick up his grandparents at the airport.

Ⓐ angry

Ⓑ tranquil

Ⓒ unsure

Ⓓ unapologetic

10. The intellectual edifice of art history has **accrued** over many years through the work of artists and scholars.

Ⓐ happened

Ⓑ prospered

Ⓒ wavered

Ⓓ decreased

Choose the best way to complete each sentence or answer each question. Then fill in the circle next to your answer.

11. Something with an **unsavory** aroma smells

Ⓐ sweet.

Ⓑ floral.

Ⓒ unpleasant.

Ⓓ delicious.

12. Which of the following is most likely to **accrue?**

Ⓐ beach erosion

Ⓑ freshly planted flowers

Ⓒ an infected wound

Ⓓ vacation time at a job

13. Nathan **inveigled** concert money from his mother by

Ⓐ flattery.

Ⓑ struggling.

Ⓒ threatening.

Ⓓ reasoning.

14. A **revelation** makes what was unknown

Ⓐ hidden.

Ⓑ forgotten.

Ⓒ irrelevant.

Ⓓ known.

15. **Purporting** to be related to someone means to

Ⓐ doubt your kinship.

Ⓑ suspect your kinship.

Ⓒ imply your kinship.

Ⓓ deny your kinship.

© 331 • MAY BE DUPLICATED

Standardized Test Preview/Practice

In this passage, some of the words from this lesson are in bold. Read the passage and then answer the questions.

Parents of toddlers often have a difficult time doing basic tasks such as grocery shopping because their children are still learning how to behave in public. Toddlers are known for their **histrionic** temper tantrums and other **improprieties** that
5 cause people around them to cringe or complain—particularly people who don't have children of their own and don't remember what it was like to be a child. That is why you see many parents **inveigling** their toddlers into being quiet with the promise of treats or giving them a toy to play with as they
10 shop.

It may help for parents to be as **explicit** as possible about the rules for their child. For example, just before going to a grocery store, a parent might explain, "We use only quiet voices in this store." However, toddlers are not old enough
15 to fully understand the **repercussions** of their actions. Their experience of the world is still very limited, and when they are tired and cranky, after being told "no" a lot, they tend to ignore rules.

1. In line 4, **histrionic** means
   - Ⓐ historical.
   - Ⓑ electronic.
   - Ⓒ dramatic.
   - Ⓓ unhelpful.

2. The word **improprieties** (line 4) most nearly means
   - Ⓐ inappropriate behaviors.
   - Ⓑ arguments.
   - Ⓒ loud noises.
   - Ⓓ unwise decisions.

3. In line 8, **inveigling** most nearly means
   - Ⓐ luring.
   - Ⓑ asking.
   - Ⓒ lying to.
   - Ⓓ ensuring.

4. The meaning of **explicit** (line 11) is
   - Ⓐ inappropriate.
   - Ⓑ clear.
   - Ⓒ strict.
   - Ⓓ flexible.

5. In line 15, **repercussions** means
   - Ⓐ meanings.
   - Ⓑ purposes.
   - Ⓒ consequences.
   - Ⓓ decisions.

© SSI • MAY BE DUPLICATED

Lesson 6 Test

Find a SYNONYM for each bold word. Then fill in the circle next to your answer.

1. The father **assuaged** his baby's teething pain with some numbing drops.

    (A) understood
    (B) noticed
    (C) angered
    (D) relieved

2. The party's **convivial** atmosphere put Jacob right at ease.

    (A) uncomfortable
    (B) carnival
    (C) sociable
    (D) secretive

3. Jessie had her **eclectic** music collection to thank for landing her the DJ job.

    (A) large
    (B) specific
    (C) varied
    (D) ethnic

4. Charities rely on **munificent** contributions from private citizens as well as endowments from corporations.

    (A) generous
    (B) yearly
    (C) steady
    (D) public

5. His mother was known in the neighborhood for her **perspicacity** when advising on difficult matters.

    (A) shrewdness
    (B) bluntness
    (C) understanding
    (D) reassurance

Find an ANTONYM for each bold word. Then fill in the circle next to your answer.

6. There is something **intrinsic** to human biology that makes language possible for us, but not for chimpanzees.

    (A) essential
    (B) peripheral
    (C) important
    (D) valuable

7. Julian's **inveterate** tardiness angered his boss.

    (A) inconsiderate
    (B) bold
    (C) occasional
    (D) repeated

© SSI • MAY BE DUPLICATED

8. The plant's plentiful blooms were a **propitious** indication of Claire's potential as a gardener.

   Ⓐ ominous
   Ⓑ promising
   Ⓒ useless
   Ⓓ possible

9. Ringing cell phones were **anathema** to the theater's patrons.

   Ⓐ forbidden
   Ⓑ accessories
   Ⓒ distasteful
   Ⓓ welcome

10. The ointment **assuaged** the inflammation on Tim's skinned knee.

    Ⓐ increased
    Ⓑ disinfected
    Ⓒ soothed
    Ⓓ erased

Choose the best way to complete each sentence or answer each question. Then fill in the circle next to your answer.

11. To **expound** upon one's value system is to

    Ⓐ refuse to talk about it.
    Ⓑ use it for an argument.
    Ⓒ explain it in detail.
    Ⓓ expose its flaws.

12. Which of the following is most likely to be described as **nascent?**

    Ⓐ an adult
    Ⓑ a mountain
    Ⓒ a seedling
    Ⓓ a ripe apple

13. When George quoted an **epigram** of Oscar Wilde's, he repeated

    Ⓐ a speech.
    Ⓑ a lengthy poem.
    Ⓒ a biographic detail.
    Ⓓ a short saying.

14. Mr. Caddie's **philistine** attitude about the closing of the museum indicates that he is likely

    Ⓐ a museum supporter.
    Ⓑ interested in the arts.
    Ⓒ interested in the museum's fate.
    Ⓓ ignorant of artistic values.

15. The veterinarian calmed our fears with her **perspicacious** advice about the surgical procedure. The advice was

    Ⓐ confusing.
    Ⓑ late.
    Ⓒ clear-sighted.
    Ⓓ condescending.

© SSI • MAY BE DUPLICATED

Standardized Test Preview/Practice

In this passage, some of the words from this lesson are in bold. Read the passage and then answer the questions.

The school board meeting did not get off to a **propitious** start. Mr. Henry, a business **mogul** known for his wildly popular fleet of food trucks, was running for an open position on the school board. He had hoped for support from the community
5   but found himself facing a lot of opposition.

"You're just a **philistine** who can't understand the **intrinsic** value of education!" said one very angry parent, her hands on her hips. "I am tired of businesspeople thinking that they can come into our communities and run everything—even our
10 schools—like a business," she added, looking around the room before sitting down and letting out a frustrated breath.

Mr. Henry raised a hand and asked politely, "May I speak?" He then stood to face the woman and others sitting next to her.

"I understand your concerns," the **avuncular**
15 businessperson said warmly, patting his teenage son's shoulder, "but I am just a parent like you, and I want my son and all our kids to get the best education possible."

1. The meaning of **propitious** (line 1) is

    Ⓐ peaceful.

    Ⓑ encouraging.

    Ⓒ uneventful.

    Ⓓ exciting.

2. In line 2, the phrase "business **mogul**" most nearly means

    Ⓐ wealthy businessperson.

    Ⓑ employer.

    Ⓒ local celebrity.

    Ⓓ worker.

3. The word **philistine** (line 6) most nearly means

    Ⓐ money-oriented person.

    Ⓑ business owner.

    Ⓒ person who doesn't respect education.

    Ⓓ ambitious person.

4. In line 6, **intrinsic** means

    Ⓐ monetary.

    Ⓑ social.

    Ⓒ potential.

    Ⓓ essential.

5. The meaning of **avuncular** (line 14) is

    Ⓐ mean and aggressive.

    Ⓑ rude and inappropriate.

    Ⓒ kind and good-humored.

    Ⓓ reserved and shy.

© SSI • MAY BE DUPLICATED

Name _____ Date _____

Lesson

7 Test

Find a SYNONYM for each bold word. Then fill in the circle next to your answer.

1. Hal was not convinced he needed new tires until his car **careened** off a wet road.

    Ⓐ stalled
    Ⓑ swerved
    Ⓒ turned
    Ⓓ sped

2. Unusual behavior in animals has been known to **presage** earthquakes.

    Ⓐ predict
    Ⓑ prevent
    Ⓒ alleviate
    Ⓓ cause

3. The small sailboat **careened** in the rough sea.

    Ⓐ sank
    Ⓑ leaned
    Ⓒ swerved
    Ⓓ steadied

4. Even though his parents were adventurous cooks, Joe was **repulsed** by exotic foods.

    Ⓐ intrigued
    Ⓑ enchanted
    Ⓒ admired
    Ⓓ disgusted

5. Winning the lottery had **seismic** repercussions on Luke's life.

    Ⓐ powerful
    Ⓑ depressing
    Ⓒ tiny
    Ⓓ unforeseen

Find an ANTONYM for each bold word. Then fill in the circle next to your answer.

6. Because he had already decided to quit his job, Terry had a **cavalier** attitude towards punctuality.

    Ⓐ strict
    Ⓑ polite
    Ⓒ carefree
    Ⓓ humble

7. Astrophysics is a **recondite** subject of study for all but a few.

    Ⓐ simple
    Ⓑ complex
    Ⓒ popular
    Ⓓ collegiate

8. Anna **repulsed** the swarm of bees with a fumigator.

   Ⓐ killed
   Ⓑ attracted
   Ⓒ disgusted
   Ⓓ tamed

9. A crowd gathered to watch the wrecking ball **pulverize** the old apartment building.

   Ⓐ touch
   Ⓑ construct
   Ⓒ demolish
   Ⓓ damage

10. Ethel and Irving have visited all forty-eight **contiguous** states in their RV.

    Ⓐ shared
    Ⓑ close
    Ⓒ separated
    Ⓓ different

Choose the best way to complete each sentence or answer each question. Then fill in the circle next to your answer.

11. **Kinetic** energy is most related to

    Ⓐ the sun.
    Ⓑ water.
    Ⓒ motion.
    Ⓓ gravity.

12. After something is **pulverized,** what is most likely to remain?

    Ⓐ evidence
    Ⓑ garbage
    Ⓒ liquid
    Ⓓ dust

13. Warping from **upheaval** generally comes from what direction?

    Ⓐ below
    Ⓑ behind
    Ⓒ above
    Ⓓ sideways

14. How is a flag that is **undulating** moving?

    Ⓐ falling
    Ⓑ waving
    Ⓒ whipping
    Ⓓ snapping

15. How did Carolyn behave as she **repulsed** Allan's flirtatious advances?

    Ⓐ cool
    Ⓑ friendly
    Ⓒ cheerful
    Ⓓ flattered

© 551 • MAY BE DUPLICATED

Standardized Test Preview/Practice

In this passage, some of the words from this lesson are in bold. Read the passage and then answer the questions.

There is a group of volcanic islands in the Pacific Ocean off the coast of Papua New Guinea called the Bismarck **Archipelago.** The islands are on the "Pacific Ring of Fire," a horseshoe-shaped area with a lot of **seismic** activity. Many
5　earthquakes hit the area and Papua New Guinea every year. However, earthquakes are not the only natural disaster common in that country. There is a strong **correlation** between earthquakes and tsunamis. The word *tsunami* comes from the Japanese words *tsu,* meaning "harbor," and *nami,*
10　meaning "wave." Reading the word's **etymology** may lead you to picture something fairly harmless—a "harbor wave"—but tsunamis are destructive, even when people are prepared for them, and they can be deadly. The last major tsunami to hit Papua New Guinea took the lives of over two thousand people,
15　and the destruction caused weeks of **upheaval** and millions of dollars' worth of damage.

1. The word **archipelago** (line 3) most nearly means

    Ⓐ area of water.

    Ⓑ country.

    Ⓒ group of islands.

    Ⓓ volcano.

2. The phrase "**seismic** activity" (line 4) most nearly means

    Ⓐ fiery explosions.

    Ⓑ weather-related disasters.

    Ⓒ earthquakes.

    Ⓓ political activity.

3. In line 7, **correlation** most nearly means

    Ⓐ distinction.

    Ⓑ connection.

    Ⓒ distance.

    Ⓓ position.

4. In line 10, **etymology** means

    Ⓐ meaning of a word.

    Ⓑ spelling of a word.

    Ⓒ history of a word.

    Ⓓ part of speech.

5. The word **upheaval** (line 15) most nearly means

    Ⓐ turmoil and disorder.

    Ⓑ oppression.

    Ⓒ action.

    Ⓓ improvement.

© SSI • MAY BE DUPLICATED

Lesson

8 Test

Find a SYNONYM for each bold word. Then fill in the circle next to your answer.

1. Though some doubted their authenticity, scholars have verified Mark Twain's lost writings and included them in his **canon.**

   Ⓐ estate
   Ⓑ writing
   Ⓒ library
   Ⓓ catalog

2. Grandmother hoped that James would ask Mari to be his **betrothed.**

   Ⓐ fiancée
   Ⓑ mentor
   Ⓒ roommate
   Ⓓ date

3. The **cadence** of dozens of joggers moving together helps Dan stay energized for the long race.

   Ⓐ sound
   Ⓑ rhythm
   Ⓒ excitement
   Ⓓ distraction

4. During surgery, the patient will be **insensate.**

   Ⓐ energized
   Ⓑ swollen
   Ⓒ unaware
   Ⓓ sensitive

5. Justin found it difficult to adjust to the **strictures** of military life.

   Ⓐ limitations
   Ⓑ routine
   Ⓒ opportunities
   Ⓓ challenges

Find an ANTONYM for each bold word. Then fill in the circle next to your answer.

6. After staying awake all night studying, Morris was **insensate** when the time came to take the test.

   Ⓐ tired
   Ⓑ dizzy
   Ⓒ sleeping
   Ⓓ aware

7. Many accused the students of **blasphemy** for painting graffiti over the stained glass window in the church.

   Ⓐ crimes
   Ⓑ disrespect
   Ⓒ reverence
   Ⓓ insanity

© SSI • MAY BE DUPLICATED

8. Detecting a rift among the cabinet ministers, the general decided to use force to **usurp** power from the civilian authority.

Ⓐ restore

Ⓑ seize

Ⓒ win

Ⓓ challenge

9. Molly was never timid with her **strictures** about trends in fashion.

Ⓐ objections

Ⓑ opinions

Ⓒ criticisms

Ⓓ endorsements

10. In his closing argument, the attorney offered a **soliloquy** about his theory of the crime.

Ⓐ dialogue

Ⓑ apology

Ⓒ oration

Ⓓ description

Choose the best way to complete each sentence or answer each question. Then fill in the circle next to your answer.

11. In which class are you most likely to discuss a **denouement?**

Ⓐ literature

Ⓑ geography

Ⓒ biology

Ⓓ geometry

12. Where are you most likely to find a **soliloquy?**

Ⓐ in a vault

Ⓑ in a garage

Ⓒ in an archive

Ⓓ in a play

13. Which of the following is most likely to be described as a **renegade?**

Ⓐ a farmer

Ⓑ an entrepreneur

Ⓒ a double agent

Ⓓ a journalist

14. Which of the following most closely describes an **edict?**

Ⓐ request

Ⓑ command

Ⓒ threat

Ⓓ guideline

15. A **votary** of a cause has what relationship to that cause?

Ⓐ devotion

Ⓑ indifference

Ⓒ leadership

Ⓓ administrative

© SSI • MAY BE DUPLICATED

Standardized Test Preview/Practice

In this passage, some of the words from this lesson are in bold. Read the passage and then answer the questions.

It is not illegal to wear religious **vestments** and claim to represent a religion or church. It is illegal, however, to **usurp** the identity of a religious leader to trick people out of money. That's fraud, and it's a crime. Unfortunately, history is full of
5   examples of this type of criminal activity.

Cult leaders are just one example of individuals who use religious faith as a tool to cheat people out of money. People who join cults often become **enamored** with cult leaders and become convinced that they must give away all their
10 possessions to achieve spiritual peace. A false representative of a religion may study and memorize the **canons** of that faith to gain the trust of the people they want to steal from.

Because religion and money are so important to people, this kind of crime is cruel and **insensate,** particularly when the
15 targets are vulnerable people searching for help.

1. The word **vestments** (line 1) most nearly means
   - Ⓐ clothing.
   - Ⓑ hats.
   - Ⓒ expressions.
   - Ⓓ jewelry.

2. The meaning of **usurp** (line 2) is
   - Ⓐ deny.
   - Ⓑ take over.
   - Ⓒ move.
   - Ⓓ complicate.

3. In line 8, the phrase "**enamored** with" most nearly means
   - Ⓐ involved with.
   - Ⓑ connected with.
   - Ⓒ ignored by.
   - Ⓓ captivated by.

4. In line 11, **canons** means
   - Ⓐ rules.
   - Ⓑ people.
   - Ⓒ buildings.
   - Ⓓ symbols.

5. The word **insensate** (line 14) most nearly means
   - Ⓐ alone.
   - Ⓑ unaware.
   - Ⓒ brutal.
   - Ⓓ helpful.

© SSI • MAY BE DUPLICATED

Name _____ Date _____

Lesson 9 Test

Find a SYNONYM for each bold word. Then fill in the circle next to your answer.

1. The loops of the roller coaster made me **queasy.**

   Ⓐ frightened
   Ⓑ nauseous
   Ⓒ angry
   Ⓓ quiet

2. After enjoying the hospitality of friends, it is nice to **reciprocate** as soon as possible.

   Ⓐ repay
   Ⓑ thank
   Ⓒ praise
   Ⓓ ignore

3. Eduardo enjoyed **fabricating** model airplanes from kits.

   Ⓐ flying
   Ⓑ buying
   Ⓒ building
   Ⓓ displaying

4. Jake's reluctance to fly borders on being a **phobia.**

   Ⓐ quirk
   Ⓑ fear
   Ⓒ aversion
   Ⓓ allergy

5. It requires a great deal of **bravado** to participate in professional wrestling.

   Ⓐ skill
   Ⓑ strength
   Ⓒ bravery
   Ⓓ resilience

Find an ANTONYM for each bold word. Then fill in the circle next to your answer.

6. Charlotte annoyed her friends by being **blasé** about meeting the president.

   Ⓐ excited
   Ⓑ indifferent
   Ⓒ calm
   Ⓓ secretive

7. Even though he deserved it, Robbie was **queasy** at the thought of asking for a raise.

   Ⓐ nervous
   Ⓑ calm
   Ⓒ arrogant
   Ⓓ ill

© SSI • MAY BE DUPLICATED

8. We **relegated** the matter of dispersing the budget surplus to the subcommittee for a vote.

   Ⓐ assigned
   Ⓑ demoted
   Ⓒ mentioned
   Ⓓ withheld

9. Maria and Lou worked out a **reciprocal** agreement that allowed them both one night of babysitting and one night of leisure every weekend.

   Ⓐ balanced
   Ⓑ unfair
   Ⓒ one-sided
   Ⓓ secret

10. Mr. Anderson's **proclivity** for essay assignments made him an intimidating teacher for some students.

    Ⓐ inclination
    Ⓑ aversion
    Ⓒ talent
    Ⓓ fondness

Choose the best way to complete each sentence or answer each question. Then fill in the circle next to your answer.

11. Which saying best reflects **reciprocity?**

    Ⓐ Do unto others as you would have them do unto you.
    Ⓑ A stitch in time saves nine.
    Ⓒ A bird in the hand is worth two in the bush.
    Ⓓ An ounce of prevention is worth a pound of cure.

12. Which of the following is the best example of a **domicile?**

    Ⓐ a library
    Ⓑ an apartment
    Ⓒ a gym
    Ⓓ an office

13. To make something appear **lilliputian** is to make it seem

    Ⓐ tiny.
    Ⓑ fierce.
    Ⓒ fast.
    Ⓓ important.

14. Trey looked for a **projectile** to scare the approaching badger. Trey wanted something to

    Ⓐ burn.
    Ⓑ brandish.
    Ⓒ eat.
    Ⓓ throw.

15. If a club's membership is **disparate,** it is most likely

    Ⓐ small.
    Ⓑ diverse.
    Ⓒ widespread.
    Ⓓ unif

© SSI • MAY BE DUPLICATED

Standardized Test Preview/Practice

In this passage, some of the words from this lesson are in bold. Read the passage and then answer the questions.

My dad's eccentric sister Marlene came over the other night for dinner. She told us that upon the **advent** of adulthood, we should leap into homeownership.

"Don't ever rent. As soon as you turn eighteen, buy your
5 own place—even if you buy a tiny studio apartment in a basement," she insisted. Marlene was known for being an **itinerant** and had never owned a home. Her **domiciles** had included a loft apartment with a spiral staircase that caused her **vertigo,** and a **lilliputian** studio apartment with a sloping
10 roof that couldn't accommodate the height of taller guests. She was now staying in an apartment over a garage and complained about toxic fumes.

My dad lifted an eyebrow and then winked at us before asking his sister, "Are they supposed to start earning money for
15 a down payment now, while they're in high school?"

"But of course," said Marlene. "That's exactly right."

We all silently exhaled, tried not to smile, and changed the subject.

1. The word **advent** (line 2) most nearly means

   (A) beginning.

   (B) calendar.

   (C) end.

   (D) type.

2. In line 7, **itinerant** most nearly means

   (A) poor person.

   (B) wanderer.

   (C) resident.

   (D) complainer.

3. The meaning of **domiciles** (line 7) is

   (A) cars.

   (B) areas.

   (C) relationships.

   (D) living spaces.

4. In line 9, **vertigo** means

   (A) joy.

   (B) sadness.

   (C) fear.

   (D) dizziness.

5. The word **lilliputian** (line 9) most nearly means

   (A) very small.

   (B) inexpensive.

   (C) wooden.

   (D) ugly.

© SSI • MAY BE DUPLICATED

Name _____ Date _____

Lesson 10 Test

Find a SYNONYM for each bold word. Then fill in the circle next to your answer.

1. Her sister suggested that flowers might **appease** Tomiko's anger.

   Ⓐ pacify
   Ⓑ increase
   Ⓒ defer
   Ⓓ remove

2. Raphael is an award-winning **equestrian.**

   Ⓐ journalist
   Ⓑ designer
   Ⓒ rider
   Ⓓ fundraiser

3. Because of her efforts to catch up, Pia's absences were **expunged** from the records.

   Ⓐ erased
   Ⓑ worsened
   Ⓒ average
   Ⓓ changed

4. Many people lost their savings in the stock market **debacle.**

   Ⓐ struggle
   Ⓑ failure
   Ⓒ controversy
   Ⓓ rumor

5. After being caught cheating in the student government election, Loren experienced **opprobrium** from her teachers and classmates.

   Ⓐ loss
   Ⓑ embarrassment
   Ⓒ contempt
   Ⓓ lessons

Find an ANTONYM for each bold word. Then fill in the circle next to your answer.

6. Brandy **upbraided** Michele for her selfishness.

   Ⓐ thanked
   Ⓑ scolded
   Ⓒ ignored
   Ⓓ praised

7. Billboards **sullied** what used to be a beautiful, scenic drive.

   Ⓐ dotted
   Ⓑ improved
   Ⓒ ruined
   Ⓓ developed

© SSI • MAY BE DUPLICATED

8. After a long day's hike, our team reached the **vertex** of Mount Rainier.

   (A) summit

   (B) middle

   (C) slope

   (D) base

9. The **attrition** of technology jobs in the slowing economy led to increased unemployment claims.

   (A) difficulty

   (B) addition

   (C) loss

   (D) salaries

10. The tour manager attempted to **appease** the restless crowd by bringing out the opening act.

   (A) enrage

   (B) repay

   (C) usurp

   (D) excite

Choose the best way to complete each sentence or answer each question. Then fill in the circle next to your answer.

11. My cousin Ladarius has **amnesia** from his head injury and can tell us

   (A) details about the accident.

   (B) nothing about the accident.

   (C) everything about the accident.

   (D) his memories about the accident.

12. Which of the following is most likely to appear **verdant?**

   (A) a clear sky

   (B) a mud puddle

   (C) vanilla ice cream

   (D) a field of clover

13. With what is a **tactile** sensation most likely experienced?

   (A) your imagination

   (B) your hands

   (C) your eyes

   (D) your nose

14. In a struggle of **attrition,** one side tries to defeat the other through what means?

   (A) harassment

   (B) reason

   (C) lies

   (D) the law

15. **Equestrian** sports involve

   (A) guns.

   (B) ice.

   (C) endurance.

   (D) horses.

© SSI • MAY BE DUPLICATED

Standardized Test Preview/Practice

In this passage, some of the words from this lesson are in bold. Read the passage and then answer the questions.

"You want me to **defoliate** this bush?" asked Graciela, holding the heavy gardening shears unsteadily in gloved hands. Tía Valentina laughed. They were in her aunt's **verdant** backyard, which had an impressive number of bushes in it.

5 Graciela had agreed to help with yard work with the **proviso** that they stop for lemonade at least once an hour.

"No, don't cut off *all* the leaves. Here, just watch me," her aunt said, clipping precisely and gently with her own shears.

"Okay—but these old shears you gave me are heavy. This

10 is going to be hard work. Remember what I said about the lemonade?" Graciela said, smiling.

"Of course I remember! I didn't suddenly get **amnesia!** The lemonade is in the fridge," Tía Valentina said.

Graciela took a deep breath and wrenched open the

15 unwieldy shears, trying to save time by whacking off two branches at a time.

Her aunt gave her a warning look. "Just remember the saying, 'Everything grows with love,' and don't do it too quickly or carelessly," she said seriously. "That's not just a **hackneyed**

20 expression. It's true."

1. The word **defoliate** (line 1) most nearly means
   Ⓐ scrub.
   Ⓑ remove the leaves from.
   Ⓒ dig around.
   Ⓓ work on.

2. The meaning of **verdant** (line 3) is
   Ⓐ private.
   Ⓑ enclosed.
   Ⓒ hot.
   Ⓓ lush with greenery.

3. In line 5, **proviso** most nearly means
   Ⓐ condition.
   Ⓑ request.
   Ⓒ objection.
   Ⓓ hope.

4. In line 12, **amnesia** means
   Ⓐ fever.
   Ⓑ gap.
   Ⓒ memory loss.
   Ⓓ sickness.

5. The word **hackneyed** (line 19) most nearly means
   Ⓐ trite.
   Ⓑ emotional.
   Ⓒ false.
   Ⓓ gardening.

Read the passage. Choose the best answer for each sentence or question about a bold word. Then fill in the circle next to your answer.

Extra, Extra! Read All About It!

In Renaissance Europe, handwritten newsletters circulated privately among merchants who passed along information about everything from wars and economic conditions to social customs and stories of human interest. With the **advent** of the printing press came the first printed forerunners of the newspaper. These documents appeared in Germany in the late 1400s in the form of news pamphlets called "broadsides." The earliest American newspapers developed to spread news of colonial political concerns as well as to report on events of local interest. These early newspapers were produced for **opulent,** highly educated people who could afford the yearly subscriptions.

The growth of colonial newspapers **correlated** with the growing belief that information should be independent from governmental control. Newspaper publishers in the seventeenth and eighteenth centuries played more than just a **peripheral** role in the colonies' decision to break from England. The struggle of the colonies to be free from English control helped shape the concept of an independent press. As early as 1690, colonial newspapers sought **autonomy,** yet publishers relied on the **munificence** of Britain for printing the paper. The council of the Massachusetts Bay Colony approved all content. The British government found the idea of an independent colonial newspaper **disconcerting.** In 1721, Benjamin Franklin's older brother James published items in his paper, *The New-England Courant,* without the official seal of the government. The British government considered him a **renegade** and jailed him like a common criminal.

In 1833, Benjamin Day created the first successful "penny paper"—a newspaper that published advertising to decrease the cost to customers. Day's paper, the *New York Sun,* published sensationalized news and reported local gossip. Readers could now buy papers daily rather than pay the one lump sum of a subscription. Day also hired newsboys, who would employ **histrionics** to interest people in the news. People would buy papers from newsboys, who stood on busy street corners and shouted the headlines to passersby.

Many early newspapers failed, but **perspicacious** investors could see the potential for growth in the industry. Newspaper publishing ventures soon turned profitable as the popularity of newspapers spread to communities of immigrants and people on the frontier. In the antebellum South and beyond, African American newspapers expressed the need for social change. Ethnic and Native American newspapers met the needs of a growing America. Specialty papers like the *North Star,* founded by abolitionist leader Frederick Douglass, became voices against the **thralldom** of African Americans and women.

The **nascent** women's movement gained a minor toehold in the beginning of the eighteenth century. In 1738, Elizabeth Timothy took over editing responsibilities for the

South Carolina Gazette after the death of her husband, and she is recognized today as the first female American newspaper editor. Other notable examples of female pioneers in the publishing industry include Anna Zenger, a proponent of free press, and journalist Ida B. Wells, a crusader for civil rights.

Newspapers have played an important role in America's social environment since colonial times, when the colonial press led the quest for national independence by **inculcating** the public with strident messages of political injustice and unrest. Two hundred years later, social activists of the 1960s resurrected the idea of newspapers as a voice of the downtrodden in America. Even today, in an era of high-speed electronic communication, newspapers still create a sense of community for the people they serve.

1. Which of the following would be least likely to be described as **peripheral?**

    Ⓐ whole
    Ⓑ center
    Ⓒ edge
    Ⓓ boundary

2. In the fifth paragraph, **nascent** is a SYNONYM for all of the following EXCEPT which?

    Ⓐ budding
    Ⓑ emerging
    Ⓒ arising
    Ⓓ dwindling

3. **Histrionics** is most closely related to behavior that is

    Ⓐ laudable.
    Ⓑ theatrical.
    Ⓒ calming.
    Ⓓ dignified.

4. Which of the following is most closely related to **thralldom?**

    Ⓐ freedom
    Ⓑ fascination
    Ⓒ slavery
    Ⓓ illness

© SSI • MAY BE DUPLICATED

5. Who are people least likely to be described as **opulent,** as the word is used in the passage?

   Ⓐ royalty

   Ⓑ tycoons

   Ⓒ servants

   Ⓓ celebrities

6. As used in the passage, **perspicacious** means

   Ⓐ selfish.

   Ⓑ apt.

   Ⓒ wealthy.

   Ⓓ shrewd.

7. If two things are **correlated,** they are

   Ⓐ different.

   Ⓑ related.

   Ⓒ similar.

   Ⓓ complex.

8. As used in paragraph two, **disconcerting** most closely means

   Ⓐ upsetting.

   Ⓑ engaging.

   Ⓒ understanding.

   Ⓓ intriguing.

9. All of the following are SYNONYMS for the word **renegade,** as it is used in the passage, EXCEPT which?

   Ⓐ rebel

   Ⓑ criminal

   Ⓒ traitor

   Ⓓ hero

10. An ANTONYM for **munificence** is

    Ⓐ selfishness.

    Ⓑ influence.

    Ⓒ generosity.

    Ⓓ stinginess.

© SSI • MAY BE DUPLICATED

Standardized Test Preview/Practice

1. In the first paragraph, **advent** most nearly means

   Ⓐ arrival.

   Ⓑ popularity.

   Ⓒ changes.

   Ⓓ promises.

   Ⓔ problems.

2. To teach by **inculcating** most likely involves what?

   Ⓐ experiments

   Ⓑ debate

   Ⓒ memorization

   Ⓓ repetition

   Ⓔ essays

3. **Autonomy** most closely means

   Ⓐ independence.

   Ⓑ reliance.

   Ⓒ possibility.

   Ⓓ intelligence.

   Ⓔ embellishment.

4. A character that plays a **peripheral** role in a drama is

   Ⓐ driving the action.

   Ⓑ affected by the action.

   Ⓒ not central to the action.

   Ⓓ opposed to the action.

   Ⓔ a victim of the action.

5. Which of the following pairs is most likely to be found to have a **correlation?**

   Ⓐ height and eye color

   Ⓑ nutrition and health

   Ⓒ rhythm and blues

   Ⓓ apples and oranges

   Ⓔ wealth and happiness

© SSI • MAY BE DUPLICATED

Name _____   Date _____

Midterm Test 2

Read the passage. Choose the best answer for each sentence or question about a bold word. Then fill in the circle next to your answer.

The United Nations Fights for Peace

The history of mankind has been a history of military, social, and economic battles between groups of people. For thousands of years, clans have fought clans, tribes have fought tribes, and nations have fought nations for control of important resources. In the early 20th century, however, Europe was devastated by World War I. This war was so destructive and horrific that heads of state and the general populace alike began to press for peaceful cooperation among the countries of the world.

The first attempt at international cooperation was the formation of the League of Nations. The League was established in 1919 under the Treaty of Versailles, which ended World War I. Unfortunately, the League of Nations failed to prevent World War II, another catastrophic war. This **debacle** encouraged the U.S. and its allies to establish the United Nations. The name "United Nations" was first used by United States President Franklin D. Roosevelt in January 1942 during the war, when representatives of 26 nations pledged their governments' support in the fight against the Axis powers. The UN was created to stabilize international relations, secure rules of warfare, and promote and develop policies for settling crises peacefully.

In Moscow on October 30, 1943, the **disparate** governments of the Soviet Union, the United Kingdom, the United States, and China called for an early establishment of an international organization to maintain peace and security. That goal was reaffirmed at the meeting of the leaders of the United States, the Soviet Union, and the United Kingdom in Tehran on December 1, 1943. The United Nations charter was ratified on October 24, 1945. The organization officially **convened** on January 24, 1946. Amid the threat of nuclear war, **strictures** from world leaders, and seemingly endless conflicts caused by those trying to **usurp** power, peacekeeping has become an overriding concern of the United Nations. Dictators who **ensconce** themselves in the halls of power and then violate their citizens' rights can expect to face censure from the UN. The UN has been instrumental in trying to help the world achieve peace and security.

In its relatively brief history, the United Nations has had many decorated leaders. From 1997 to 2006, the UN was led by Secretary-General Kofi Annan. A native of Ghana, Annan was the first diplomat to rise to secretary-general from within the international civil service. He was also the first African elected to the post. During his career, Annan had been **indoctrinated** in UN policy, performing important assignments in the field and at duty stations throughout the world, beginning with a position in the World Heath Organization in 1962. As Secretary-General, Kofi Annan was instrumental in bringing new life to an organization previously **relegated** largely to ceremonial displays. Annan's first major initiative was his plan for reform, "Renewing the United Nations." The plan emphasized improving coherence and coordination in the organization. It was Annan's goal to ensure that the **edicts**

© SSI • MAY BE DUPLICATED

of the United Nations were binding on all members, and that the UN's power to promote peace and economic development was not undermined by the aggression of a single country.

Annan was succeeded in 2007 by Ban Ki-moon, the Minister of Foreign Affairs and Trade for the Republic of South Korea. Mr. Ban had worked for the UN in several capacities. He had served as chairman of the Preparatory Commission for the Nuclear Test Ban treaty of 2001–2002. He also headed the South Korean Republic's Presidency of the General Assembly. In the latter role Mr. Ban was instrumental in leading the official UN condemnation of the 2001 attacks on the World Trade Center in New York City.

With the **denouement** of the Cold War and the rise in terrorism around the world, the UN has been called on to more fully perform its mission to provide a forum for conflict resolution. That said, the United Nations and its family of agencies are still engaged in an **eclectic** array of work that touches every aspect of people's lives around the world. Primary initiatives of this office include providing adequate health care and nutrition to needy world citizens, protecting human rights, and maintaining the environment.

In addressing environmental concerns, Ban Ki-moon presided over the historic 2009 climate change conference in Copenhagen, Denmark. His message for the conference was direct. "Now is the time to act," he said. "Seldom in history has a choice been so clear. We can move toward a future of sustainable green growth, or we can continue down the road to ruin."

The UN remains determined to meet the world's economic, social, and environmental challenges. It will continue to tackle the issues of health and medical research, environmental protection, and human rights. As **votaries** of peace, then-leader Kofi Annan and the United Nations received the Nobel Peace Prize on December 10, 2001, "for their work for a better organized and more peaceful world."

1. As used in the second paragraph, all of the following are SYNONYMS for **debacle** EXCEPT

   Ⓐ failure.

   Ⓑ downfall.

   Ⓒ collapse.

   Ⓓ setback.

2. As used in the third paragraph, **disparate** refers to what kinds of things?

   Ⓐ allied

   Ⓑ similar

   Ⓒ different

   Ⓓ warring

3. As used in the third paragraph, a SYNONYM for **convened** is

   Ⓐ organized.

   Ⓑ gathered.

   Ⓒ dissolved.

   Ⓓ opened.

© SSI • MAY BE DUPLICATED

4. As used in the third paragraph, **strictures** is most closely related to

   Ⓐ requests.

   Ⓑ objections.

   Ⓒ demands.

   Ⓓ criticisms.

5. As used in this passage, a SYNONYM for **usurp** is

   Ⓐ share.

   Ⓑ abdicate.

   Ⓒ seize.

   Ⓓ win.

6. As used in the fourth paragraph, all of the following are SYNONYMS for **indoctrinated** EXCEPT

   Ⓐ instilled.

   Ⓑ taught.

   Ⓒ trained.

   Ⓓ brainwashed.

7. As used in this passage, **ensconce** is most closely related to being

   Ⓐ uncomfortable.

   Ⓑ secure.

   Ⓒ hesitant.

   Ⓓ shy.

8. **Relegated,** as used in the fourth paragraph, is most closely related to being

   Ⓐ demoted.

   Ⓑ assigned.

   Ⓒ promoted.

   Ⓓ concerned.

9. As used in the sixth paragraph, **denouement** most nearly means

   Ⓐ horror.

   Ⓑ triumph.

   Ⓒ end.

   Ⓓ outcome.

10. As used in the sixth paragraph, **eclectic** refers to all of the following except

   Ⓐ assortment.

   Ⓑ variety.

   Ⓒ uniformity.

   Ⓓ range.

© SSI • MAY BE DUPLICATED

Standardized Test Preview/Practice

1. In the eighth paragraph, **votaries** is least related to

   Ⓐ commitment.

   Ⓑ devotion.

   Ⓒ fickleness.

   Ⓓ loyalty.

   Ⓔ allegiance.

2. As used in the fourth paragraph, an **edict** is most closely related to

   Ⓐ a pact.

   Ⓑ a treaty.

   Ⓒ a letter.

   Ⓓ a guide.

   Ⓔ a decree.

3. Which of the following is most likely to describe a **debacle?**

   Ⓐ sudden

   Ⓑ minor

   Ⓒ gradual

   Ⓓ partial

   Ⓔ destroyed

4. Which of the following is most likely to be **convened?**

   Ⓐ a movie

   Ⓑ a sporting event

   Ⓒ a vacation

   Ⓓ a party

   Ⓔ a meeting

5. Which of the following is least likely to contain an **eclectic** assortment of things?

   Ⓐ a fruit basket

   Ⓑ a department store

   Ⓒ a tire shop

   Ⓓ a backpack

   Ⓔ a museum

© SSI • MAY BE DUPLICATED

Lesson
11 **Test**

Find a SYNONYM for each bold word. Then fill in the circle next to your answer.

1. Covering her mouth and nose with a scarf, Lori tried to **attenuate** the harshness of the bitter cold air.

   Ⓐ decrease
   Ⓑ warm
   Ⓒ increase
   Ⓓ avoid

2. Sunday noise ordinances **impinged** on residents' rights to tend to their yards during their time off from work.

   Ⓐ allowed
   Ⓑ overlooked
   Ⓒ threatened
   Ⓓ encroached

3. It struck Raul as an **oxymoron** when Shana told him to "act naturally."

   Ⓐ contradiction
   Ⓑ impossibility
   Ⓒ joke
   Ⓓ insult

4. Chris annoyed his friends by assuming "Work now; play later" was a **postulate** they all accepted.

   Ⓐ ethic
   Ⓑ guideline
   Ⓒ goal
   Ⓓ principle

5. Jason only makes his famous peach pie in late summer, because he refuses to use fruit that is not perfectly **succulent.**

   Ⓐ grown
   Ⓑ juicy
   Ⓒ ready
   Ⓓ aromatic

Find an ANTONYM for each bold word. Then fill in the circle next to your answer.

6. The chef's skilled fingers made it look effortless to **attenuate** the dough into long ropes to be cut into spaghetti.

   Ⓐ stretch
   Ⓑ shape
   Ⓒ fatten
   Ⓓ roll

7. Rumors that his death was faked circulated for a century before the family allowed his body to be **disinterred** and proven to be that of Jesse James.

   Ⓐ disturbed
   Ⓑ buried
   Ⓒ tested
   Ⓓ identified

© SSI • MAY BE DUPLICATED

8. When it came to appeasing Nat's sweet tooth, ice cream would **prevail** over cake every time.

Ⓐ win

Ⓑ dominate

Ⓒ lose

Ⓓ weaken

9. When Juan's parents asked if he would like to spend his junior year abroad, he responded with an **unequivocal** "yes."

Ⓐ ambiguous

Ⓑ ungrateful

Ⓒ emotional

Ⓓ hysterical

10. Diana was accustomed to her small car, and she found it difficult to adjust to driving a **behemoth** like her friend's van.

Ⓐ vehicle

Ⓑ size

Ⓒ car

Ⓓ miniature

Choose the best way to complete each sentence or answer each question. Then fill in the circle next to your answer.

11. A large tree **impinged** on our porch roof during the storm. The tree

Ⓐ threatened it.

Ⓑ blew off it.

Ⓒ crashed on it.

Ⓓ cast a shadow on it.

12. How much do you have when you have a **plenitude** of something?

Ⓐ a shortage

Ⓑ enough

Ⓒ an abundance

Ⓓ an excess

13. What can be said of a trend that **prevails?**

Ⓐ It is widespread.

Ⓑ It is new.

Ⓒ It is weakening.

Ⓓ It is over.

14. Which sense is offended by something that has **putrefied?**

Ⓐ sight

Ⓑ smell

Ⓒ touch

Ⓓ hearing

15. Which of the following most nearly relates to **vicissitudes?**

Ⓐ incisions

Ⓑ food

Ⓒ fluctuations

Ⓓ travel

© SSI • MAY BE DUPLICATED

Standardized Test Preview/Practice

In this passage, some of the words from this lesson are in bold. Read the passage and then answer the questions.

The benefits of exercise include better quality of sleep, improved mental health, increased bone density, and a longer life span. There are many forms of exercise, but the **multifarious** options can be organized into three main

5   categories: flexibility, strength, and cardio.

Exercises focusing on flexibility, such as yoga, involve stretching, toning, and lengthening muscles. One of the **salubrious** effects of increased flexibility is the prevention of injuries.

10   Strength training is beneficial because it has been proven to increase bone density. Ancient bones **disinterred** by archeologists show how important weight-bearing exercise is for bone health; before humans began farming, they did more heavy lifting, and their bones were thicker and stronger than

15   those of modern-day humans.

Cardiovascular exercise strengthens the heart and lungs. Although many are aware of cardio's benefits, some feel that the idea of "enjoyable cardio" is an **oxymoron.** This may be because it takes several weeks to build up endurance; in the

20   meantime, being out of breath is definitely uncomfortable.

You can overcome the initial discomfort of exercise by using your imagination. While running around the block, for example, you can pretend you are running across the Siberian **tundra,** trying to get home before you freeze.

1. The word **multifarious** (line 4) most nearly means

    Ⓐ hidden.

    Ⓑ confusing.

    Ⓒ various.

    Ⓓ correct.

2. The meaning of **salubrious** (line 8) is

    Ⓐ side.

    Ⓑ scientific.

    Ⓒ unintended.

    Ⓓ healthful.

3. In line 11, **disinterred** most nearly means

    Ⓐ studied.

    Ⓑ dug up.

    Ⓒ classified.

    Ⓓ photographed.

4. In line 18, **oxymoron** means

    Ⓐ wise saying.

    Ⓑ quotation by experts.

    Ⓒ contradictory combination of words.

    Ⓓ piece of advice.

5. The word **tundra** (line 24) most nearly means

    Ⓐ border.

    Ⓑ path.

    Ⓒ boundary.

    Ⓓ arctic plain.

© SSI • MAY BE DUPLICATED

Lesson 12 Test

Find a SYNONYM for each bold word. Then fill in the circle next to your answer.

1. Organizers were surprised at the **amity** with which former rivals worked when trying to achieve a common goal.

   Ⓐ difficulty
   Ⓑ hostility
   Ⓒ friendship
   Ⓓ friction

2. Emperor Commodus of Rome sought to **exalt** himself by giving himself twelve titles, then renaming the months of the year with those titles.

   Ⓐ glorify
   Ⓑ humiliate
   Ⓒ immortalize
   Ⓓ publicize

3. Though she was a millionaire many times over, Mitzi clung to her **penurious** ways.

   Ⓐ decadent
   Ⓑ careless
   Ⓒ evil
   Ⓓ stingy

4. Though the professional world knew her as Melissa Banks, Esq., she would never stop responding to the old family **sobriquet** "Mimi" when she was at home.

   Ⓐ nickname
   Ⓑ joke
   Ⓒ slogan
   Ⓓ cheer

5. While his father found the **bucolic** cabin restful, Adnan only considered it dull.

   Ⓐ cozy
   Ⓑ pastoral
   Ⓒ tiny
   Ⓓ remote

Find an ANTONYM for each bold word. Then fill in the circle next to your answer.

6. Jenna grew weary of Beth's constant **animadversions** and wished she would focus her energy on constructive comments.

   Ⓐ compliments
   Ⓑ criticisms
   Ⓒ gossip
   Ⓓ whining

7. Javin's ambition was to someday join the **exalted** ranks of the Nobel laureates.

   Ⓐ public
   Ⓑ secret
   Ⓒ lofty
   Ⓓ lowly

© SSI • MAY BE DUPLICATED

8. Marcia looked forward to graduating and getting a job, and the end of her **penurious** life as a college student.

Ⓐ modest

Ⓑ opulent

Ⓒ frivolous

Ⓓ innocent

9. Although they had not seen each other in almost five years, the **amity** between the cousins was as if they had never parted.

Ⓐ hostility

Ⓑ resemblance

Ⓒ familiarity

Ⓓ alienation

10. Jacob's friends would not let him forget his **craven** reaction to seeing the mouse run across the kitchen floor.

Ⓐ animated

Ⓑ brave

Ⓒ comical

Ⓓ stunned

Choose the best way to complete each sentence or answer each question. Then fill in the circle next to your answer.

11. When one person is another's **antithesis,** those people are each other's

Ⓐ neighbors.

Ⓑ family.

Ⓒ friends.

Ⓓ opposites.

12. Someone who is **craven** would be most likely to

Ⓐ bake a cake.

Ⓑ slay a dragon.

Ⓒ hide from danger.

Ⓓ build a tree house.

13. To **impugn** one's honesty is to

Ⓐ call it into question.

Ⓑ confirm it.

Ⓒ make note of it.

Ⓓ test it.

14. An **introspective** person is likely to be aware of his or her

Ⓐ surroundings.

Ⓑ feelings.

Ⓒ enemies.

Ⓓ belongings.

15. **Throes** are most likely to come from which of the following?

Ⓐ pitchers

Ⓑ surprises

Ⓒ struggles

Ⓓ windfalls

© SSI • MAY BE DUPLICATED

Standardized Test Preview/Practice

In this passage, some of the words from this lesson are in bold. Read the passage and then answer the questions.

Bhalu didn't like camping. One reason he didn't like it was the **privation.** Why go without things like electricity, running water, a toilet that flushes, and a nice soft mattress to sleep on? Bhalu just didn't understand the appeal of "roughing it."

5 After some **introspection,** Bhalu realized that the other reason he didn't like camping was because of bad memories. On a three-day camping trip in fourth grade, Bhalu was put in a cabin with boys he didn't know very well. One **bellicose** boy, Ming, had made fun of him and threatened to beat him up.

10 Ming had convinced the other boys to play tricks on Bhalu that weren't funny at all. They had dunked his sneakers in water, taken the batteries out of his flashlight, and put dirt on his toothbrush.

When Bhalu had complained to the camp counselor, a

15 college student, she just patted him on his head, told him to "toughen up," and sent him back to the cabin to deal with the bullies on his own. Whatever her real **métier** was, it must not have involved working with kids or helping them resolve their problems. What she had done to Bhalu had been **tantamount**

20 to putting a small fish into a tank full of mean, hungry sharks.

1. The word **privation** (line 2) most nearly means

   Ⓐ situation.

   Ⓑ lack of privacy.

   Ⓒ insecurity.

   Ⓓ lack of comforts.

2. The phrase "after some **introspection**"(line 5) most nearly means

   Ⓐ after examining his own thoughts and feelings.

   Ⓑ after analyzing the idea of camping.

   Ⓒ after taking some time.

   Ⓓ after learning new information.

3. In line 8, **bellicose** most nearly means

   Ⓐ strong.

   Ⓑ combative.

   Ⓒ older.

   Ⓓ funny.

4. In line 17, **métier** means

   Ⓐ problem.

   Ⓑ decision at that moment.

   Ⓒ most suitable profession.

   Ⓓ thought process.

5. In line 19, the phrase "had been **tantamount** to" most nearly means

   Ⓐ was the same as.

   Ⓑ was in preparation for.

   Ⓒ was not similar to.

   Ⓓ was opposed to.

© SSI • MAY BE DUPLICATED

Name _____   Date _____

Lesson 13 Test

Find a SYNONYM for each bold word. Then fill in the circle next to your answer.

1. The actress could not choose between the prestigious Broadway part and her regular television role, so she opted to appear in both of the **concurrent** productions.

    Ⓐ popular
    Ⓑ disparate
    Ⓒ simultaneous
    Ⓓ demanding

2. Tabloid newspapers often change the meaning of a statement by presenting it without providing the **context** in which it originally occurred.

    Ⓐ circumstances
    Ⓑ mood
    Ⓒ meaning
    Ⓓ reaction

3. Liz declined the invitation, since she knew the heat of Ceylonese **cuisine** was more than she could take.

    Ⓐ beaches
    Ⓑ theaters
    Ⓒ saunas
    Ⓓ cooking

4. A traffic citation **enjoins** the recipient to pay a fine or to appear in court.

    Ⓐ forbids
    Ⓑ commands
    Ⓒ requests
    Ⓓ prohibits

5. The **genesis** for Erik's business idea was when Pat mentioned that he did not want a pet, but that he wanted a dog to run with.

    Ⓐ origin
    Ⓑ outcome
    Ⓒ result
    Ⓓ success

Find an ANTONYM for each bold word. Then fill in the circle next to your answer.

6. Though the same could not necessarily be said of his business practices, Andrew Carnegie's private **altruism** was legendary.

    Ⓐ selfishness
    Ⓑ generosity
    Ⓒ immaturity
    Ⓓ charity

7. Since Martin could not seem to refrain from making **crass** comments, I decided not to bring him to the wedding.

    Ⓐ serious
    Ⓑ loud
    Ⓒ tasteless
    Ⓓ delicate

© SSI • MAY BE DUPLICATED

8. Rather than **debase** the office with a long, sordid inquiry, Rachel chose to resign quietly.

   Ⓐ expose
   Ⓑ glorify
   Ⓒ cheapen
   Ⓓ preoccupy

9. Kathryn could not seem to **reconcile** herself to the fact that her mother's promotion meant changing schools for her senior year.

   Ⓐ resist
   Ⓑ accept
   Ⓒ admit
   Ⓓ realize

10. Padraig would remember the emergency of the mudslide as the **genesis** of his career in medicine.

    Ⓐ inspiration
    Ⓑ end
    Ⓒ highlight
    Ⓓ birth

Choose the best way to complete each sentence or answer each question. Then fill in the circle next to your answer.

11. If students are **enjoined** from leaving campus during school hours, that means that they are

    Ⓐ permitted to leave campus.
    Ⓑ encouraged to leave campus.
    Ⓒ forbidden to leave campus.
    Ⓓ discouraged from leaving campus.

12. Before an **extemporaneous** speech, which of the following is Cherrie most likely to do?

    Ⓐ clear her throat
    Ⓑ prepare note cards
    Ⓒ rehearse with a friend
    Ⓓ memorize the outline

13. When Janice is experiencing a **malaise,** she feels

    Ⓐ joyful.
    Ⓑ energetic.
    Ⓒ ill.
    Ⓓ elated.

14. If neighbors need to **reconcile,** then they are currently

    Ⓐ amicable.
    Ⓑ feuding.
    Ⓒ cordial.
    Ⓓ blaming.

15. The stock market crash of 1929 led to a decade of **travail.** Which of the following least describes **travail?**

    Ⓐ suffering
    Ⓑ anguish
    Ⓒ hardship
    Ⓓ inactivity

Standardized Test Preview/Practice

In this passage, some of the words from this lesson are in bold. Read the passage and then answer the questions.

Wedding celebrations are social occasions that vary all over the world, but a few things appear to be common to many. For example, in the social **context** of a wedding, **platitudes** are not frowned upon or seen as a bad thing. In
5 fact, they are almost always encouraged; nearly everyone wishes the newly married couple "the best," "a lifetime of happiness," or warns them "never to take each other for granted." Many platitudes focus on the importance of couples sticking together in difficult times and not allowing the
10 relationship to be **sundered.** You will hear long-married couples give advice such as "never go to bed angry" or "be one another's best friend."

In addition to platitudes, another standard part of many wedding celebrations is sharing food and drink. Guests
15 can expect special **libations** to be served and often enjoy traditional music and **cuisine** associated with the cultural heritage of the bride and groom.

1. The word **context** (line 3) most nearly means

   Ⓐ written passage.

   Ⓑ rules.

   Ⓒ circumstances.

   Ⓓ ceremonies.

2. The meaning of **platitudes** (line 4) is

   Ⓐ overused sayings.

   Ⓑ polite attitudes.

   Ⓒ expressions of anger.

   Ⓓ displays of affection.

3. In line 10, **sundered** most nearly means

   Ⓐ continued.

   Ⓑ changed.

   Ⓒ emotional.

   Ⓓ broken apart.

4. In line 15, **libations** means

   Ⓐ cakes.

   Ⓑ drinks.

   Ⓒ appetizers.

   Ⓓ desserts.

5. The word **cuisine** (line 16) most nearly means

   Ⓐ dancing.

   Ⓑ food specific to a culture.

   Ⓒ rituals.

   Ⓓ formalities.

© SSI • MAY BE DUPLICATED

Lesson 14 Test

Find a SYNONYM for each bold word. Then fill in the circle next to your answer.

1. Ross **buttressed** his argument that he deserved a promotion by charting sales increases in the years since he was first hired.

   Ⓐ proved
   Ⓑ strengthened
   Ⓒ illustrated
   Ⓓ punctuated

2. To enhance cultural awareness, the community center set up an **ecumenical** center and encouraged discussions there.

   Ⓐ international
   Ⓑ open
   Ⓒ selective
   Ⓓ universal

3. No matter what shock she encountered in her work as a counselor, Coretta kept it hidden behind her blasé **facade.**

   Ⓐ appearance
   Ⓑ smile
   Ⓒ personality
   Ⓓ eyeglasses

4. The advent of World War II made the debate about whether it was appropriate for women to work outside the home **moot.**

   Ⓐ irrelevant
   Ⓑ heated
   Ⓒ important
   Ⓓ accelerate

5. Wayne chose not to battle the storm, but he vowed to see the **pinnacle** of Mt. Everest someday.

   Ⓐ snow
   Ⓑ view
   Ⓒ base
   Ⓓ peak

Find an ANTONYM for each bold word. Then fill in the circle next to your answer.

6. Barry was a hindrance to the group's progress, as he tended to be **dilatory** in completing his part of the work.

   Ⓐ thorough
   Ⓑ prompt
   Ⓒ dedicated
   Ⓓ sloppy

7. The topic of Claudia's curfew is **mooted** at the dinner table at least once weekly.

   Ⓐ discussed
   Ⓑ suggested
   Ⓒ debated
   Ⓓ decided

© 331 • MAY BE DUPLICATED

8. Summer classes were in **abeyance** while the school's boiler was brought up to code.

Ⓐ disrepair

Ⓑ use

Ⓒ suspension

Ⓓ uncertainty

9. The city of Jerusalem is **sacrosanct** to Christians, Muslims, and Jews.

Ⓐ exotic

Ⓑ common

Ⓒ secular

Ⓓ sacred

10. A **tenet** of the practice of medicine is to do no harm.

Ⓐ rule

Ⓑ option

Ⓒ lie

Ⓓ suggestion

Choose the best way to complete each sentence or answer each question. Then fill in the circle next to your answer.

11. When she was offered a salary "**commensurate** with her experience," how did Sara expect to be paid?

Ⓐ at a higher rate than her last job

Ⓑ at a lower rate than she deserved

Ⓒ without regard to her experience

Ⓓ proportionately with her experience

12. Which way is a building's **facade** most likely to face?

Ⓐ toward the street

Ⓑ toward the pool

Ⓒ toward the setting sun

Ⓓ toward the neighboring building

13. Which of the following best describes a **gargoyle?**

Ⓐ charming

Ⓑ grotesque

Ⓒ functional

Ⓓ warm

14. When Aunt Iva reflected on the **pinnacle** of her career, she was thinking about its

Ⓐ beginning.

Ⓑ low point.

Ⓒ high point.

Ⓓ end.

15. Upon what does something **sensuous** act?

Ⓐ a stage

Ⓑ the intellect

Ⓒ the senses

Ⓓ a weakness

© SSI • MAY BE DUPLICATED

Standardized Test Preview/Practice

In this passage, some of the words from this lesson are in bold. Read the passage and then answer the questions.

"Could I have a few dollars to get a snack to eat on the bus?" asked Yinge, tapping her grandmother on the shoulder. Her grandmother was watching television.

"Shhh—listen," her grandmother said, directing her
5   attention to the TV. She was watching a funeral service taking place in a beautiful, grand cathedral with arching **buttresses.** People walked beneath the stone arches, dressed in black.

"What am I supposed to be listening to?" Yinge asked, a little annoyed.

10   "The **requiem,**" her grandmother said. "Don't you hear that beautiful music? Close your eyes and listen." She grabbed hold of Yinge's hand to keep her there.

Yinge obediently closed her eyes. As she listened to the music, something happened. She **transcended** the moment.
15   She was no longer in her living room. She was in the cathedral seeing candles being lit, smelling incense burning, and looking through beautiful stained-glass windows. In her mind she was reliving the **sensuous** experience of visiting the Washington National Cathedral, a place she had seen only once when she
20   was six years old.

When the music stopped, Yinge's eyes fluttered open. Her grandmother gestured toward the cathedral on the screen.

"That's the kind of **venue** I want for *my* funeral service!" she joked, finally handing Yinge money for her snack.

1. The word **buttresses** (line 6) means

    Ⓐ birds that nest inside cathedrals.
    Ⓑ structures supporting a wall.
    Ⓒ religious symbols.
    Ⓓ stained-glass windows.

2. The meaning of **requiem** (line 10) is

    Ⓐ poetry spoken at a funeral.
    Ⓑ music played to honor the dead.
    Ⓒ sound on television.
    Ⓓ respectful silence.

3. In line 14, **transcended** most nearly means

    Ⓐ waited for.
    Ⓑ enjoyed.
    Ⓒ went beyond.
    Ⓓ concentrated on.

4. In line 18, **sensuous** means

    Ⓐ enjoyable to the senses.
    Ⓑ serious.
    Ⓒ unforgettable.
    Ⓓ calming.

5. The word **venue** (line 23) most nearly means

    Ⓐ scene of a crime.
    Ⓑ location.
    Ⓒ television coverage.
    Ⓓ atmosphere.

© SSI • MAY BE DUPLICATED

Name _____   Date _____

Lesson 15 Test

Find a SYNONYM for each bold word. Then fill in the circle next to your answer.

1. Pam enjoyed her office role as the **arbiter** of grammatical correctness.

   Ⓐ advocate
   Ⓑ expert
   Ⓒ judge
   Ⓓ guardian

2. Less-experienced coworkers were intimidated by the **coterie** of the company's top salespeople.

   Ⓐ clique
   Ⓑ confidence
   Ⓒ success
   Ⓓ talent

3. The **graphic** violence in the film made Elena queasy.

   Ⓐ understated
   Ⓑ terrible
   Ⓒ vivid
   Ⓓ implied

4. Lars considered it an **inimical** act when David drove across the flowerbeds that lined the driveway.

   Ⓐ aggressive
   Ⓑ accidental
   Ⓒ clumsy
   Ⓓ hostile

5. With the **inordinate** demands work and school were putting on her time lately, Cassie was beginning to miss her friends.

   Ⓐ unpredictable
   Ⓑ constant
   Ⓒ excessive
   Ⓓ frequent

Find an ANTONYM for each bold word. Then fill in the circle next to your answer.

6. Scientists believe there is a correlation between recent increases in average annual temperatures and the **concomitant** shrinkage of the polar ice caps.

   Ⓐ unrelated
   Ⓑ accompanying
   Ⓒ coincidental
   Ⓓ exaggerated

7. When it came time to vote on the proposal, Richard **demurred,** saying he preferred to wait until all the facts were in.

   Ⓐ acquiesced
   Ⓑ withdrew
   Ⓒ abstained
   Ⓓ disagreed

© SSI • MAY BE DUPLICATED

8. Wearing a seatbelt has been shown to drastically reduce the **inimical** effects of traffic accidents.

   Ⓐ harmful
   Ⓑ beneficial
   Ⓒ costly
   Ⓓ psychological

9. Ally found Jim's intention to cheat on the midterm **repugnant.**

   Ⓐ harmless
   Ⓑ distasteful
   Ⓒ offensive
   Ⓓ agreeable

10. Accustomed to eating in front of the television, Julie was afraid she would embarrass herself at a function as **genteel** as an afternoon tea.

   Ⓐ amusing
   Ⓑ pretentious
   Ⓒ stuffy
   Ⓓ vulgar

Choose the best way to complete each sentence or answer each question. Then fill in the circle next to your answer.

11. To prepare for Jorge's surprise party, a **conclave** of friends and family

   Ⓐ spoke often.
   Ⓑ discussed it casually.
   Ⓒ met secretly.
   Ⓓ spread the news.

12. An **enticing** invitation is least likely to do which of the following?

   Ⓐ intrigue
   Ⓑ allure
   Ⓒ persuade
   Ⓓ repulse

13. Someone with **genteel** manners is most likely to be described as

   Ⓐ polite.
   Ⓑ crass.
   Ⓒ arrogant.
   Ⓓ snobbish.

14. Which of the following best describes an **oligarchy?**

   Ⓐ a commune
   Ⓑ a democracy
   Ⓒ a business
   Ⓓ a government

15. Derrick **flaunted** his perfect score, rather than sparing his classmates' egos by being less

   Ⓐ shy.
   Ⓑ conspicuous.
   Ⓒ cruel.
   Ⓓ rude.

© SSI / MAY BE DUPLICATED

Standardized Test Preview/Practice

In this passage, some of the words from this lesson are in bold. Read the passage and then answer the questions.

Every year the entire school community looked forward to the Spring Fun Fest, which included putting the **redoubtable** and beloved school principal, Mr. Kingsley, in the **ludicrous** position of being dunked in a dunk tank.

5 If you donated three dollars to the "Improve Our School" fund, you got to throw a softball at a target that released a lever and dunked Mr. Kingsley. This always caused an **inordinate** amount of laughter, especially for the younger students who sometimes saw him as an **inimical** figure,

10 despite his helpful and approachable personality. Seeing their principal emerge from the water, sputtering, his hair plastered across his forehead, soaking wet in his suit jacket and tie, always caused massive amounts of giggles.

For weeks afterward students would talk about seeing

15 Mr. Kingsley being dunked, describing it in **graphic** detail and sometimes acting it out so they could laugh about it again.

1. The word **redoubtable** (line 2) most nearly means

   Ⓐ ridiculous.

   Ⓑ unworthy.

   Ⓒ highly respected.

   Ⓓ doubted.

2. The meaning of **ludicrous** (line 3) is

   Ⓐ enviable.

   Ⓑ odd.

   Ⓒ ridiculous.

   Ⓓ perfect.

3. In line 8, the phrase "an **inordinate** amount" most nearly means

   Ⓐ a specific amount.

   Ⓑ more than the usual amount.

   Ⓒ less than the usual amount.

   Ⓓ the usual amount.

4. In line 9, **inimical** means

   Ⓐ comical.

   Ⓑ unfriendly.

   Ⓒ warm.

   Ⓓ authority.

5. The word **graphic** (line 15) most nearly means

   Ⓐ artistic.

   Ⓑ precise.

   Ⓒ imprecise.

   Ⓓ fuzzy.

© SSI • MAY BE DUPLICATED

Lesson 16 Test

Find a SYNONYM for each bold word. Then fill in the circle next to your answer.

1. After taking his exams, Diego loaded all his **chattels** into his truck and headed home for summer vacation.

   Ⓐ responsibilities
   Ⓑ property
   Ⓒ friends
   Ⓓ cousins

2. The pep squad did their best to counteract the **listlessness** of the fans at the football game.

   Ⓐ apathy
   Ⓑ anger
   Ⓒ disgust
   Ⓓ energy

3. Eager to explore life beyond the pasturelands, Chuck applied to colleges at every **metropolis** in the country.

   Ⓐ hamlet
   Ⓑ city
   Ⓒ village
   Ⓓ suburb

4. We **sequestered** ourselves all weekend to meet the Monday deadline.

   Ⓐ punished
   Ⓑ admonished
   Ⓒ amused
   Ⓓ secluded

5. Hal tried to **subvert** the school dress code by printing and circulating his own version of the rules.

   Ⓐ ridicule
   Ⓑ endorse
   Ⓒ undermine
   Ⓓ overrule

Find an ANTONYM for each bold word. Then fill in the circle next to your answer.

6. A high fever left Moira so **listless** that she hardly left her bedroom for four days.

   Ⓐ indifferent
   Ⓑ weak
   Ⓒ spiritless
   Ⓓ enthusiastic

7. Since she was a generally tidy person, all Ellie's house needed was a **perfunctory** straightening to prepare for visitors.

   Ⓐ major
   Ⓑ quick
   Ⓒ thorough
   Ⓓ surface

© SSI • MAY BE DUPLICATED

8. Ward's father threatened to **sequester** the car all weekend if he delayed painting the living room any longer.

   Ⓐ bestow

   Ⓑ seize

   Ⓒ hide

   Ⓓ enjoy

9. Barbara and Taria stopped at the gas station, the grocery store, the florist, the bakery, and the card shop before arriving at the hospital, the **terminus** of their odyssey.

   Ⓐ periphery

   Ⓑ layover

   Ⓒ purpose

   Ⓓ beginning

10. Max was unprepared for the **virulent** criticism he received at his first writers' workshop meeting.

   Ⓐ endless

   Ⓑ benevolent

   Ⓒ constructive

   Ⓓ passionate

Choose the best way to complete each sentence or answer each question. Then fill in the circle next to your answer.

11. Which of the following is least related to **chattel?**

   Ⓐ furniture

   Ⓑ livestock

   Ⓒ real estate

   Ⓓ appliances

12. Which of the following is most likely to be described as **commodious?**

   Ⓐ a bathroom

   Ⓑ a ballroom

   Ⓒ a bedroom

   Ⓓ a broom closet

13. **Limbo** has the least to do with which of the following?

   Ⓐ attention

   Ⓑ neglect

   Ⓒ transition

   Ⓓ disregard

14. Which of the following is least likely to describe a **virulent** outbreak of food poisoning?

   Ⓐ deadly

   Ⓑ dangerous

   Ⓒ widespread

   Ⓓ harmless

15. A **metropolitan** city is most likely to be described as

   Ⓐ important.

   Ⓑ scary.

   Ⓒ polluted.

   Ⓓ crowded.

© SSI • MAY BE DUPLICATED

Standardized Test Preview/Practice

In this passage, some of the words from this lesson are in bold. Read the passage and then answer the questions.

Genealogy—the study of one's family history and **lineage**—has become increasingly popular as genealogical records have become digitized and available in searchable online databases. People used to have to visit dusty old

5 **archives** in libraries to find information about their long-dead relatives, or search in their own attics and basements for items such as birth certificates and marriage licenses. It's very rare to find a **pristine** record of family history in a private home, however, because many items are damaged or lost over time.

10 Fortunately, the digitizing of family records avoids future loss due to **conflagration** or other disasters such as flooding.

Although most genealogical searches online are intended simply to learn more about a family's history, some people search for specific reasons, such as finding evidence

15 of **subversive** activities during the Civil War, for example, or evidence of a crime. Certain pieces of information aren't necessarily passed down through storytelling within a family. Due to technology, it's now easier than ever to discover both things that might make a family proud, and things they'd

20 rather hide.

1. The word **lineage** (line 2) most nearly means
   Ⓐ length.
   Ⓑ ancestry.
   Ⓒ documents.
   Ⓓ health.

2. The meaning of **archives** (line 5) is
   Ⓐ bookshelves.
   Ⓑ rooms.
   Ⓒ containers.
   Ⓓ historical records.

3. In line 8, **pristine** most nearly means
   Ⓐ complete.
   Ⓑ undamaged.
   Ⓒ digital.
   Ⓓ old.

4. In line 11, **conflagration** means
   Ⓐ hurricanes.
   Ⓑ humidity.
   Ⓒ fire.
   Ⓓ mold.

5. The word **subversive** (line 15) most nearly means
   Ⓐ insubordinate.
   Ⓑ heroic.
   Ⓒ defensive.
   Ⓓ illegal.

© SSI • MAY BE DUPLICATED

Lesson 17 Test

Find a SYNONYM for each bold word. Then fill in the circle next to your answer.

1. Josef Stalin, premier of the Soviet Union from 1941 until 1953, was a powerful **autocrat** who dealt harshly with anyone who opposed him.

   Ⓐ politician
   Ⓑ mockery
   Ⓒ lunatic
   Ⓓ tyrant

2. One **caustic** comment from Enrique was enough to make his sensitive siblings cry.

   Ⓐ challenging
   Ⓑ sarcastic
   Ⓒ silly
   Ⓓ inappropriate

3. Shannon admired her brother's **felicitous** manner in everything from casual cookouts to formal business meetings.

   Ⓐ appropriate
   Ⓑ awkward
   Ⓒ competent
   Ⓓ knowledgeable

4. Wilson was stunned to learn that Beth was so **mercenary** that she expected to be paid for her summer internship at the women's shelter.

   Ⓐ poor
   Ⓑ optimistic
   Ⓒ naive
   Ⓓ greedy

5. Eliza knew she could survive the layoff, since she had been raised by a **parsimonious** father who showed her how to stretch every dollar.

   Ⓐ indulgent
   Ⓑ frugal
   Ⓒ patient
   Ⓓ clever

Find an ANTONYM for each bold word. Then fill in the circle next to your answer.

6. Mobutu Sese Seko ruled Zaire as an **autocracy** from 1965 until 1997.

   Ⓐ dictatorship
   Ⓑ triumvirate
   Ⓒ democracy
   Ⓓ monarchy

7. Russ's illness had **debilitated** him so badly that he had to rest every few minutes.

   Ⓐ empowered
   Ⓑ embarrassed
   Ⓒ trapped
   Ⓓ prepared

© SSI • MAY BE DUPLICATED

8. Andrea believed that, more than money or status, the most important thing was to lead a **felicitous** life.

   Ⓐ pleasant
   Ⓑ diligent
   Ⓒ unfortunate
   Ⓓ carefree

9. Soldiering has always been a career, but rather than being paid to be loyal and ready, as in modern armies, **mercenaries** used to fight for whichever side was prepared to pay.

   Ⓐ peasants
   Ⓑ knights
   Ⓒ officers
   Ⓓ volunteers

10. Being the granddaughter of a Wild West train robber gave Annie a **notoriety** that she would have happily done without.

    Ⓐ power
    Ⓑ popularity
    Ⓒ anonymity
    Ⓓ reputation

Choose the best way to complete each sentence or answer each question. Then fill in the circle next to your answer.

11. Which of the following is most likely to be **caustic?**

    Ⓐ oil
    Ⓑ butter
    Ⓒ aloe
    Ⓓ bleach

12. Which of the following people most needs to be **forthright?**

    Ⓐ a doctor
    Ⓑ a salesperson
    Ⓒ a librarian
    Ⓓ an entertainer

13. Someone who is **impecunious** is most likely to lack what?

    Ⓐ talent
    Ⓑ manners
    Ⓒ money
    Ⓓ friends

14. Which of the following is least associated with having a **jaundiced** attitude?

    Ⓐ jealousy
    Ⓑ even-handedness
    Ⓒ hostility
    Ⓓ resentment

15. Karen had incurred thousands of dollars in credit card debt through foolishness, which she now intended to pay off through **parsimony.** What is Karen's lifestyle most likely to be?

    Ⓐ joyless
    Ⓑ whimsical
    Ⓒ opulent
    Ⓓ penurious

© SSI • MAY BE DUPLICATED

Standardized Test Preview/Practice

In this passage, some of the words from this lesson are in bold. Read the passage and then answer the questions.

"The **precept** 'live and let live' should never apply to dictators," Ary said during her opinion speech in front of her class. Her grandparents were from Cambodia. Ary's topic was Pol Pot, an **autocratic** dictator whose **ouster** from Cambodia
5 in 1979 had been a boon to that country. He had been responsible for approximately one million deaths.

Ary explained that Pol Pot had come to power because he had been **duplicitous** and had made his followers believe that society could begin again at "year zero." He had convinced
10 them that brutality and violence were necessary and would ultimately lead to a peaceful and powerful new future for Cambodia.

"After Pol Pot fell, many Cambodians—my grandparents included—had a **jaundiced** view of politicians," Ary said. She
15 explained that they felt hopeless that there were honorable leaders anywhere, finding it hard to trust anyone who wanted to lead their country. "The terror my grandparents felt will never go away, but over time they have learned that truly good leaders do exist in the world."

1. The word **precept** (line 1) most nearly means

Ⓐ words.

Ⓑ promise.

Ⓒ general principle.

Ⓓ commitment.

2. The meaning of **autocratic** (line 4) is

Ⓐ self-limiting.

Ⓑ completely controlling.

Ⓒ understanding.

Ⓓ entertaining.

3. In line 4, **ouster** most nearly means

Ⓐ celebration.

Ⓑ election.

Ⓒ political action.

Ⓓ removal from power.

4. In line 8, **duplicitous** means

Ⓐ deceptive.

Ⓑ evil.

Ⓒ well meaning.

Ⓓ important.

5. The word **jaundiced** (line 14) most nearly means

Ⓐ yellow.

Ⓑ bitter.

Ⓒ informed.

Ⓓ ignorant.

© SSI • MAY BE DUPLICATED

Lesson 18 Test

Find a SYNONYM for each bold word. Then fill in the circle next to your answer.

1. His friends **derided** Eduardo for sacrificing his weekend to study for an exam that was still two weeks away.

   Ⓐ congratulated
   Ⓑ helped
   Ⓒ admired
   Ⓓ ridiculed

2. Uncle Tommy had the **effrontery** to suggest that the children should eat dinner on the back porch because they were wearing clothes he didn't like.

   Ⓐ cleverness
   Ⓑ audacity
   Ⓒ wisdom
   Ⓓ thoughtlessness

3. Afraid of being accused of **hypocrisy,** the author of the popular weight-loss book was careful to dispose of her cupcake wrappers several blocks away from her office.

   Ⓐ falseness
   Ⓑ sincerity
   Ⓒ dedication
   Ⓓ carelessness

4. The Gales braced for the **impending** tornado underground in the storm cellar.

   Ⓐ violent
   Ⓑ unpredictable
   Ⓒ routine
   Ⓓ imminent

5. Originality is one of several **criteria** judges use to determine which entry will win the grand prize at the science fair.

   Ⓐ precedent
   Ⓑ destruction
   Ⓒ gravity
   Ⓓ standards

Find an ANTONYM for each bold word. Then fill in the circle next to your answer.

6. Though it was supposed to be a political satire, local critics dismissed the experimental drama as being **bereft** of social conscience.

   Ⓐ trained
   Ⓑ stripped
   Ⓒ packed
   Ⓓ devoid

7. The detective needed to gather all the **pertinent** facts as he reconstructed the events on the night of the break-in.

   Ⓐ irrelevant
   Ⓑ interesting
   Ⓒ important
   Ⓓ illicit

© SSI • MAY BE DUPLICATED

8. Although the poisoning was an accident, Vicki feared **retribution** when the old oak trees on her street died.

   Ⓐ reward

   Ⓑ punishment

   Ⓒ notoriety

   Ⓓ recognition

9. Gandhi **espoused** nonviolent resistance to oppression, a philosophy later adopted by Martin Luther King Jr.

   Ⓐ embraced

   Ⓑ rejected

   Ⓒ advocated

   Ⓓ denied

10. Dormitory rules **proscribe** loud music after 10:00 P.M. on weeknights.

   Ⓐ govern

   Ⓑ tolerate

   Ⓒ prohibit

   Ⓓ encourage

Choose the best way to complete each sentence or answer each question. Then fill in the circle next to your answer.

11. When a suggestion meets with **derision,** how do people most likely feel about it?

   Ⓐ intimidated

   Ⓑ scornful

   Ⓒ attracted

   Ⓓ suspicious

12. Which of the following is most likely to be considered a **hypocrite?**

   Ⓐ a doctor who smokes

   Ⓑ a teacher who reads

   Ⓒ a criminal who lies

   Ⓓ a dentist who flosses

13. Once something is **promulgated,** it is least likely to be

   Ⓐ accepted.

   Ⓑ newsworthy.

   Ⓒ understood.

   Ⓓ secret.

14. The right to petition the government for **redress** of grievances means that Americans can ask their government to

   Ⓐ repeat wrongs.

   Ⓑ deny wrongs.

   Ⓒ correct wrongs.

   Ⓓ admit wrongs.

15. A **regime** is most closely related to which of the following?

   Ⓐ a corporation

   Ⓑ a military

   Ⓒ a government

   Ⓓ a charity

© SSI • MAY BE DUPLICATED

Standardized Test Preview/Practice

In this passage, some of the words from this lesson are in bold. Read the passage and then answer the questions.

Sunday morning is supposed to be a relaxed time for our family, but then my dad began to **promulgate** the "mug rule." The mug rule goes like this: You choose one mug that is yours, and yours alone. You can pick any mug, but once you've picked
5   it, it is your responsibility. No one else gets to drink from that mug, but no one else has to wash it either. He told us he wouldn't get so upset about dirty mugs anymore because each mug would have an "owner."

He thought this rule would bring peace to our Sundays,
10 but it did not. First of all, he was **hypocritical.** Not only did he break the rule and fail to limit himself to one mug, but he would get **incensed** when he saw any mug "lying around" unclean, even if the mug's owner hadn't had the chance to wash it yet. He acted **bereft** and moody when anyone else
15 picked the biggest mug before he could, because he thought it should belong to him. My little brothers would leave dirty mugs around, and Dad would angrily hunt us all down, one by one, questioning us to try to **substantiate** who had done this. We couldn't stop laughing at him. All Sunday. Every Sunday.
20   I was so glad when his rule was abolished.

1. The word **promulgate** (line 2) most nearly means

   Ⓐ write down.

   Ⓑ complain about.

   Ⓒ announce.

   Ⓓ decide to end.

2. The meaning of **hypocritical** (line 10) is

   Ⓐ not following the rules you say you believe in.

   Ⓑ angry and unreasonable.

   Ⓒ duplicitous.

   Ⓓ unreasonable.

3. In line 12, **incensed** most nearly means

   Ⓐ worried.

   Ⓑ saddened.

   Ⓒ intensely angry.

   Ⓓ mildly upset.

4. In line 14, **bereft** means

   Ⓐ angry.

   Ⓑ deprived.

   Ⓒ relieved.

   Ⓓ concerned.

5. The word **substantiate** (line 18) most nearly means

   Ⓐ verify.

   Ⓑ punish.

   Ⓒ scold.

   Ⓓ interview.

© 331 • MAY BE DUPLICATED

Lesson 19 Test

Find a SYNONYM for each bold word. Then fill in the circle next to your answer.

1. Many Italian artists worked under the **aegis** of the powerful Borgia family.

   Ⓐ attention
   Ⓑ sponsorship
   Ⓒ ire
   Ⓓ fear

2. Even though their value was entirely sentimental, Aunt Mildred cherished the **baubles** she had collected from her admirers through the years.

   Ⓐ forks
   Ⓑ trinkets
   Ⓒ letters
   Ⓓ proposals

3. My grandmother was very superstitious and considered even the most common daily occurrences to be **portentous.**

   Ⓐ ominous
   Ⓑ insignificant
   Ⓒ interesting
   Ⓓ entertaining

4. Because of his children's illness, Mr. Tate gave us a **reprieve** on our deadline.

   Ⓐ escape
   Ⓑ respite
   Ⓒ option
   Ⓓ hint

5. Lewis and Clark's mission was to find a **viable** route to the Pacific Ocean.

   Ⓐ actual
   Ⓑ safe
   Ⓒ workable
   Ⓓ convoluted

Find an ANTONYM for each bold word. Then fill in the circle next to your answer.

6. Trey's approval of forming a neighborhood watch was **consolidated** when his garden statuary was vandalized.

   Ⓐ disregarded
   Ⓑ reversed
   Ⓒ destroyed
   Ⓓ strengthened

7. Leigh decided to **consolidate** the contents of many small bags into one main bag.

   Ⓐ unite
   Ⓑ combine
   Ⓒ separate
   Ⓓ remove

© SSI • MAY BE DUPLICATED

8. While studying for her pre-med finals, LaTasha had an **epiphany** that her true calling was the law.

   Ⓐ fear

   Ⓑ awareness

   Ⓒ message

   Ⓓ suspicion

9. The nominee was gifted with so **stentorian** a voice that she could captivate large groups without the need for amplification.

   Ⓐ monotonous

   Ⓑ commanding

   Ⓒ charismatic

   Ⓓ quiet

10. Erika preferred to wear **pendulous** jewelry because she felt that it was particularly dramatic.

    Ⓐ immobile

    Ⓑ expensive

    Ⓒ understated

    Ⓓ flowing

Choose the best way to complete each sentence or answer each question. Then fill in the circle next to your answer.

11. Which of the following best describes an **epiphany?**

    Ⓐ evolutionary

    Ⓑ vague

    Ⓒ gradual

    Ⓓ sudden

12. A **portent** is most related to things in the

    Ⓐ pantry.

    Ⓑ library.

    Ⓒ future.

    Ⓓ subconscious.

13. Which of the following is most related to **tenure?**

    Ⓐ pay rate

    Ⓑ time period

    Ⓒ authority

    Ⓓ hobbies

14. Which of the following professions most needs to be **pragmatic?**

    Ⓐ poet

    Ⓑ philosopher

    Ⓒ general

    Ⓓ historian

15. Which of the following is least likely to describe a **reprieve** from a responsibility?

    Ⓐ inconvenient

    Ⓑ temporary

    Ⓒ welcome

    Ⓓ relief

© SSI • MAY BE DUPLICATED

Standardized Test Preview/Practice

In this passage, some of the words from this lesson are in bold. Read the passage and then answer the questions.

To maintain **viable** and thriving rain forests around the world, governments must stop making decisions **unilaterally** to protect these fragile environments from illegal logging, and instead work together to end the destruction. The continued

5 **depredation** of rain forests is not something we can afford to be **complaisant** about, because the loss of rain forests affects us all. Millions of different species are in danger of being wiped out, including unique animals such as the proboscis monkey of Borneo, whose distinctive **pendulous** nose gives it

10 its name—*proboscis* is the word for a mammal's nose. Unless governments work together to enforce laws to protect rain forests, these precious natural habitats will be lost.

1. The word **viable** (line 1) most nearly means

   Ⓐ large.

   Ⓑ able to be protected.

   Ⓒ capable of living.

   Ⓓ wet.

2. The meaning of **unilaterally** (line 2) is

   Ⓐ individually, without consulting others.

   Ⓑ against their own interests.

   Ⓒ quickly and decisively.

   Ⓓ without disagreement.

3. In line 5, **depredation** most nearly means

   Ⓐ identification.

   Ⓑ study.

   Ⓒ analysis.

   Ⓓ destruction.

4. The phrase "be **complaisant** about" (line 6) means

   Ⓐ agree to go along with.

   Ⓑ decide to believe in.

   Ⓒ refuse to participate in.

   Ⓓ pay for.

5. The word **pendulous** (line 9) most nearly means

   Ⓐ red.

   Ⓑ sharply pointed.

   Ⓒ probing.

   Ⓓ loosely hanging.

© SSI • MAY BE DUPLICATED

Lesson 20 Test

Find a SYNONYM for each bold word. Then fill in the circle next to your answer.

1. Robert rushed home from school, knowing his mother would **excoriate** him if his room was still a mess by the time she got home from work.

   Ⓐ forgive
   Ⓑ punish
   Ⓒ berate
   Ⓓ deride

2. One of Anna's **idiosyncratic** habits was that she always served dessert first.

   Ⓐ quirky
   Ⓑ unfortunate
   Ⓒ grisly
   Ⓓ flawed

3. Ms. Morse's **pedagogical** talents were such that she could make calculus accessible to even the most confused.

   Ⓐ mathematical
   Ⓑ intimidating
   Ⓒ teaching
   Ⓓ illustrative

4. Even after watching the debate, Greg did not develop a **stance** on capital punishment.

   Ⓐ justification
   Ⓑ opinion
   Ⓒ grip
   Ⓓ objection

5. Though she wanted to continue studying, Dawn feared the **deleterious** effects of staying up all night on her ability to concentrate during the exam.

   Ⓐ intellectual
   Ⓑ creative
   Ⓒ somnolent
   Ⓓ harmful

Find an ANTONYM for each bold word. Then fill in the circle next to your answer.

6. His uncle's **grisly** war stories gave Patrick nightmares.

   Ⓐ typical
   Ⓑ unbelievable
   Ⓒ horrible
   Ⓓ pleasant

7. Thanksgiving at the McKinleys' house was a daylong parade of family **idiosyncrasies.**

   Ⓐ recipes
   Ⓑ stories
   Ⓒ habits
   Ⓓ normalities

© SSI • MAY BE DUPLICATED

8. The pharmacist warned Alex that the antibiotics could **negate** the effectiveness of other medicine he might be taking.

   Ⓐ enhance

   Ⓑ reduce

   Ⓒ obstruct

   Ⓓ affect

9. Ginnie continued to send handwritten thank-you notes, even though her friends assured her that e-mail had made them **passé.**

   Ⓐ unnecessary

   Ⓑ fashionable

   Ⓒ pretentious

   Ⓓ outmoded

10. Sam hid his **antipathy** to parsnips so as not to offend his hostess.

    Ⓐ disgust

    Ⓑ allergy

    Ⓒ fondness

    Ⓓ aversion

Choose the best way to complete each sentence or answer each question. Then fill in the circle next to your answer.

11. **Ambidextrous** writers can write with

    Ⓐ their mouth.

    Ⓑ their left hand.

    Ⓒ either hand.

    Ⓓ their feet.

12. Which of the following is most likely to be a **pedagogue?**

    Ⓐ a dairy farmer

    Ⓑ a scoutmaster

    Ⓒ a shopkeeper

    Ⓓ a pastry chef

13. A **preponderance** is least related to

    Ⓐ the majority.

    Ⓑ superiority.

    Ⓒ importance.

    Ⓓ surprises.

14. A **stance** is most closely related to which of the following?

    Ⓐ feet

    Ⓑ arms

    Ⓒ head

    Ⓓ eyes

15. A **grisly** scene is least likely to be described as

    Ⓐ grim.

    Ⓑ ghastly.

    Ⓒ attractive.

    Ⓓ harsh.

© SSI • MAY BE DUPLICATED

Standardized Test Preview/Practice

In this passage, some of the words from this lesson are in bold. Read the passage and then answer the questions.

No car ride, no matter how short, was safe from arguments. Shay's younger brothers, Tyrese and Jackson, were nine and eleven years old. They always got on each other's nerves when they sat next to each other in the backseat.

5 At some point during each trip, Shay would hear Jackson **excoriate** Tyrese for doing something like touching his leg or looking at him the wrong way. Then Tyrese would **negate** any kind of accusation, swearing he'd done nothing and was entirely innocent. Things would settle down for a few minutes,

10 and then Jackson would start complaining about something else, usually **imputing** evil intentions on Tyrese's part.

"Tyrese just ate the last granola bar! Then he drank from my water bottle!"

It was difficult to **extrapolate** what had actually

15 happened by looking at them in the backseat. Usually there was no evidence of any wrongdoing to be found—just two very upset boys.

During one of their typical arguments, Shay's mother decided to interrupt with a warning.

20 "I **propound** that you two remain silent for the rest of this car trip. Give me and your sister some peace!" she said loudly.

I love my mother.

1. The word **excoriate** (line 6) most nearly means
   Ⓐ highly praise.
   Ⓑ calmly blame.
   Ⓒ sharply criticize.
   Ⓓ whisper to.

2. The meaning of **negate** (line 7) is
   Ⓐ deny.
   Ⓑ return.
   Ⓒ complain about.
   Ⓓ insist on.

3. In line 11, **imputing** most nearly means
   Ⓐ ascribing.
   Ⓑ understanding.
   Ⓒ yelling.
   Ⓓ suggesting.

4. In line 14, **extrapolate** means
   Ⓐ assign blame.
   Ⓑ figure out from the evidence.
   Ⓒ restrain.
   Ⓓ investigate.

5. The word **propound** (line 20) most nearly means
   Ⓐ demand.
   Ⓑ put forth an idea.
   Ⓒ foresee.
   Ⓓ encourage.

© SSI • MAY BE DUPLICATED

Lessons 1–20 Final Test 1

Read the passage. Choose the best answer for each sentence or question about a bold word. Then fill in the circle next to your answer.

What's in a Name?

Who wrote your favorite book? Are you sure? There is a good chance that the real writer of your favorite book has a name you do not recognize. There are myriad reasons for writers to want to mask their identities, and when they opt to do so, the first thing they reach for is a pen name. Adopting a pen name, also called a pseudonym or a *nom de plume,* is a perfectly legal and widely accepted practice in publishing. Authors' **duplicity** when they **purport** to be someone other than their true selves is considered minor. Pseudonyms are probably as old as the printed word. The reasons to **fabricate** one may be personal or professional, practical or utterly unfathomable. An **altruistic** author with a shocking true story to tell may choose a pseudonym in order to spare his or her family any embarrassment at being associated with the name.

One common reason authors have for using a pseudonym is that they fear they lack the professional credibility for their work to be taken seriously. By disguising the work's true source, the writers hope to **entice** a publisher to accept it on its own merit. In the early 1700s, a teenaged Ben Franklin, a printer's apprentice with practically no formal education, began submitting essays to his brother's newspaper under the name "Silence Dogood." The popular features would never have been published had the editor known his own little brother was responsible for writing them. Historically, many women writers published under male names either because it was considered improper for ladies to write novels or because some people thought it inconceivable that they could. Some notable female writers who used pseudonyms to **transcend** gender **disparities** in publishing were George Eliot (Mary Ann Evans) and Currer, Ellis, and Acton Bell (Charlotte, Emily, and Anne Brontë).

Another reason writers have assumed pen names is so that their success in one field or genre would not interfere with their credibility in another. The author of the children's fantasy classic *Alice's Adventures in Wonderland* wrote fiction under the name Lewis Carroll because as Charles Lutwidge Dodgson, he held **tenure** at England's Oxford University and published books on mathematics. Mystery master Agatha Christie wrote romantic novels as Mary Westmacott, so as not to disappoint fans who picked up a love story expecting a thriller.

Another issue of credibility that may be solved by a pen name is not in the writer's credentials but in the name itself. Writers often choose a name that reflects the subject matter of their story. That way, audiences will feel that the author has a **propensity** for writing particular subject matter. Writers who focus on historical fiction set in a particular locale may be more believable if their names support the idea that they should have particular knowledge about that place. For example, a writer of Westerns might feel the name Tex Masterson has more "authenticity" on the cover of a book than a name like Cyril Higginbotham.

© SSI • MAY BE DUPLICATED

The desire to protect their own privacy may also be responsible for some people's choosing pseudonyms. Authors who **espouse** controversial ideas or reveal family secrets may choose a pseudonym to avoid publicity or **antipathy** from the audience. While most writers dream of becoming famous, some wish to avoid the **thrall** of celebrity. Some practical business considerations may also make the use of a pen name necessary. Using a pen name may allow writers to continue working on other projects if a contract prohibits them from publishing under a certain name. For others, hiding their true identity is mandated by the terms of the publishing contract; some publishers require their authors to use a pen name.

Then there are those pen names that are well known to most people, but for which the reason for adoption remains a mystery. Classic American **raconteur** Mark Twain was born Samuel Clemens. He adopted the pseudonym as a young journalist in Nevada because it reminded him of his favorite times traveling on the Mississippi River by riverboat. The boat's leadsmen would periodically check distance between the bottom of the steamboat and the riverbed, and when the depth was the dangerously shallow twelve feet, he would sound the alert by shouting, "By the mark, twain!" It may be that Samuel Clemens needed an alter ego more than a pen name.

Our enjoyment of a work is often closely tied to what we believe to be the source of that work. Writers and publishers understand this. They try to manipulate our impressions accordingly. A book's writer may be as fictional as the book itself, but how much does that matter if you enjoy the read? Remember the adage, "You can't judge a book by its cover"? Perhaps we should add, "You can't judge a book by its author."

1. As used in the second paragraph, to **entice** means to do what?

   Ⓐ placate
   Ⓑ extort
   Ⓒ persuade
   Ⓓ deceive

2. As used in this passage, an ANTONYM for **espouse** is

   Ⓐ support.
   Ⓑ preserve.
   Ⓒ discuss.
   Ⓓ oppose.

3. As used in the fifth paragraph, a SYNONYM for **antipathy** is

   Ⓐ aversion.
   Ⓑ tolerance.
   Ⓒ stalking.
   Ⓓ invasion.

© SSI • MAY BE DUPLICATED

4. As used in the second paragraph, **disparities** is most closely related to

   Ⓐ prejudices.

   Ⓑ preferences.

   Ⓒ differences.

   Ⓓ aptitudes.

5. As used in this passage, **propensity** is most closely related to what type of tendency?

   Ⓐ natural

   Ⓑ practiced

   Ⓒ knowledgeable

   Ⓓ learned

6. As used in the first paragraph, an ANTONYM for **fabricate** is

   Ⓐ invent.

   Ⓑ reveal.

   Ⓒ destroy.

   Ⓓ deny.

7. As used in the third paragraph, **tenure** is most closely related to

   Ⓐ position.

   Ⓑ prestige.

   Ⓒ power.

   Ⓓ pay.

8. Which is a SYNONYM for **altruistic?**

   Ⓐ greedy

   Ⓑ selfish

   Ⓒ selfless

   Ⓓ harmless

9. Which of the following is NOT a SYNONYM for **transcend?**

   Ⓐ exceed

   Ⓑ fight

   Ⓒ surpass

   Ⓓ rise above

10. As used in the first paragraph, **duplicity** refers to all of the following except

    Ⓐ deceit.

    Ⓑ publicity.

    Ⓒ secrecy.

    Ⓓ dishonesty.

© SSI • MAY BE DUPLICATED

Standardized Test Preview/Practice

1. In the first paragraph, **purport** is least related to

   Ⓐ claim.

   Ⓑ imply.

   Ⓒ assert.

   Ⓓ deny.

   Ⓔ profess.

2. As used in the sixth paragraph, **raconteur** is most closely related to

   Ⓐ songs.

   Ⓑ stories.

   Ⓒ lectures.

   Ⓓ trends.

   Ⓔ demoted.

3. As used in paragraph five, **thrall** is a state of

   Ⓐ powerlessness.

   Ⓑ confusion.

   Ⓒ bliss.

   Ⓓ publicity.

   Ⓔ control.

4. Which of the following is most likely to **espouse** something?

   Ⓐ an accountant

   Ⓑ a student

   Ⓒ an advocate

   Ⓓ a police officer

   Ⓔ an actor

5. Which of the following is most likely to engage in **duplicity?**

   Ⓐ a judge

   Ⓑ a minister

   Ⓒ a student

   Ⓓ a con artist

   Ⓔ a merchant

© SSI • MAY BE DUPLICATED

Final Test 2

Read the passage. Choose the best answer for each sentence or question about a bold word. Then fill in the circle next to your answer.

Name That Hurricane

A hurricane belongs to the **triumvirate** of storms that also includes tropical cyclones and typhoons. Hurricanes are known to exist only in the Atlantic Ocean, typhoons are found in the Pacific Ocean, and tropical cyclones are found in the Indian Ocean. A hurricane begins as a weak storm system that forms over warm, tropical waters. As the strength of the winds increases, the storm is first called a tropical depression, then a tropical storm, then a hurricane. It takes days for a full-force hurricane to develop from its **incipient** stage, if it develops at all. Unlike earthquakes or tornadoes, hurricanes give people in the path of the storm time to protect themselves.

The severe winds of a hurricane revolve around a central "eye," a relatively **listless** area. Around this "eye" area, storm clouds move in a counter-clockwise motion as they cause the sea below to **undulate** wildly. The word *hurricane* is thought to be from the West Indian word meaning "big wind." Others believe the **etymology** is related to the Indian word *huracan* (evil spirit) or from the Mayan word *huraken* (bad weather).

Beginning in 1873, the Army Signal Corps attempted to issue storm warnings, although there was no **viable** tracking system in the U.S. until 1890. The practice of naming hurricanes began to help identify storms and track them as they move across the ocean. Military weather forecasters began giving women's names to significant storms during World War II after George R. Stewart used a woman's name for a storm in his 1941 novel, *Storm*. Then in 1950, the World Meteorological Organization (WMO) agreed to an alphabetical system, using a code created by the military. The first Atlantic hurricane named according to this system was Able, in 1950. After careful consideration, officials soon realized the naming procedure would be less **utilitarian** if more than one powerful hurricane met the **criteria** in the same order in a season. So, in 1953 the organization adopted a rotating series of women's names. Names of **notorious** storms were retired.

The practice of exclusively using female names ended to **appease** groups that objected to these forces of destruction always being thought of as women. In 1978, male and female names were used to name storms in the eastern Pacific. A year later, an alternating male/female naming process was included in lists for the Atlantic and the Gulf of Mexico. The name lists include international names because hurricanes affect many nations and are tracked by the weather services of many countries. Twenty-one names are reserved each year and the names are recycled every six years. When a name is retired, the WMO chooses a new name to replace it. The letters Q, U, X, Y, and Z are not included because of the scarcity of names beginning with those letters.

Hurricanes are categorized according to the strength of their winds, using the Saffir-Simpson Hurricane Scale. A Category 1 storm has the lowest wind speeds, while a Category 5 hurricane has the most **frenetic.** The Tropical Prediction Center near Miami, Florida, keeps a

© SSI • MAY BE DUPLICATED

constant watch on oceanic storm-breeding grounds. Hurricane season officially runs from the beginning of June to the end of November. Once a system with counter-clockwise rotation and wind speeds of 39 miles per hour or greater is detected, the Center considers it a tropical storm and gives it a name from the list for the current year. If its winds reach sustained speeds of 74 miles per hour, it then becomes classified as a hurricane.

Hurricanes usually affect the areas of the North Atlantic, the Caribbean **archipelago,** the Gulf of Mexico, and the Eastern Pacific. Hurricane Andrew, which hit the U.S. in 1992, produced an estimated $26 billion in damage and left 180,000 homeless in Florida. Prediction models now **portend** that, after Miami and New Orleans, New York City is the third most likely location for a hurricane catastrophe in a **metropolitan** area. If it happens, residents' safety will depend on the information we now know about hurricanes.

1. As used in the second paragraph, **etymology** is a SYNONYM for

   Ⓐ science.
   Ⓑ history.
   Ⓒ definition.
   Ⓓ pronunciation.

2. As used in the second paragraph, **undulate** is most closely related to

   Ⓐ waves.
   Ⓑ temperature.
   Ⓒ rotation.
   Ⓓ surface.

3. As used in the third paragraph, a SYNONYM for **viable** is

   Ⓐ popular.
   Ⓑ workable.
   Ⓒ acceptable.
   Ⓓ reliable.

4. To say a storm is **notorious** means that it is

   Ⓐ named for the cities it damaged.
   Ⓑ particularly powerful.
   Ⓒ common to all areas.
   Ⓓ remembered for the damage it caused.

5. As used in the fourth paragraph, **appease** most closely means

   Ⓐ taunt.
   Ⓑ pacify.
   Ⓒ honor.
   Ⓓ submit.

© SSI • MAY BE DUPLICATED

6. An ANTONYM for **frenetic,** as used in paragraph five, is

   Ⓐ calm.

   Ⓑ excited.

   Ⓒ happy.

   Ⓓ frenzied.

7. As used in the third paragraph, a SYNONYM for **utilitarian** is

   Ⓐ practical.

   Ⓑ useful.

   Ⓒ beautiful.

   Ⓓ confusing.

8. As used in the sixth paragraph, **portend** most nearly means

   Ⓐ indicate.

   Ⓑ guess.

   Ⓒ threaten.

   Ⓓ doubt.

9. The word **archipelago** refers to

   Ⓐ islands.

   Ⓑ regions.

   Ⓒ nations.

   Ⓓ continents.

10. Which of the following most applies to a city described as **metropolitan?**

   Ⓐ big

   Ⓑ crowded

   Ⓒ important

   Ⓓ imposing

© SSI • MAY BE DUPLICATED

Standardized Test Preview/Practice

1. In the second paragraph, **listless** implies a lack of

   Ⓐ restraint.

   Ⓑ rain.

   Ⓒ fury.

   Ⓓ energy.

   Ⓔ danger.

2. To **portend** is most closely related to what type of events?

   Ⓐ future

   Ⓑ current

   Ⓒ desirable

   Ⓓ unlikely

   Ⓔ historical

3. What best captures the meaning of the word **incipient** in the first paragraph?

   Ⓐ insignificant

   Ⓑ dangerous

   Ⓒ final

   Ⓓ harmless

   Ⓔ beginning

4. In the third paragraph, **criteria** most nearly means

   Ⓐ standards.

   Ⓑ reasons.

   Ⓒ levels.

   Ⓓ speed.

   Ⓔ notoriety.

5. A **triumvirate** relates to what?

   Ⓐ rotation

   Ⓑ number

   Ⓒ strength

   Ⓓ size

   Ⓔ family

© 331 • MAY BE DUPLICATED

Lessons 1–20 **Final Test 3**

Read the passage. Choose the best answer for each sentence or question about a bold word. Then fill in the circle next to your answer.

A Friend in Need

The **genesis** of the Saint Bernard dog breed is inextricably bound to the mountain pass and the monastery that bear the same name. In the sixteenth century, the Saint Bernard Pass provided a route between Switzerland and Italy through the Alps. In 57 B.C.E. Julius Caesar attempted to secure safe passage over the Alps, but it was not until 7 or 6 B.C.E. that the Roman legions conquered the Alpine region and secured the pass. What would come to be known as the Saint Bernard Pass provided the most **expedient** route to the newly conquered province, Britannia. Later, the small path was improved to accommodate travelers and their carriages crossing the Alps.

The pass fell out of use for several hundred years before the monastery was built. It regained importance in medieval times, but was plagued by **marauders** who preyed on those using the pass. The Saint Bernard monastery was established in the pass about a millennium after the Romans first used it. Legend **postulates** that the Holy Saint Bernard of Montjou banished evil spirits and founded the monastery around 950. However, historical records of a meeting Saint Bernard had in 1086 renders that story unlikely. Experts believe that the monastery was actually founded around the year 1050. It included a hospice where travelers would receive three days' free meals and lodging.

Traders traveling through the pass brought dogs to the monastery until the 1100s. Then the route was largely unused for several hundred years, and no new dogs entered the Saint Bernard Monastery. It was during this time that the Saint Bernard breed arose. Records from 1700 note the first mountain guides assigned to accompany travelers to the other side of the pass. The Saint Bernard's **metier** was to accompany guides, as the dogs' excellent sense of direction proved most beneficial. Their broad chests were well suited to help clear paths for travelers, and the dogs also possessed an uncanny ability to maneuver through heavy fog and snowstorms, which have a **deleterious** effect on safe travel.

During the 200 years that the dogs served on the Saint Bernard Pass, approximately 2,000 **itinerants** were rescued. The dogs' sense of direction, compassion for humans, and adaptations to the harsh weather combined in a **proclivity** for rescue that saw hundreds of thousands of travelers safely through the **travails** of the pass. The last documented rescue dates from 1897, when a twelve-year-old boy was found nearly frozen and was awakened by a dog. The feature most often associated with the Saint Bernard, along with the oversized build and red-and-white coloring, is the barrel strapped beneath the dog's neck. The barrel, however, appears to be nothing more than a **fabrication** of some imaginative author.

The Saint Bernard was established as a pure breed with standards by Heinrich Schumacher in Switzerland in the 1850s. Many of today's Saint Bernards can trace their

© SSI • MAY BE DUPLICATED

lineage to the dogs bred by Schumacher. Saint Bernards have plenty to offer aside from their skill as lifesavers. The monks seem to think—and families in cooler climates around the world have come to agree—that the faithfulness, gentleness, and intelligence of this **redoubtable** breed makes Saint Bernards welcome additions to any household.

1. As used in the first paragraph, **genesis** is least related to

    Ⓐ legend.

    Ⓑ beginning.

    Ⓒ origin.

    Ⓓ creation.

2. An ANTONYM for **expedient,** as used in the first paragraph, is

    Ⓐ dangerous.

    Ⓑ useful.

    Ⓒ inconvenient.

    Ⓓ practical.

3. As used in the second paragraph, **marauders** is most closely related to

    Ⓐ combatants.

    Ⓑ bullies.

    Ⓒ vagabonds.

    Ⓓ criminals.

4. To **postulate** most nearly means to

    Ⓐ assume.

    Ⓑ proclaim.

    Ⓒ know.

    Ⓓ doubt.

5. As used in paragraph three, **metier** is most closely related to

    Ⓐ talent.

    Ⓑ work.

    Ⓒ reward.

    Ⓓ instinct.

© SSI • MAY BE DUPLICATED

6. As used in the third paragraph, an ANTONYM for **deleterious** is

   Ⓐ gradual.

   Ⓑ blinding.

   Ⓒ harmless.

   Ⓓ dangerous.

7. As used in the fourth paragraph, **itinerants** are most closely related to

   Ⓐ freezing.

   Ⓑ fleeing.

   Ⓒ begging.

   Ⓓ traveling.

8. Which is a SYNONYM for **proclivity?**

   Ⓐ inclination

   Ⓑ passion

   Ⓒ talent

   Ⓓ duty

9. Which of the following does not describe **travails?**

   Ⓐ difficult

   Ⓑ enjoyable

   Ⓒ arduous

   Ⓓ burdensome

10. As used in the fourth paragraph, **fabrication** most nearly means

    Ⓐ illustration.

    Ⓑ description.

    Ⓒ invention.

    Ⓓ fantasy.

© SSI • MAY BE DUPLICATED

Standardized Test Preview/Practice

1. In the fifth paragraph, **lineage** is least related to

   Ⓐ descent.

   Ⓑ ancestry.

   Ⓒ family.

   Ⓓ parentage.

   Ⓔ nobility.

2. As used in the fifth paragraph, **redoubtable** is most closely related to

   Ⓐ energy.

   Ⓑ fear.

   Ⓒ trouble.

   Ⓓ respect.

   Ⓔ society.

3. Which of the following is most closely related to a person's **genesis?**

   Ⓐ birthday

   Ⓑ graduation

   Ⓒ anniversary

   Ⓓ retirement

   Ⓔ death

4. Which of the following is most likely to be described as **deleterious?**

   Ⓐ a thunderstorm

   Ⓑ poison

   Ⓒ the ocean

   Ⓓ ice

   Ⓔ a headache

5. Which of these is most likely to be an **itinerant?**

   Ⓐ an office manager

   Ⓑ a police officer

   Ⓒ a traveling salesman

   Ⓓ a local politician

   Ⓔ a bakery owner

© SSI • MAY BE DUPLICATED

Lessons 1–20   Final Test 4

Read the passage. Choose the best answer for each sentence or question about a bold word. Then fill in the circle next to your answer.

Salt Shakes an Empire

Until the mid-twentieth century, India was under the rule of the **behemoth** known as the British Empire. Mohandas "Mahatma" Gandhi, the father of India's independence from the Empire, pioneered civil disobedience to bring about India's freedom. An important **tenet** of Gandhi's teaching was that protesters utilize nonviolence as a show of strength to bring about change. The Salt March of 1930 was a historic campaign Gandhi led to protest the injustices imposed on the Indian people by the British Government—in this case, the issue was salt.

Salt was vital to the health and economy of India, and British taxes on salt had an **inordinate** impact on the most impoverished sectors of Indian society. Not only did the salt laws force people out of commercial trade, but Indian citizens also had to pay a tax on the salt required for food preservation and preparation. Even the salt required for **sacrosanct** cultural rituals was subject to taxation.

Over many years, resentment against the British grew, and citizens across India increasingly disapproved of the British government's practices. Gandhi decided these injustices should be endured no longer and found tremendous support for his cause. Before talk of protest, Gandhi tried to **reconcile** the people's differences with the government by writing about their displeasure to Lord Irwin, Viceroy of India. He wrote of the inequities of British colonial rule and of his intentions to peacefully break the salt laws.

The resulting Salt March attracted **disparate** participants from all sections of Indian society, drawing people from large cities as well as from the **bucolic** Indian countryside. Setting out from Gandhi's religious retreat near Ahmedabad in the spring of 1930, the march began with Gandhi and seventy-eight **zealous** followers who began the long 240-mile walk to Dandi on the Arabian Sea. At the beginning of the march, Gandhi had only a few hundred followers, but as they made their way toward Dandi, thousands more joined them. Local officials even resigned to show their support. When they arrived at the western shore of India, Gandhi made his own salt from the seawater, as had always been the practice in India, in an act of civil disobedience against the British rule.

The march sparked widespread acts of protest across the country in opposition to the salt laws. As the protest grew along both coastlines, the British **flaunted** their power with violent attacks on activists. As people scooped up handfuls of salt all along the coasts, police considered their actions **tantamount** to revolt and used clubs to knock the salt from protesters' hands. When force failed, thousands of *satyagrahis* (soldiers of civil disobedience) were arrested, but others continued. To suppress the strength of the movement, Gandhi was woken from his sleep while staying in a village near the sea where he and his followers continued to make salt and was arrested on May 4, 1930. However, the incarceration of the

© SSI • MAY BE DUPLICATED

movement's leader did not bring about the **abeyance** of defiance the British government had hoped for, nor did the arrest of over sixty thousand Indians for their acts of civil disobedience during the Salt March.

Gandhi was eventually released in 1931. After his release, the **imperturbable** activist continued to work tirelessly toward Indian independence. India finally became a sovereign nation once again in August 1947. Gandhi died a mere five months later. His message of nonviolent protest has reverberated around the world and has been a strategy successfully employed during the United States civil-rights movement and proponents of freedom everywhere.

1. As used in the first paragraph, **behemoth** is least related to

   Ⓐ antiquity.

   Ⓑ hugeness.

   Ⓒ vastness.

   Ⓓ power.

2. All of the following are SYNONYMS for **tenet** EXCEPT

   Ⓐ principle.

   Ⓑ belief.

   Ⓒ suggestion.

   Ⓓ truth.

3. As used in the second paragraph, **inordinate** is most closely related to

   Ⓐ punitive.

   Ⓑ excess.

   Ⓒ lack.

   Ⓓ subtlety.

4. As used in this passage, **sacrosanct** most nearly means

   Ⓐ holy.

   Ⓑ culinary.

   Ⓒ casual.

   Ⓓ mundane.

5. As used in the third paragraph, to **reconcile** is most closely related to

   Ⓐ discussing plans.

   Ⓑ repairing communication.

   Ⓒ achieving independence.

   Ⓓ reaching agreement.

© 551 • MAY BE DUPLICATED

6. As used in the fourth paragraph, an ANTONYM for **disparate** is

    Ⓐ impassioned.

    Ⓑ different.

    Ⓒ solemn.

    Ⓓ similar.

7. As used in paragraph four, **bucolic** most closely means

    Ⓐ sophisticated.

    Ⓑ rustic.

    Ⓒ dusty.

    Ⓓ lush.

8. Which of the following is NOT a SYNONYM for **zealous?**

    Ⓐ enthusiastic

    Ⓑ insane

    Ⓒ fervent

    Ⓓ passionate

9. Which of the following is NOT a SYNONYM for **flaunted,** as used in the fifth paragraph?

    Ⓐ exhibited

    Ⓑ displayed

    Ⓒ paraded

    Ⓓ disguised

10. As used in the fifth paragraph, an ANTONYM for **tantamount** is

    Ⓐ opposite.

    Ⓑ equivalent.

    Ⓒ the same as.

    Ⓓ comparable.

© SSI • MAY BE DUPLICATED

Standardized Test Preview/Practice

1. In the fifth paragraph, **abeyance** is most closely related to

   Ⓐ starting.

   Ⓑ interrupting.

   Ⓒ ending.

   Ⓓ stopping.

   Ⓔ continuing.

2. As used in the sixth paragraph, **imperturbable** is least related to being

   Ⓐ calm.

   Ⓑ composed.

   Ⓒ serene.

   Ⓓ emotional.

   Ⓔ stoic.

3. Which of the following is most likely to be described as a **behemoth?**

   Ⓐ a goldfish

   Ⓑ a shark

   Ⓒ a salmon

   Ⓓ a dolphin

   Ⓔ a whale

4. Which of the following is most likely to be considered **sacrosanct?**

   Ⓐ books

   Ⓑ pets

   Ⓒ vows

   Ⓓ fruit

   Ⓔ hobbies

5. Which of the following is most likely to be considered **zealous?**

   Ⓐ a dog catcher

   Ⓑ a campaign manager

   Ⓒ a pastry chef

   Ⓓ a fact checker

   Ⓔ a racecar driver

© SSI • MAY BE DUPLICATED

Answer Keys

Lesson 1

1A Understanding Meanings p. 3

(Possible answers; students' sentences may vary.)

1. C
2. An **imperturbable** person is very difficult to upset.
3. C
4. C
5. A **subterfuge** is a plan intended to deceive.
6. C
7. C
8. A **raconteur** is skilled at telling stories.
9. C
10. C
11. To **mortify** someone is to thoroughly embarrass that person.
12. **Levity** is a lack of seriousness.
13. C
14. C
15. An **apocryphal** event is one of dubious authenticity.

1B Using Words p. 4

1. a. exuded
   c. exuded
2. a. mortified
   b. mortified
3. c. vacillated
4. a. raconteur
   c. raconteur
5. c. gesticulated
6. c. apocryphal
7. a. expedient
   b. expedient
   c. expedient
8. b. convened
   c. convened

1C Word Study: Similar Meanings p. 6

1. vacillate
2. waver
3. —
4. exudes
5. emits
6. —
7. —
8. mysterious
9. arcane
10. spurious
11. apocryphal
12. —
13. expedient
14. —
15. convenient

1D Images of Words p. 7

1. b
2. b, c
3. b, c
4. b
5. a, c
6. a, b, c
7. No sentence suggests **vacillate.**
8. a, c
9. a, b
10. b, c

1E Vocabulary in Context p. 8

(Possible answers; students' sentences may vary.)

1. A storyteller may take too much time away from the auction and from selling the items.
2. Several schools for auctioneers exist. One of the oldest **convenes** four times a year, with courses lasting for several days.
3. It would be important for an auctioneer to be calm when the bidders **exude** excitement or when the bids are in very large amounts of money.
4. It describes the story as **apocryphal.**
5. Both need to develop good **peripheral** vision.
6. A good auctioneer adds **levity** by telling amusing stories.
7. They **reiterate** the last bid in their chants, along with the next price they want to hear.
8. There is a lot more **gesticulating** in a public auction. A private art auction has less overt gesturing by the bidders.
9. Sample response: One embarrassing experience might be **vacillating** too long to make a bid and losing something one wants. Another might be paying a very large sum for something that turns out to be of little value.
10. An auctioneer often employs **subterfuges** to keep the auction interesting.
11. The few details given suggest that you need to become informed of how things work to participate successfully in fine art auction houses.
12. Bidders might make some gesture that they have prearranged with the auctioneer to mean they are stopping their bids on a certain item.

Lesson 2

2A Determining Precise Meaning p. 15

1. b
2. a
3. a
4. a
5. b
6. a
7. a
8. b
9. a
10. b
11. b
12. a
13. b
14. a
15. b

2B Understanding Word Relationships p. 16

1. b, c, d
2. b, c
3. a, b, d
4. b, c
5. b, d
6. a, c
7. a, b, c
8. b
9. c, d
10. a, c

2C Word Study: Synonyms and Antonyms p. 18

1. center, periphery — A
2. propensity, tendency — S
3. reduction, increment — A
4. therapeutic, detrimental — A
5. accessories, accoutrements — S
6. phlegmatic, choleric — A
7. vacillate, waver — S
8. convene, summon — S
9. imperturbable, excitable — A
10. placated, aggrieved — A

2D Understanding Contextual Meanings p. 19

(Possible answers; students' sentences may vary.)
1. The kitchen had a **utilitarian** design with no extras.
2. C
3. The moderator **interposed** herself between the two candidates.
4. C
5. C
6. Manuel's dignified **comportment** during his interview impressed the board of admissions.
7. C
8. I would like to go to Madagascar to see the **fauna** on the island.
9. C
10. C

2E Vocabulary in Context p. 20

(Possible answers; students' sentences may vary.)
1. Llamas' success as family pets, pack animals, and caddies for golfers shows that llamas feel attracted to humans.
2. Sample response: Llamas would probably carry tents, sleeping bags, and food.
3. Llamas will **interpose** themselves between the sheep they are protecting and **marauding** animals.
4. They **comport** themselves well as caddies.
5. Llamas may spit if they are upset.
6. The llama became part of the North American **fauna** in the early 1900s.
7. Because of their soft padded feet, llamas cause a **modicum** of damage to the environment.
8. The **utilitarian** tasks llamas were able to accomplish broadened their appeal.
9. The passage says that **choleric** golfers tend to calm down and that people with mental illnesses are comfortable around llamas.
10. Llamas are widespread as family pets. They are used to perform many routine jobs. They have moved beyond being creatures available only to the very rich.

Lesson 3

3A Understanding Meanings p. 26

(Possible answers; students' sentences may vary.)
1. C
2. C
3. A **regimen** is a structured program.
4. C
5. An **emolument** is a payment for services rendered.
6. C
7. A **vibrant** sound vibrates or causes vibration.
8. A **martinet** rigidly enforces a set of rules.
9. C
10. To **atrophy** is to waste away.
11. C
12. C
13. An **incipient** plan is in its beginning stage.
14. A **stoic** attitude is one that is unaffected by pleasure or pain.
15. C

3B Using Words p. 27

1. b. regimen
2. a. vibrant
   b. vibrant
   c. vibrant
3. b. inculcate
4. a. lackluster
   b. lackluster
   c. lackluster
5. a. efficacy
   b. efficacy
   c. efficacy
6. b. inestimable
   c. inestimable
7. b. prodigious
   c. prodigious
8. a. zealous
   b. zealous

3C Word Study: Analogies p. 29

1. d   6. a
2. c   7. d
3. d   8. d
4. a   9. b
5. c   10. c

3D Images of Words p. 30

1. a, b   6. a, b, c
2. a   7. b, c
3. a, b   8. a, b
4. c   9. a
5. a   10. a, b

3E Vocabulary in Context p. 31

(Possible answers; students' sentences may vary.)
1. Rudolph's mother clearly had a lot of vigor and energy to make the **prodigious** effort she did in caring for her daughter during her first ten years.
2. The passage says she practiced her exercises **zealously.**
3. She is described as being **stoic** about the difficulties she faced.
4. Rudolph was born with an **incipient** form of polio.
5. As a child she couldn't walk because her leg muscles had **atrophied.**
6. She made sure her daughter exercised and got leg massages several times a day.
7. Their efforts were effective because by age eleven Rudolph was able to walk.
8. The ideas that Mrs. Hoskins drummed into her students were ones of self-reliance and determination. When Rudolph hurt her ankle before several important races, these ideas may have made her reluctant to quit without trying.
9. Rudolph gave a **stellar** performance.
10. She might have gotten **emoluments** from big corporations for being a famous athlete.
11. Rudolph overcame great physical problems and set amazing records in track.
12. Answers will vary.

Lesson 4

4A Determining Precise Meaning   p. 38

1. b	9. b
2. a	10. a
3. a	11. a
4. b	12. b
5. a	13. b
6. a	14. a
7. b	15. a
8. a	

4B Understanding Word Relationships   p. 39

1. d	6. a, b, d
2. b, c	7. a, c
3. a, b	8. c
4. a, b, c	9. b, c
5. b, d	10. c, d

4C Word Study: Word Parts   p. 41

(Definitions are examples; students' answers may vary.)

1. stellar; of or relating to a star
2. autonomy; the state of being self-governing
3. interpose; to put between
4. convene; to come or bring together
5. incognito; with one's identity not known
6. atrophy; to waste away
7. circumspect; careful to make sure all is as it should be
8. levity; a lack of seriousness
9. utilitarian; useful rather than merely decorative
10. apocryphal; probably not true or authentic

4D Understanding Contextual Meanings   p. 42

(Possible answers; students' sentences may vary.)

1. C
2. I quickly regained my **composure** after forgetting my lines in the play.
3. C
4. C
5. The purpose of the assembly is to **indoctrinate** new students with the school's rules.
6. The **edifice** will be sixty stories high when completed.
7. C
8. C
9. A sudden loud noise woke me from my **reverie**.
10. C

4E Vocabulary in Context   p. 43

(Possible answers; students' sentences may vary.)

1. They showed caution in concealing their identities and their purpose from the boy's family. They arrived **incognito** and had a series of tests for the little boy.
2. His grave manner and perfect **composure** were noticeable.
3. He was taught the fundamental knowledge he needed to become leader of his people.
4. No, it is the traditional residence of the ruler of Tibet.
5. It gave precise details about the house and surroundings of the little boy.
6. The invading soldiers were not unfortunate. They had powerful forces and attacked Tibet from eight different fronts.
7. Not really. During that **interim** the Chinese army took control of the country and destroyed many of the buildings. There was little the Dalai Lama could do.
8. Quotation marks are used to show that what the Chinese were doing is the opposite of liberation.
9. The Chinese soldiers **pillaged** and destroyed most of the **monasteries** and libraries of Tibet. They sold the nation's cultural and religious objects.
10. He established himself there to be able to continue leading his people. He felt he might be imprisoned by the Chinese if he remained in Tibet.
11. The Tibetans are still in **thrall** to China.
12. He probably wishes for the return of **autonomy** to Tibet.

Lesson 5

5A Understanding Meanings   p. 51

(Possible answers; students' sentences may vary.)

1. C
2. C
3. C
4. **Repercussions** are the results of an action.
5. C
6. **Probity** is honesty and trustworthiness.
7. C
8. C
9. C
10. **Histrionics** are theatrical displays of emotion.
11. C
12. C
13. To **besmirch** someone is to damage that person's reputation.
14. C
15. C

5B Using Words   p. 52

1. a. impropriety
   b. impropriety
   c. impropriety
2. a. purport
   b. purport
3. a. accrue
   b. accrue
4. a. explicit
   b. explicit
   c. explicit
5. a. unsavory
   b. unsavory
   c. unsavory
6. a. inveigled
   b. inveigled
   c. inveigled
7. a. acquiesce
   c. acquiescence
8. a. besmirched
   c. besmirched

5C Word Study: Synonyms and Antonyms   p. 53

1. strengthen, atrophy   A
2. circumspect, audacious   A
3. arcane, abstruse   S
4. prodigious, puny   A
5. heinous, commendable   A
6. submit, acquiesce   S
7. efficacious, effective   S
8. fortunate, hapless   A
9. accumulate, accrue   S
10. lackluster, vibrant   A

5D Images of Words   p. 54

1. c
2. b, c
3. a, c
4. a, b, c
5. No sentence suggests **acquiescence.**
6. a, b, c
7. b
8. a
9. b
10. a, b, c

5E Vocabulary in Context   p. 56

(Possible answers; students' sentences may vary.)

1. There was a **surfeit** of quiz shows modeled after the successful TV program, *The $64,000 Question*.
2. The questions they posed in the early rounds were less **abstruse** than those in the later rounds.
3. The contestants were **purporting** to hear the questions for the first time.
4. The passage says viewers were **inveigled** by the contestants' furrowed brows and anguished looks.
5. He should have become suspicious when the producers' hints about questions became more **explicit.**
6. Sample response: They might have become upset because they knew the game was fixed.
7. Sample response: People may be less surprised today to hear of cheating.
8. Sample response: He caused people to doubt his **probity.**
9. Twenty-one people were charged with perjury. Van Doren was fired from his job as a television consultant and resigned from Columbia University.
10. He **penitently** expressed his regret at having deceived the public, his friends, and his family.
11. This event may have **besmirched** the reputation of other teachers.

Lesson 6

6A Determining Precise Meaning   p. 62

1. a
2. a
3. b
4. a
5. a
6. b
7. a
8. a
9. b
10. a
11. b
12. a
13. a
14. a
15. b

6B Understanding Word Relationships   p. 63

1. b, c, d
2. a, b, d
3. b, c
4. a, b, c
5. b, d
6. a, c
7. a, c, d
8. b
9. c, d
10. b, d

6C Word Study: Analogies   p. 65

1. a
2. c
3. d
4. b
5. a
6. b
7. d
8. a
9. b
10. c

6D Understanding Contextual Meanings   p. 66

(Possible answers; students' sentences may vary.)

1. C
2. The **eclectic** store sells a variety of goods from many different countries.
3. Samaira can **expound** for hours on the joys of bicycling.
4. C
5. We spent a **convivial** evening with good friends.
6. C
7. C
8. Brussels sprouts are **anathema** to Lola.
9. C
10. C

6E Vocabulary in Context   p. 67

(Possible answers; students' sentences may vary.)

1. Vogel is described as a stocky, **avuncular** man with a twinkle in his eye.
2. They would have probably agreed. By donating their art to the National Gallery, they guaranteed that these works will be appreciated for generations to come.
3. They satisfied their hunger by devoting all of Herbert's salary to the acquisition of art.
4. The 1960s were a favorable time because **nascent** movements like pop art and minimalism were developing in New York where the Vogels lived. Also, young artists were selling their pieces at an affordable price.
5. The Vogels were **perspicacious** in selecting works from talented, young artists.
6. The Vogels became **inveterate** collectors, living frugally to purchase more works, and spending their leisure time learning about the art world.
7. The idea of attaching a price to artwork was **anathema** to the Vogels.
8. Their **munificent** gift can be enjoyed by everyone because the gallery is open to the public at no cost.
9. Visitors might assume that the Vogels were business or industry **moguls.**
10. The Vogels had **eclectic** tastes. A variety of artists and styles attracted their attention.
11. The Vogels had a deep appreciation of art and believed in its **intrinsic** worth.

Lesson 7

7A Understanding Meanings   p. 73

(Possible answers; students' sentences may vary.)
1. To **pulverize** rock is to grind it into powder.
2. C
3. A **cavalier** response is one that shows little or no concern.
4. C
5. To **presage** an event is to foretell its occurrence.
6. C
7. **Kinetic** energy is energy related to motion.
8. C
9. C
10. C
11. To **career** is to move rapidly, lurching and swaying.
12. **Etymology** is the study of word origins.
13. **Contiguous** sections are those sharing a common border.
14. A **frenetic** movement is frantic and frenzied.
15. C

7B Using Words   p. 74

1. a. pulverize
   b. pulverized
2. a. undulate
   b. undulate
   c. undulate
3. a. cavalier
   b. cavalier
   c. cavalier
4. a. repulse
   c. repulsed
5. b. careened
   c. careened
6. a. correlation
   c. correlation
7. a. presage
   c. presage
8. b. contiguous

7C Word Study: Similar Meanings   p. 76

1. repulsed
2. —
3. repelled
4. —
5. assuage
6. satisfy
7. acquiesce
8. comply
9. —
10. —
11. penitent
12. sorry
13. intervene
14. interpose
15. —

7D Images of Words   p. 77

1. c
2. a, b, c
3. a
4. a, b, c
5. c
6. a, b
7. b, c
8. b, c
9. a, b
10. a, b

7E Vocabulary in Context   p. 78

(Possible answers; students' sentences may vary.)
1. It is a combination of two Japanese words meaning *harbor* and *wave*.
2. All three are **contiguous** to the Pacific Ocean and are vulnerable to earthquakes.
3. The Pacific is an area of great **seismic** activity.
4. If the plates grind against each other, it can cause an **upheaval.** If this occurs on the ocean floor, a tsunami may be created.
5. The **kinetic** energy of a tsunami can be tremendous, creating waves that travel hundreds of miles per hour and walls of water a hundred feet high.
6. The **kinetic** energy is distributed through the depth of the ocean waters, causing only mild **undulations.**
7. Seismologists monitor a large area and **correlate** the data they obtain about earthquakes to predict in which direction the waves might go. Because there are so many variables, this science seems like it would be difficult to understand.
8. Sample response: People who are dismissive of the danger probably won't help with evacuation efforts and may influence others to ignore warnings as well.
9. When the needles on the sensing instruments show **frenetic** activity, seismologists know an earthquake has occurred somewhere.
10. Seawalls may be able to **repulse** some of the water, but with a powerful tsunami, the walls themselves may be **pulverized.**

Lesson 8

8A Determining Precise Meaning   p. 85

1. a
2. a
3. a
4. b
5. a
6. a
7. b
8. b
9. a
10. b
11. b
12. a
13. b
14. b
15. a

8B Understanding Word Relationships   p. 86

1. b, c
2. a, c
3. c, d
4. a, b
5. b, c
6. c, d
7. b, c, d
8. b, c
9. b, c, d
10. a, c, d

8C Word Study: Word Parts   p. 87

(Definitions are examples; students' answers may vary.)
1. explicit, fully and clearly expressed
2. triumvirate, a powerful group of three
3. convivial, enjoying being with lively company
4. munificent, extremely generous
5. nascent, beginning to exist
6. perspicacious, clear-sighted
7. archipelago, a large group of islands
8. contiguous, close together or touching
9. soliloquy, a speech giving a character's thoughts
10. etymology, the history of words

8D Understanding Contextual Meanings p. 89

(Possible answers; students' sentences may vary.)

1. Billy the Kid was a **renegade** and has been the subject of many movies.
2. The **strictures** heaped on the mogul's offensive rhetoric were well deserved.
3. C
4. Eli delivered the **soliloquy** to an enthralled audience.
5. C
6. C
7. C
8. C
9. The priest addressed his **votaries** at the prayer session.
10. C

8E Vocabulary in Context p. 90

(Possible answers; students' sentences may vary.)

1. Polyneices tried to **usurp** Creon's throne. He was breaking the law.
2. Creon refused burial to another human being.
3. Creon refuses to change his **edict.**
4. Antigone hangs herself.
5. No. Because Prometheus was a god himself, his action of giving fire to humans was not violating something sacred.
6. Antigone was not a follower or devotee of Creon's ideas.
7. Medea murders her children.
8. Sophocles modified the **vestments** of his actors to express mourning for his colleague.
9. Sophocles expanded the number of actors, he added scenery, and his characters were very human.
10. Aeschylus's language in his dramas had a stately and noble **cadence.**
11. In the early works, the leader of the chorus and an actor spoke in **soliloquies.** Euripedes used several actors speaking in dialogue.
12. These three playwrights had a powerful influence on drama for hundreds of years after their time.

Lesson 9

9A Understanding Meanings p. 99

(Possible answers; students' sentences may vary.)

1. C
2. A **phobia** is an intense, irrational fear.
3. C
4. To **fabricate** a story is to invent or make it up.
5. A **proclivity** is a strong inclination toward a thing.
6. **Itinerant** musicians are those who travel from place to place.
7. The **advent** of something is its arrival.
8. C
9. C
10. A **projectile** is an object propelled by force through the air.
11. C
12. C
13. A **domicile** is a person's house or place of residence.
14. **Vertigo** is a state of dizziness.
15. C

9B Using Words p. 100

1. a. proclivity
   b. proclivity
2. a. reciprocate
   c. reciprocate
3. a. lilliputian
   b. lilliputian
   c. lilliputian
4. a. advent
   b. advent
5. a. fabricate
   b. fabricate
   c. fabricate
6. b. relegate
   c. relegate
7. a. queasy
   b. queasy
8. a. projectile

9C Word Study: Parts of Speech p. 102

1. autonomous
2. incremental
3. peripheral
4. opulent
5. efficacious
6. undulation
7. reciprocity
8. fabrication
9. acquiescence
10. correlation
11. penitence
12. reciprocity
13. perspicacity
14. munificence
15. disparity

9D Images of Words p. 103

1. a, c
2. b
3. a, c
4. b
5. a, b
6. a, c
7. b
8. b, c
9. a, b
10. b, c

9E Vocabulary in Context p. 104

(Possible answers; students' sentences may vary.)

1. A person with a fear of heights would not be calm or unimpressed while looking down from one of the world's tallest buildings. On the contrary, that person would probably panic or become hysterical.
2. The Dominion Bridge Steel Company offered employment to the Mohawks in exchange for the right to build on their land.
3. The Mohawks were **relegated** to unskilled labor positions, which paid much less than the jobs for skilled workers.
4. The Mohawks' fascination with heights was not an arrogant show of bravery. They had a **proclivity** for this kind of work.
5. Ironworkers would appear **lilliputian** to people on the ground.
6. The Mohawks helped **fabricate** some of the most famous buildings of the twentieth century.
7. The **advent** of the skyscraper boom provided the Mohawks with continuous, localized work for many decades.
8. After the boom, the Mohawks returned to **domiciles** in Canada and northern New York state.
9. If the fear reaches extreme degrees, it might be considered a **phobia.**
10. One may feel **queasy** or experience **vertigo.**

Lesson 10

10A Determining Precise Meaning   p. 109

1. b
2. b
3. b
4. a
5. a
6. b
7. a
8. a
9. b
10. b
11. b
12. a
13. a
14. b
15. a

10B Understanding Word Relationships   p. 111

1. a, b, c
2. a, c, d
3. b
4. b, c
5. b, c, d
6. a, b
7. c
8. a, b, d
9. c
10. a, b

10C Word Study: Synonyms and Antonyms   p. 112

1. nascent, incipient   S
2. munificent, stingy   A
3. hackneyed, original   A
4. upbraid, praise   A
5. appease, provoke   A
6. fabrication, falsehood   S
7. usurp, relinquish   A
8. enthralled, enamored   S
9. abstruse, recondite   S
10. presage, foreshadow   S

10D Understanding Contextual Meanings   p. 113

(Possible answers; students' sentences may vary.)
1. C
2. C
3. The **verdant** hills of Ireland can be found in many of the artist's paintings.
4. C
5. He suffered **amnesia** for a short time after his concussion.
6. Inappropriate words have been **expunged** from the public record.
7. C
8. C
9. The broadcasting antenna was placed at the **vertex** of the building.
10. C

10E Vocabulary in Context   p. 114

(Possible answers; students' sentences may vary.)
1. Using highly toxic chemicals, the army **defoliated** much of the vegetation to aid in the bombing.
2. The end of the war is described as a sudden collapse, a **debacle,** not as a series of concessions.
3. Each side hoped to force the other into giving up by taking more lives. This was a slow, drawn-out process.
4. People were unwilling to acknowledge the war because it brought back too many painful memories.
5. Many civilians refused to welcome returning soldiers or show support for them. Some even **upbraided** the soldiers for their actions.

6. Their names would be located midway between the **vertices (vertexes)** of the two walls.
7. Being able to touch the wall where the names are might give people a chance to begin healing and to begin **expunging** some of the terrible memories.
8. By building the wall into the ground and not glorifying the dead, critics felt she had **sullied** their memory.
9. The veterans who had raised money for the memorial requested that the memorial express no political view of the war.
10. Sample response: Yes. By copying this format (a **tactile** surface with names), others could make it seem commonplace or unoriginal.

Lesson 11

11A Understanding Meanings   p. 119

(Possible answers; students' sentences may vary.)
1. C
2. C
3. A **behemoth** is an enormous and powerful person.
4. C
5. **Vicissitudes** are changes of fortune.
6. C
7. The **tundra** is a flat, treeless area in the Arctic regions.
8. C
9. To **putrefy** is to rot, producing a strong odor.
10. C
11. C
12. To **attenuate** something is to make it smaller or weaker.
13. C
14. C
15. C

11B Using Words   p. 121

1. b. impinge
   c. impinge
2. a. prevail
   b. prevail
   c. prevail
3. b. unequivocal
   c. unequivocal
4. a. succulent
   c. succulent
5. b. disinterred
6. a. attenuated
   b. attenuated
   c. attenuated
7. a. putrefy
8. b. tundra
   c. tundra

11C Word Study: Analogies   p. 122

1. c
2. d
3. d
4. b
5. a
6. b
7. d
8. c
9. d
10. c

11D Images of Words p. 123

1. b
2. c
3. c
4. a, b, c
5. No sentence suggests **succulent**.
6. a, c
7. b, c
8. a, b
9. a, b
10. a, b

11E Vocabulary in Context p. 125

(Possible answers; students' sentences may vary.)

1. The tundra has little **succulent** plant life.
2. Scientists speculate that these **behemoths** developed over time to survive attacks by predators.
3. How can something enormous be described as tiny? That statement expresses the contradictory meaning of an **oxymoron.**
4. It allowed humans to travel into areas that earlier they could not. They began killing the mammoths.
5. Scientists **postulate** that the rising water from the melting ice cap cut Wrangel Island off from the mainlands, allowing the mammoths to live with a decreased threat of predators.
6. Mammoths served **multifarious** purposes for humans, providing food, shelter, and clothing.
7. Because the remains were frozen, they had not **putrefied** and did not give off an unpleasant odor.
8. Scientists **postulate** that the island provided abundant vegetation for the mammoths and protection from predators.
9. Sample response: Because scientific knowledge is always changing, theories that **prevail** one day may be disproved the next.

Lesson 12

12A Determining Precise Meaning p. 131

1. a
2. b
3. a
4. b
5. a
6. a
7. b
8. b
9. a
10. b
11. a
12. a
13. b
14. a
15. a

12B Understanding Word Relationships p. 132

1. c, d
2. b, c, d
3. b, d
4. a, b
5. a, c, d
6. c, d
7. b
8. b, d
9. a, b, c
10. a, b

12C Word Study: Similar Meanings p. 134

1. expunge
2. —
3. erase
4. arrival
5. advent
6. —
7. craven
8. cowardly
9. —
10. —
11. assume
12. postulate
13. fear
14. phobia
15. —

12D Understanding Contextual Meanings p. 135

(Possible answers; students' sentences may vary.)

1. C
2. C
3. Not telling her what happened is **tantamount** to lying.
4. C
5. C
6. His **introspective** mien made him seem intelligent.
7. C
8. **Penurious** patients were put on the hospital's long-term payment plan.
9. C
10. The warm sunshine today is the **antithesis** of the snowstorm yesterday.

12E Vocabulary in Context p. 136

(Possible answers; students' sentences may vary.)

1. He called racial justice into question because he saw unequal treatment based on race everywhere.
2. During the 1960s the country was in the **throes** of war and civil unrest. The sides were quite polarized, so the atmosphere was not peaceful or friendly.
3. Woodstock was a gathering of people who **exalted** the opposite point of view. They sought peace and cooperation.
4. During her visit to North Vietnam, Joan Baez shared the hardships of the Vietnamese by staying in makeshift shelters amidst deadly bombing.
5. She received harsh criticisms of her political views from those who held **antithetical** views.
6. As a child, Baez was **introspective** and shy.
7. Her family is described as middle class.
8. Sample response: Baez has a talent for singing, writing, and performing, as well as an ability to use these talents to express political views.
9. Baez wasn't cowardly about expressing her beliefs but rather spoke out through her actions and songs.
10. Sample response: It means someone who has attributes related to freedom and peace.

Lesson 13

13A Understanding Meanings p. 143

(Possible answers; students' sentences may vary.)

1. C
2. C
3. **Cuisine** is a style of cooking.
4. **Crass** behavior shows lack of sensitivity to others' feelings.
5. C
6. C
7. A **libation** is a drink used especially for a celebration or ritual.
8. C
9. **Concurrent** events take place simultaneously.
10. C
11. **Platitudes** are trite statements.
12. C
13. **Extemporaneous** remarks are those made with little or no preparation.
14. C
15. C

13B Using Words   p. 144

1. a. debase
   b. debase
   c. debase
2. b. platitude
3. b. enjoined
   c. enjoined
4. a. concurrent
   c. concurrent
5. a. travail
   c. travail
6. a. context
   b. context
7. a. reconcile
   b. reconcile
   c. reconcile
8. a. sunder
   b. sunder
   c. sunder

13C Word Study: Word Parts   p. 145

(Definitions are examples; students' answers may vary.)

1. advent, a coming or arrival
2. proclivity, a strong leaning toward something
3. itinerant, traveling from place to place
4. opprobrium, scornful treatment or contempt
5. unequivocal, leaving no room for misunderstanding
6. domicile, one's home or place of residence
7. antithetical, being in direct opposition
8. attrition, a gradual reduction in strength
9. reconcile, to reestablish a friendly relationship
10. multifarious, having many forms

13D Images of Words   p. 147

1. a, c
2. b, c
3. a, b
4. a, b, c
5. a, b
6. a, c
7. b, c
8. a, c
9. a, b, c
10. a, b

13E Vocabulary in Context   p. 148

(Possible answers; students' sentences may vary.)

1. The violent Watts riots of 1965 provided the **genesis** of Kwanzaa. Maulana Karenga felt a need for change.
2. Answers will vary.
3. For many, there was a general **malaise** that reflected both physical and spiritual deprivation.
4. People are encouraged to settle their differences with friends, family, and colleagues.
5. Sample response: Spending a lot of money would emphasize the material rather than the spiritual aspect of the holiday.
6. African American **cuisine** is served at a special meal. **Libations** are offered as part of a ceremony near the end of the festival.
7. Sample response: No, the ideas in these principles are not trite. They encourage people to think about the spiritual aspects of their lives.
8. The principles encourage positive thinking, community, and working to help others.

9. People are urged to take care of each other and leave their communities more beautiful and beneficial than they were before.
10. No, the feast occurs on the sixth day, but the candle lighting occurs on the first.

Lesson 14

14A Determining Precise Meaning   p. 154

1. b
2. a
3. a
4. b
5. b
6. a
7. a
8. a
9. b
10. a
11. b
12. a
13. a
14. b
15. b

14B Understanding Word Relationships   p. 155

1. a, c
2. b, d
3. c
4. a, b, c
5. b, d
6. a, b
7. a, c, d
8. c, d
9. a, c
10. b, c

14C Word Study: Synonyms and Antonyms   p. 157

1. dilatory, prompt   A
2. belief, tenet   S
3. origin, genesis   S
4. unite, sunder   A
5. penurious, affluent   A
6. amity, friendship   S
7. pugnacious, bellicose   S
8. ambiguous, unequivocal   A
9. wholesome, salubrious   S
10. disinter, bury   A

14D Understanding Contextual Meanings   p. 158

(Possible answers; students' sentences may vary.)

1. C
2. C
3. C
4. Political-party disagreements had to be **transcended** before the railroad could be built.
5. C
6. C
7. The holy ground is **sacrosanct** to the church.
8. Nashville is the **venue** for many musical events.
9. The mountain climbers reached the **pinnacle** in less than an hour.
10. C

14E Vocabulary in Context   p. 159

(Possible answers; students' sentences may vary.)

1. The absence of a state religion is a major **tenet** of the constitution.
2. Yes, his idea was universal because he described it as a great church that would be open to all.
3. Washington, D.C., was a **venue** where all people in the nation could worship.

4. The idea was suggested in 1793 but remained **moot** for a hundred years because of the issue of separating church and state.
5. Flying **buttresses** were used to support the walls, and **gargoyles** were used as decorative elements.
6. No, a **requiem** service was held for President Eisenhower and for others before it was completely finished.
7. Hart's sculpture is described as a **sensuous** composition of male and female figures.
8. The passage says that the cathedral is the world's sixth largest cathedral.
9. The church has no local congregation, and it is open to people of all faiths.
10. The cathedral is built on the highest point of land in Washington, D.C., Mount St. Alban.

Lesson 15

15A Understanding Meanings p. 164

(Possible answers; students' sentences may vary.)
1. C
2. C
3. **Concomitant** events accompany a main event.
4. C
5. An **oligarchy** is a government controlled by a privileged elite.
6. To **entice** someone is to attract that person by arousing desire.
7. C
8. An **inordinate** amount is one that is excessive.
9. C
10. C
11. A **repugnant** suggestion offends or repulses its recipients.
12. C
13. C
14. A **redoubtable** scholar is one whose credentials are worthy of respect.
15. An **arbiter** is one whose decisions are accepted as final.

15B Using Words p. 166

1. b. repugnant
   c. repugnant
2. b. inordinate
   c. inordinate
3. a. demur
   b. demur
4. a. entice
   c. entice
5. a. redoubtable
6. a. inimical
   b. inimical
   c. inimical
7. a. flaunted
   b. flaunted
   c. flaunted
8. a. graphic
   b. graphic
   c. graphic

15C Word Study: Analogies p. 167

1. b	6. a
2. b	7. a
3. d	8. c
4. b	9. b
5. d	10. a

15D Images of Words p. 168

1. b, c	6. c
2. b, c	7. b, c
3. a	8. a, b, c
4. b, c	9. No sentence suggests **demur.**
5. a	10. a, b, c

15E Vocabulary in Context p. 170

(Possible answers; students' sentences may vary.)
1. These women were part of an **oligarchy** because they came from old, well-to-do families that possessed social and economic power and could easily exert an influence over city government.
2. Her friends viewed her as an **arbiter** of fashion and followed her advice. Those who **demurred** were ostracized from the group.
3. Sample response: If politeness, delicacy, and elegance were more important to Hemenway, she probably wouldn't have concerned herself with the origin of the aigrettes.
4. The article gave **graphic** details about the slaughter of birds.
5. The industry was excessive and inhumane in its treatment of birds, slaughtering close to five million of them each year.
6. **Concomitant** with the laws would be the need for women to boycott the use of feathered adornments.
7. They said it would cause an **inordinate** amount of hardship to workers in the feather industry.
8. The senator was **inimical** to the proposal.
9. They were not an exclusive group, but rather one that hoped to **entice** many people into joining their cause.
10. People are more aware of the threat to different species and would be offended to see them killed for frivolous purposes.

Lesson 16

16A Determining Precise Meaning p. 175

1. a	6. b	11. a
2. a	7. b	12. b
3. b	8. a	13. a
4. a	9. b	14. b
5. a	10. b	15. a

16B Understanding Word Relationships p. 177

1. b, c	6. a, c
2. b, c, d	7. d
3. a, b	8. c, d
4. a, d	9. a, b
5. c, d	10. b, d

16C Word Study: Similar Meanings   p. 178

1. —
2. beginning
3. genesis
4. severed
5. sundered
6. —
7. —
8. sequestered
9. secluded
10. surpass
11. —
12. transcend
13. —
14. deadly
15. virulent

16D Understanding Contextual Meanings   p. 179

(Possible answers; students' sentences may vary.)
1. C
2. The political process was in **limbo** until the court handed down a decision.
3. C
4. An old, **ramshackle** bridge was the only means of crossing the river.
5. C
6. The **archives** can be found in the basement of the old library.
7. C
8. C
9. England's Prince Charles can trace his **lineage** back to William the Conqueror.
10. The report was so **perfunctory,** it might as well not have been written.

16E Vocabulary in Context   p. 180

(Possible answers; students' sentences may vary.)
1. Many immigrants chose to settle in the **metropolis** of New York City.
2. Ellis Island's buildings have been restored and are now in **pristine** condition.
3. Ellis Island had a **commodious** harbor for ocean-going ships to enter, and its location allowed for people with contagious illnesses to be **sequestered.**
4. Answers will vary.
5. **Listlessness** is not always a sign of sickness. Today, inspectors have more sophisticated methods of checking for contagious illnesses.
6. Answers will vary.
7. People who had **virulent** illnesses or were considered politically **subversive** were not permitted to stay.
8. The buildings deteriorated after 1954 because they were no longer used. After 1954, the majority of immigrants came by plane rather than ship.
9. They can check the **archives** for records of their ancestors.
10. Native Americans are the only people whose **lineage** begins in this country.

Lesson 17

17A Understanding Meanings   p. 189

(Possible answers; students' sentences may vary.)
1. C
2. A **pejorative** term is belittling or unpleasant.
3. C
4. C
5. A **mercenary** is a person, especially a soldier, who works strictly for money.

6. C
7. A **caustic** substance is corrosive and causes chemical burns.
8. An **autocrat** is a domineering person, one with complete control.
9. C
10. C
11. C
12. **Duplicity** is deceptive behavior.
13. C
14. An **emissary** is a representative sent on a special mission.
15. C

17B Using Words   p. 190

1. b. debilitated
   c. debilitated
2. b. impecunious
3. a. parsimonious
   b. parsimonious
   c. parsimonious
4. a. notorious
   c. notorious
5. a. jaundiced
   b. jaundiced
   c. jaundiced
6. a. oust
   b. oust
   c. ouster
7. a. caustic
   b. caustic
8. a. felicitous
   b. felicitous

17C Word Study: Word Parts   p. 192

(Definitions are examples; students' answers may vary.)
1. commensurate, corresponding in size, degree, or amount
2. impecunious, being habitually without money
3. transcend, to go beyond
4. metropolis, a city of great size and importance
5. dilatory, slow to act
6. oligarchy, rule by a small, elite group
7. concomitant, accompanying or existing at the same time
8. demur, to raise objections
9. conclave, a meeting held behind closed doors
10. pinnacle, a tall, slender pointed top

17D Images of Words   p. 193

1. a, b
2. a, b, c
3. b
4. c
5. a
6. a, b, c
7. b
8. b, c
9. a
10. No sentence suggests **impecunious.**

17E Vocabulary in Context   p. 194

(Possible answers; students' sentences may vary.)
1. Under de' Medici, the arts flourished, so he probably supported artists' projects. This would be a fortunate time for artists to be working.

2. Florence under de' Medici was an **autocracy**; the government after that was a republic, which allowed people to choose their leaders.
3. They express his ideas in a **forthright** way.
4. The passage says de' Medici spent money on the arts. Machiavelli urged **parsimonious** ways to rulers because of de' Medici's "extravagances." This suggests that de' Medici may have spent Florence's money excessively, leaving it poor.
5. Sample responses: He organized a citizen army to replace the one made up of **mercenaries.** He was an **emissary** for his government.
6. Answers will vary.
7. He was **ousted** from his political position and put in jail. He eventually retired to his home outside the city.
8. They found his **precepts** shocking.
9. He lived and worked in government at a time when leaders used **duplicity** all the time.
10. Answers will vary.

Lesson 18

18A Determining Precise Meaning   p. 200

1. a	6. a	11. b
2. a	7. a	12. a
3. b	8. b	13. b
4. b	9. a	14. a
5. a	10. a	15. a

18B Understanding Word Relationships   p. 201

1. b, c, d	5. a, c	8. d
2. b, c	6. b, c	9. b
3. a, d	7. c, d	10. a, c
4. a, b, d		

18C Word Study: Synonyms and Antonyms   p. 203

1. beneficial, inimical	A
2. vibrant, listless	A
3. filthy, pristine	A
4. cramped, commodious	A
5. weaken, debilitate	S
6. corrosive, caustic	S
7. munificent, parsimonious	A
8. forthright, duplicitous	A
9. ouster, appointment	A
10. adulation, derision	A

18D Understanding Contextual Meanings   p. 204

(Possible answers; students' sentences may vary.)
1. She **proscribed** us from doing anything until we knew the whole truth.
2. C
3. C
4. Mario had the **effrontery** to condemn bullying when he is the biggest bully I know.
5. C
6. The college dean **espoused** the idea of free tuition.
7. C
8. The poll results were **promulgated** on radio, TV, the Internet, and in the newspapers.
9. C
10. C

18E Vocabulary in Context   p. 205

(Possible answers; students' sentences may vary.)
1. An example of **hypocrisy** is leaders who claim to support human rights but then mistreat their citizens.
2. They **incensed** the government with their **effrontery** to speak out for freedom.
3. This is probably how Salazár viewed them.
4. The United Nations **espoused** basic human rights and wanted to protect the citizens of all countries. By proclaiming these rights, they could pressure countries to comply.
5. Without the intervention of Amnesty International, many prisoners would be **bereft** of hope.
6. Their letters ask government officials to **redress** injustices they've committed.
7. They **substantiate** each prisoner's history and circumstances to make sure he or she meets the organization's **criteria.**
8. Prisoners of conscience must be unfairly detained and must not **espouse** violence.
9. A **regime** that takes power by force is probably not likely to honor commitments to human rights.
10. Answers will vary.

Lesson 19

19A Understanding Meanings   p. 210

(Possible answers; students' sentences may vary.)
1. C
2. C
3. A **stentorian** voice is one that is loud.
4. C
5. An **epiphany** is a revelation.
6. C
7. C
8. A **unilateral** move is made without others acting in concert.
9. C
10. C
11. **Tenure** is the condition of holding an office or position.
12. A **complaisant** person is eager to please.
13. A **moratorium** is a waiting period or temporary ban.
14. C
15. C

19B Using Words   p. 212

1. a. pragmatic
   c. pragmatic
2. a. stentorian
3. a. pendulous
4. a. depredations
   b. depredations
   c. depredations
5. a. viable
   b. viable
6. a. portend
   b. portend
7. a. consolidate
   b. consolidate
   c. consolidate
8. a. complaisant
   b. complaisant

19C Word Study: Parts of Speech   **p. 213**

1. antithetical	9. derision
2. metropolitan	10. espousal
3. portentous	11. listlessness
4. parsimonious	12. altruism
5. hypocritical	13. introspection
6. indoctrination	14. notoriety
7. portent	15. autocracy
8. ouster	

19D Images of Words   **p. 214**

1. a, b	6. b, c
2. c	7. b, c
3. a, b, c	8. b, c
4. a, c	9. a, b
5. a, b, c	10. a, c

19E Vocabulary in Context   **p. 216**

(Possible answers; students' sentences may vary.)

1. A demand for ivory carvings led to a larger number of kills and **portended** the possible extinction of elephants.
2. One can hear their **stentorian** trumpeting.
3. They intertwine their **pendulous** trunks and click their tusks.
4. She had a strong connection to Africa. It felt like home, even though she had never been there before.
5. The ivory carvings are elaborate and have significant value.
6. Elephants live in family groups of several generations of females, with less mature calves under the **aegis** of a matriarch who is the oldest and often the wisest.
7. She says the **reprieve** granted to elephants can only continue if the **moratorium** on ivory sales remains strong.
8. They took a **pragmatic** view of their country's dependence on the tourist trade. This industry would remain **viable** only as long as there were elephants to see.
9. It may signal the **depredation** of huge numbers of elephants.
10. It led to a **consolidation** of action on the part of other African nations. They began to support it.

Lesson 20

20A Determining Precise Meaning   **p. 221**

1. b	9. a
2. a	10. b
3. a	11. a
4. b	12. b
5. b	13. a
6. a	14. b
7. b	15. b
8. a	

20B Understanding Word Relationships   **p. 223**

1. b, c, d	6. b, d
2. a, b, c	7. a, b
3. a, c, d	8. c, d
4. b, c	9. c
5. a, c	10. a, d

20C Word Study: Analogies   **p. 225**

1. d	6. c
2. d	7. a
3. a	8. b
4. b	9. d
5. d	10. a

20D Understanding Contextual Meanings   **p. 226**

(Possible answers; students' sentences may vary.)

1. C
2. C
3. If you **extrapolate** from a small sample, you may get faulty results.
4. C
5. People who are **ambidextrous** can write with both hands.
6. C
7. C
8. The famous movie star **excoriated** the young actor for interrupting him.
9. Try not to **impute** your friend until you know more about the situation.
10. C

20E Vocabulary in Context   **p. 227**

(Possible answers; students' sentences may vary.)

1. There has always been a **preponderance** of right-handed people.
2. Researchers had the unpleasant task of examining skulls to see which side of the head was more likely to be injured by blows.
3. Other scientists felt that **extrapolating** from such a small sample of the population might **negate** Coren and Halpern's findings.
4. The belief that left-handed people are inferior is now **passé**.
5. They would be as **maladroit** as left-handed people are when asked to use tools that are inappropriate for them.
6. If left-handed people continue to hear negative things about this characteristic, it could be psychologically **deleterious** to them.
7. Because of the **stance** they must use to pitch the ball, they are in a better position to pick off base stealers.
8. Other primates are **ambidextrous**.
9. It names several famous people who have been highly successful, in spite of their left-handedness.
10. Sample response: Perhaps people viewed left-handed people as inferior just because they were in the minority.

Lessons 1–4
Crossword Puzzle
page 48

Lessons 5–8
Hidden Message
pages 94–96

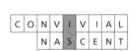

Lessons 9–12
Crossword Puzzle
page 140

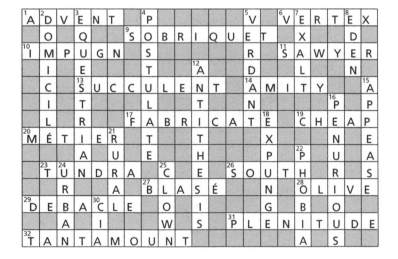

Lessons 13–16

Hidden Message
pages 184–186

```
        C R A S S
L U D I C R O U S
  C O N C O M I T A N T
        I N I M I C A L
  S E N S U O U S
  P E R F U N C T O R Y
```

```
      G R A P H I C
        C
      R E Q U I E M
    V I R U L E N T
E N J O I N
        T R A V A I L
  S U B V E R S I V E
  I N O R D I N A T E
```

```
T E R M I N U S
      C O T E R I E
  F L A U N T
      L I S T L E S S
  C O N T E X T
```

```
R E D O U B T A B L E
  A B E Y A N C E
```

```
A R B I T E R
P R I S T I N E
```

```
  L I B A T I O N
G A R G O Y L E
    V E N U E
```

```
P L A T I T U D E
    H
  L I N E A G E
```

```
S E Q U E S T E R
A R C H I V E S
  O L I G A R C H Y
      C H A T T E L
  M O O T
G E N T E E L
E C U M E N I C A L
    C O N T E X T
```

```
  F A C A D E
R E C O N C I L E
  M A L A I S E
  D I L A T O R Y
      T E N E T
  C O N C L A V E
  A L T R U I S M
  C U I S I N E
C O M M O D I O U S
    S U N D E R
```

```
S A C R O S A N C T
      F
```

```
M E T R O P O L I S
  B U T T R E S S
      D E M U R
        J
  C O N C U R R E N T
        D E B A S E
      L I M B O
P I N N A C L E
E N T I C E D
  T R A N S C E N D
```

Lessons 17–20

Crossword Puzzle
page 231

1 D	U	2 P	L	3 I	C	I	T	Y		4 P	5 A	S	S	6 É					7 E		
		R		A				8 P	N	O		9 P			P		P	10 D
		A	11 A	U	T	O	C	R	A	T	I	C		12 R	E	G	I	M	E
		G		S				O		I	K	O		P		P		R
13 I	M	P	U	T	E			S	P	S	P		14 H	A	R	D
		A		I			C		A		O	H		N		E
15 M	E	T	R	I	C		16 M	O	R	A	T	O	R	I	U	M		N		Y
		I		18 R		I	H	E	N	Y
19 I	N	20 C	E	N	S	E	D		B	Y	P	D	21 C		22 G
		E		D		E			R		23 M	A	J	O	R		I
24 O			G		R		25 A	26 E	G	I	S		C		L
27 U	N	I	L	A	T	E	R	A	L		R	E	28 C	I	T	R	U	S
S			T		S			I		V		U	L
29 T	H	E	R	E	30 S	T	A	N	C	E	31 E	M	I	S	S	A	R	Y

Lesson 1

1. arcane
2. vacillates
3. levity
4. mortified
5. peripheral
6. raconteur
7. reiterate
8. increments
9. subterfuges
10. apocryphal
11. convene
12. expedient
13. gesticulation
14. exude
15. imperturbable

Lesson 2

1. fauna
2. propensity
3. patrician
4. modicum
5. aggrieved
6. phlegmatic
7. accoutrements
8. therapeutic
9. choleric
10. comport
11. disconcerting
12. marauding
13. interpose
14. opulent
15. utilitarian

Lesson 3

1. lackluster
2. vibrant
3. atrophy
4. regimen
5. efficacy
6. inestimable
7. icon
8. inculcated
9. martinet
10. zealous
11. stellar
12. stoic
13. prodigious
14. emoluments
15. incipient

Lesson 4

1. reverie
2. circumspect
3. incognito
4. environs
5. ensconced
6. edifice
7. indoctrination
8. composure
9. thrall
10. autonomous
11. hapless
12. heinous
13. pillaged
14. mausoleum
15. interim

Lesson 5

1. unsavory
2. abstruse
3. besmirched
4. revelation
5. acquiescence
6. explicit
7. impropriety
8. accrued
9. histrionic
10. inveigled
11. probity
12. repercussions
13. purported
14. surfeit
15. penitence

Lesson 6

1. munificent
2. assuaged
3. intrinsic
4. mogul
5. anathema
6. inveterate
7. avuncular
8. convivial
9. eclectic
10. expound
11. propitious
12. nascent
13. epigram
14. philistines
15. perspicacious

Lesson 7

1. kinetic
2. pulverizes
3. careening
4. undulate
5. etymology
6. contiguous
7. archipelago
8. cavalier
9. repulse
10. recondite
11. correlate
12. seismic
13. presage
14. frenetic
15. upheaval

Lesson 8

1. triumvirate
2. votaries
3. vestments
4. blasphemy
5. cadences
6. soliloquy
7. usurped
8. denouement
9. renegade
10. canon
11. enamored
12. insensate
13. strictures
14. edict
15. betrothed

Lesson 9

1. reciprocity
2. relegated
3. blasé
4. bravado
5. proclivity
6. vertigo
7. queasy
8. phobias
9. fabrication
10. projectiles
11. advent
12. itinerants
13. disparate
14. domiciles
15. lilliputian

Lesson 10

1. sully
2. appease
3. attrition
4. expunge
5. debacle
6. defoliate
7. amnesia
8. upbraided
9. equestrian
10. proviso
11. hackneyed
12. opprobrium
13. tactile
14. verdant
15. vertex

Lesson 11

1. behemoths
2. plenitude
3. attenuated
4. tundra
5. vicissitudes
6. impinged
7. prevail
8. putrefied
9. succulent
10. disinterred
11. multifarious
12. unequivocal
13. salubrious
14. postulate
15. oxymoron

Lesson 12

1. throes
2. bucolic
3. antithetical
4. craven
5. bellicose
6. exalted
7. animadversions
8. privations
9. impugned
10. tantamount
11. penury
12. amity
13. métier
14. introspective
15. sobriquet

Lesson 13

1. travail
2. malaise
3. context
4. genesis
5. sundered
6. concurrently
7. enjoined
8. debases
9. altruistic
10. extemporaneous
11. cuisine
12. platitude
13. libation
14. crass
15. reconcile

Lesson 14

1. transcend
2. commensurate
3. abeyance
4. venue
5. requiem
6. dilatory
7. sacrosanct
8. moot
9. ecumenical
10. tenet
11. pinnacle
12. buttresses
13. sensuous
14. facade
15. gargoyles

Lesson 15

1. ludicrous
2. flaunted
3. inordinate
4. concomitant
5. genteel
6. graphic
7. conclave
8. coteries
9. arbiters
10. oligarchy
11. enticed
12. inimical
13. demurred
14. redoubtable
15. repugnant

Lesson 16

1. archives
2. lineage
3. chattels
4. commodious
5. terminus
6. sequestered
7. limbo
8. listless
9. virulent
10. perfunctory
11. metropolitan
12. conflagration
13. ramshackle
14. subversive
15. pristine

Lesson 17

1. autocracies
2. emissary
3. impecunious
4. mercenary
5. ousted
6. jaundiced
7. caustic
8. debilitate
9. felicitous
10. duplicity
11. parsimonious
12. forthright
13. pejorative
14. notoriety
15. precepts

Lesson 18

1. redress
2. retribution
3. regime
4. bereft
5. effrontery
6. promulgated
7. hypocrites
8. proscribes
9. derision
10. incensed
11. impending
12. pertinent
13. substantiate
14. criteria
15. espoused

Lesson 19

1. depredations
2. reprieve
3. baubles
4. pragmatic
5. aegis
6. complaisant
7. moratorium
8. consolidated
9. portent
10. unilateral
11. tenure
12. viable
13. stentorian
14. pendulous
15. epiphany

Lesson 20

1. ambidextrous
2. imputed
3. preponderance
4. antipathy
5. maladroit
6. deleterious
7. excoriated
8. idiosyncrasy
9. negated
10. pedagogical
11. propounded
12. extrapolate
13. grisly
14. stance
15. passé

Test Answer Key

Lesson 1

1. C
2. A
3. B
4. C
5. C
6. B
7. D
8. A
9. B
10. D
11. B
12. B
13. C
14. D
15. A

STP/P

1. C
2. A
3. D
4. B
5. B

Lesson 2

1. C
2. B
3. D
4. A
5. B
6. B
7. A
8. B
9. C
10. B
11. C
12. B
13. D
14. A
15. D

STP/P

1. B
2. C
3. D
4. A
5. C

Lesson 3

1. A
2. C
3. D
4. A
5. D
6. B
7. B
8. C
9. C
10. A
11. C
12. D
13. A
14. B
15. B

STP/P

1. C
2. A
3. B
4. A
5. B

Lesson 4

1. D
2. C
3. B
4. D
5. A
6. B
7. C
8. B
9. B
10. C
11. B
12. A
13. C
14. D
15. B

STP/P

1. B
2. D
3. B
4. D
5. B

Lesson 5

1. C
2. A
3. C
4. B
5. B
6. C
7. A
8. C
9. D
10. D
11. C
12. D
13. A
14. D
15. C

STP/P

1. C
2. A
3. A
4. B
5. C

Lesson 6

1. D
2. C
3. C
4. A
5. A
6. B
7. C
8. A
9. D
10. A
11. C
12. C
13. D
14. D
15. C

STP/P

1. B
2. A
3. C
4. D
5. C

Lesson 7

1. B
2. A
3. B
4. D
5. A
6. D
7. A
8. B
9. B
10. C
11. C
12. D
13. A
14. B
15. A

STP/P

1. C
2. C
3. B
4. C
5. A

Lesson 8

1. D
2. A
3. B
4. C
5. A
6. D
7. C
8. A
9. D
10. A
11. A
12. D
13. C
14. B
15. A

STP/P

1. A
2. B
3. D
4. A
5. C

Lesson 9

1. B
2. A
3. C
4. B
5. C
6. A
7. B
8. D
9. C
10. B
11. A
12. B
13. A
14. D
15. B

STP/P

1. A
2. B
3. D
4. D
5. A

Lesson 10

1. A
2. C
3. A
4. B
5. C
6. D
7. B
8. D
9. B
10. A
11. B
12. D
13. B
14. A
15. D

STP/P

1. B
2. D
3. A
4. C
5. A

Midterm Test 1
(Lessons 1–10)

1. B
2. D
3. B
4. C
5. C
6. D
7. B
8. A
9. D
10. D

STP/P

1. A
2. D
3. A
4. C
5. B

Midterm Test 2
(Lessons 1–10)

1. D
2. C
3. B
4. D
5. C
6. D
7. B
8. A
9. D
10. C

STP/P

1. C
2. E
3. A
4. E
5. C

Lesson 11

1. A
2. D
3. A
4. D
5. B
6. C
7. B
8. C
9. A
10. D
11. C
12. C
13. A
14. B
15. C

STP/P

1. C
2. D
3. B
4. C
5. D

Lesson 12

1. C
2. A
3. D
4. A
5. B
6. A
7. D
8. B
9. A
10. B
11. D
12. C
13. A
14. B
15. C

STP/P

1. D
2. A
3. B
4. C
5. A

Lesson 13

1. C
2. A
3. D
4. B
5. A
6. A
7. D
8. B
9. A
10. B
11. C
12. A
13. C
14. B
15. D

STP/P

1. C
2. A
3. D
4. B
5. B

Lesson 14

1. B
2. D
3. A
4. A
5. D
6. B
7. D
8. B
9. C
10. C
11. D
12. A
13. B
14. C
15. C

STP/P

1. B
2. B
3. C
4. A
5. B

Lesson 15

1. C
2. A
3. C
4. D
5. C
6. A
7. A
8. B
9. D
10. D
11. C
12. D
13. A
14. D
15. B

STP/P

1. C
2. C
3. B
4. B
5. B

Lesson 16

1. B
2. A
3. B
4. D
5. C
6. D
7. C
8. A
9. D
10. B
11. C
12. B
13. A
14. D
15. A

STP/P

1. B
2. D
3. B
4. C
5. A

Lesson 17

1. D
2. B
3. A
4. D
5. B
6. C
7. A
8. C
9. D
10. C
11. D
12. A
13. C
14. B
15. D

STP/P

1. C
2. B
3. D
4. A
5. B

Lesson 18

1. D
2. B
3. A
4. D
5. D
6. C
7. A
8. A
9. B
10. D
11. B
12. A
13. D
14. C
15. C

STP/P

1. C
2. A
3. C
4. B
5. A

Lesson 19

1. B
2. B
3. A
4. B
5. C
6. C
7. C
8. D
9. D
10. A
11. D
12. C
13. B
14. C
15. A

STP/P

1. C
2. A
3. D
4. A
5. D

Lesson 20

1. C
2. A
3. C
4. B
5. D
6. D
7. D
8. A
9. B
10. C
11. C
12. B
13. D
14. A
15. C

STP/P

1. C
2. A
3. A
4. B
5. B

Final Test 1
(Lessons 1–20)

1. C
2. D
3. A
4. C
5. A
6. C
7. A
8. C
9. B
10. B

STP/P

1. D
2. B
3. A
4. C
5. D

Final Test 2
(Lessons 1–20)

1. B
2. A
3. B
4. D
5. B
6. A
7. B
8. A
9. A
10. C

STP/P

1. D
2. A
3. E
4. A
5. B

**Final Test 3
(Lessons 1–20)**

1. A
2. C
3. D
4. A
5. B
6. C
7. D
8. A
9. B
10. C

STP/P

1. E
2. D
3. A
4. B
5. C

**Final Test 4
(Lessons 1–20)**

1. A
2. C
3. B
4. A
5. D
6. D
7. B
8. B
9. D
10. A

STP/P

1. B
2. D
3. E
4. C
5. B

Notes

Notes